PENGUIN BOOKS

FALSE STARTS

Malcolm Braly was born in Portland,
Oregon, in 1925. He is the author of four
novels, including the highly acclaimed *On
the Yard*, also published by Penguin
Books. He is now a free-lance writer and
lives in Baltimore, Maryland.

Books by Malcolm Braly

Felony Tank
Shake Him Till He Rattles
It's Cold Out There
On the Yard
False Starts

False Starts

A Memoir of San Quentin and
Other Prisons

=========by Malcolm Braly

Penguin Books

Penguin Books Ltd, Harmondsworth,
Middlesex, England
Penguin Books, 625 Madison Avenue,
New York, New York 10022, U.S.A.
Penguin Books Australia Ltd, Ringwood,
Victoria, Australia
Penguin Books Canada Limited, 2801 John Street,
Markham, Ontario, Canada L3R 1B4
Penguin Books (N.Z.) Ltd, 182–190 Wairau Road,
Auckland 10, New Zealand

First published in the United States of America by
Little, Brown and Company 1976
Reprinted by arrangement with Little, Brown and Company
Published in Penguin Books 1977

LIBRARY OF CONGRESS CATALOGING IN PUBLICATION DATA
Braly, Malcolm, 1925–
  False starts.
  Reprint of the 1976 ed. published by Little,
Brown, Boston.
  1. Braly, Malcolm, 1925–   2. Prisoners—
United States—Biography.   3. Crime and criminals—
United States—Biography.   I.   Title.
[HV9468.B68A34 1977]   365'.6'0924   [B]
ISBN 0 14 00.4454 X   77-1068

Printed in the United States of America by
Offset Paperback Mfrs., Inc., Dallas, Pennsylvania
Set in Linotype Janson

For Beverly
Steven
Anandi
and all those others
who fill these pages . . .

False Starts

My Family

==

THIS IS AN ACCOUNT of how I blundered in and out of prison for over twenty years — far more *in* than out — and how these experiences changed me. I invite you to realize this adventure with me, to see it in the form of a journey, a long and often difficult voyage through the life of our times, which, finally, finds the grace of safe harbor.

I was not entirely state-raised, the term we used to characterize those held in institutions (orphanages, foster homes, reform schools) from their earliest years, but lived with my family until I was fourteen. I'm tempted to skip this prelude simply because childhoods of every possible variety have become the familiar landscapes of our literature, and mine is not so dear to me I feel I could illuminate it in any special light. However, much that followed was so rare, such a statistical freak, that I can't just wave these early years away, because they may contain clues. The burden of my account is what happened, but I'm clearly compelled to make some effort to show *why* it happened, and the condition that this task is impossible humbles me, but doesn't depress me, and, of course, I have a few rubbery notions I've picked up here and there which I'll probably try to stretch into place.

I was born with a silver spoon in my mouth — or, at least one of sturdy nickel plate — but at age five, during the crash of '29, it was abruptly snatched and probably my mouth was torn. In my magical apprehension I was somehow half-convinced I had caused this disaster.

It's tempting to imagine the Depression robbed me, as it robbed many, of the life I might have lived, where I would have eventually gone to college, entered one of the professions, married, raised children, and passed my time on earth in a comparatively quiet contentment, but I doubt this. My intuition tells me the shadow had been cast even before the Depression. My earliest memories, the few I can summon, are unhappy, flat, and standing there in that narrow and darkening perspective I sense a shy and fearful child. I don't know why I was like that. Some say we are indelibly stamped before the end of our second year, and, if this is true, we must all be mysteries to ourselves. What happened beyond the threshold of our earliest memories? What misapprehensions form the loci for the illogical constructions which we carry, as turtles their shells, into our lives?

I was, from any beginning I can recall, a liar, a sneak, a braggart, a show-off and a thief. Common tendencies and some, refined in the light of cultural paradigm, are even honored, but, from the first, I was unable to grasp or calculate consequences. I lied in hopeless situations, where the only possible mitigation lay in telling the truth, and I took things only I could have stolen, and never imagined I could be caught.

My father was an ordinary member of a smart and successful family, who had been raised in the shadow of a brilliant older brother, dead of blood poisoning at seventeen, and when the hopes of the family shifted to him he proved unable to bear them. He was thrown out of several colleges for high spirits and low marks, and ended his pretense at education by marrying my mother who was pregnant with me. He was twenty, she was seventeen. The legend as I grasped it was that he married because he had to, and that he married beneath himself. My mother's family was poor, even in those good times, but they had managed to get their girl into college, no small thing then, and they proudly traced their lineage to William Bradford, the first governor of the Plymouth Colony.

My mother was smart, tough, and, I suspect, cold. As a child I never experienced a quiver of religious intuition and I lay that quality to her. She shot down Santa, the Easter Bunny and God with the same dispassionate coolness. My father might have been a happy man, in the support of his family. He was a musician by avocation and I can remember him playing and singing. Inked on the head of his banjo was the expression: "Oh, you kid!" and a pair of dice coming up seven. It's easy to imagine him in a porkpie hat, earmuffs and a coonskin coat, looking a little like Fred MacMurray, holding the same alto sax. On my birth certificate he gave his occupation as office manager of my grandfather's Franklin automobile agency.

Five years later Franklin collapsed and rolled off to join

the Reo, the Essex and the Star. The agency folded, and my grandfather was forced to sell his town house and retrench to his country home. My father was left looking, and he decided to look in other places. Not only might the grass be greener, but men's records didn't follow them about in those times and probably he yearned for the epiphany of a fresh start. This became a theme. There were many fresh starts.

We wandered up and down the West Coast for a number of years and lived in a dozen cities. Sometimes we stayed only a few weeks, sometimes a few months, occasionally a year, but, always, we picked up again and moved on. At first, times were desperate and my father struggled to support us selling shirts door-to-door, and I was put to selling razor blades. A sad shift. My mother took me out, selected my target, then hid herself while I went forward to try to squeeze a few nickels from my innocence. I wasn't, however, so innocent I didn't occasionally embezzle enough for a candy bar. It never occurred to me my mother must know of these small shortages and it is some measure of her distress that she never mentioned them.

My education was an apparent disaster. I entered and left so many different schools, frequently starting or stopping in the middle of the term, moving from districts with the traditional eight-grade system to those experimenting with junior high schools, and with such intricacies as Low Fourth and High Fifth that I was frequently uncertain what grade I should be in and was often expected to know things I had not yet had the chance to learn. I recall one teacher dismayed to discover I knew only the first few letters of the alphabet, and to this day there are lacunae in some of my basic skills.

I began to have trouble in school. My marks were disappointing. Twice I was left behind and, whenever possible, I was enrolled in summer sessions. This marked the beginning of my failure to understand and successfully cope with institutions. Today I would be recognized as a disadvantaged — and perhaps disturbed — child. Then they simply concluded I was slow.

All this came to a curious climax. I'm not sure why I was unable to retain basic information, but, except for an obsessive interest in history, I was a dim and uncertain student. It's been observed that most of what we learn only serves to limit us. The universal child is gradually squeezed into the sharply circumscribed and mortal adult, and in our early years we are required to integrate a number of arbitrary systems that have little value in the child's world beyond the approval reflected from the adults surrounding us. Puppies are trained with more tangible rewards.

My own rebellion began somewhere around $7 \times 9 =$ (and I still don't know unless I employ some circumnumerical device, such as taking 7×10 and then subtracting 7 from the product), but it didn't begin in tantrums — I simply slipped away. The rewards of enthusiastic cooperation were empty when placed beside the potent magic of my dreamworld. There I was, as all are, the mythic foundling, the infant Moses floating toward greatness in his cradle of reeds.

I was hiding there, playing dumb, protecting my common dreams from the acid tarnish of reality, and might have continued but for the Stanford-Binet. This IQ test was just coming into common use, bringing the awesome mystique which has hardly been questioned until the present day, and our whole school was required to take it. Our scores were privy, but mine was high enough to cause them to ask my father to come talk to my teacher, and she told him that the difference between my performance and my potential suggested I might be seriously disturbed. News to him.

The Freudian boom with its news of reversals and even more intricate psychic masquerades was beginning to sound in the intellectual centers, but my father, a basic if lapsed Presbyterian who was juggling his own mysterious failures, assumed I simply wasn't trying. And even with the considerable weight and great variety of water that has gone over the dam since, I can still sense the solid pull of his assumption. I wasn't trying.

Richard Feverel's father would have approved his solution. He ordered me to memorize the dictionary and to learn the multiplication tables up to such numerical monsters as $27 \times 29 =$, and in the evenings he gave me tests where I was required to spell and define words such as Antependium and Alsinaceous (I doubt his enthusiasm for this bizarre exercise lasted through the As) and for each mistake I was given one lash. Fortunately, he took it easy. I made many errors, often accumulating over fifty lashes, and he would have beaten me to death if he had laid on with any will. I note one thing for the light it might shed on this stubborn and convoluted kid. I was spanked a lot and whipped occasionally, and I could bear either if I knew how many times I was going to be hit. But if he wouldn't tell me what sentence he had in mind (and grasping the secret of my endurance, he learned not to) I became hysterical and tried to run away. How strange then this characteristic becomes (as if I were working some sly anterior detail into a melodrama) when you go on to consider how I spent many years in prison systems using the indeterminate sentence, where I seldom knew how long I would have to serve.

My sister, seven years younger, was born in these difficult times. When, years later, she applied for her birth certificate, she discovered a contraceptive had been used. She had somehow tricked it for her chance at life. I wonder, parenthetically, at the mind requiring such information collected on a certificate of birth.

I can imagine, if not quite remember, how unwelcome my mother's second pregnancy must have been. There was seldom enough to eat, and I can recall, in one town or another, watching through a restaurant window while my mother ate breakfast and I was doing without. She told my father, and he punished me for embarrassing her.

A few months after my sister Barbara was born, our mother left us and our father to live with another man, with whom she spent the rest of her life. I try to sense the fragrance of this new romance — she was only twenty-four — and I try to sense the anguish it must have cost her to leave her children, but nothing stirs in me, and I have often seen her as an angry Medea who murdered the normal lives we might have had. I try to believe I loved her because I think love is never lost, but as I sit here trying to feel her hand on me a certain weary and irreducible coldness tells me I didn't.

I did love my father. He was a fool, I suppose, and I think he had a mean streak, but he always tried to laugh and joke his way through our misfortunes. He lied. He cheated. He stole from those who trusted him. But his heart was often as light as his fingers. I try to remember what he was really like and I hear him repeating Émile Coué's litany of auto-suggestion: "Every day in every way I grow better and better." I know he was an optimist. How could someone less than an optimist sell used cars for his living? And at dinner I hear him say, "Pasa la plata de potatos," (pronouncing "potato" in the New England manner) and claim he was speaking Spanish. His French, which he also claimed, consisted of "Parlez-vous français in a Chevrolet coupe." And I consider the slender and motley store of French and Latin with which I sometimes patch my own conversation. He passed me his poor affectations and dowered me with his faults. I absorbed his ambitions. I recall him showing me the back of an envelope on which he had sketched his version of the Draw-This-Face ad, and I remember him struggling with the aptitude test offered by the Famous Writers' School. However, he could sometimes sell cars, and, after a few rough years, we began to live better. We had the first two-tone Buick in Portland, and when I was picked up in this splendid car it was like being called for by limousine. Typically, the Buick wasn't really ours, but belonged to the business, which soon failed and left my father running from criminal charges of embezzlement. He must have had some charm and some wit because people continued to trust him and in each new town he found work and did well for a while. A pattern I would also repeat. Sometimes when I despair of my insensitivity and my magpie's eye for the obvious, I remind myself I am the son of a used-car salesman and a failed confidence man.

The only continuity of our lives was that we had none. Always we continued to move. My father found a new wife, the daughter of Irish immigrants and a Catholic, who began to convert us. My father called her a "cat licker," but he looked away while she turned us over to the nuns. I spent several years in a Catholic boarding school, north of Seattle, and they proselytized, particularly in the Easter season, until they seemed to realize that, as much as I liked the attention, my religious intuitions were as numb as my heart and I had no intention of embracing a life of early morning mass.

I have mentioned religion twice — that room in my mansion wasn't empty, it was simply full of magic. I absorbed Hawthorne's retold Greek myths and the tales of Edgar Allan Poe, and, in the real world, only amusement parks held the power of enchantment. Particularly the tunnel rides. For years I could imagine no greater pleasure or excitement than to be alone and free in any amusement park. When I ran away, which I did often, this was the only destination I ever had.

I don't want to loiter over this, a lot of families were trashed in those years, but I should describe my first arrest. I began to steal seriously as a member of a small gang of boys. We backed into it, simply enough, by collecting milk and soda bottles to turn in for the deposits, but, after we had exhausted the vacant lots, empty fields, and town dumps, we began to sneak into garages where we sometimes found cases of quarts, worth a nickel each, and, having dared garages and survived, we next began to loot back porches, and, finally, breathlessly, we entered someone's kitchen. We took the milk bottles from the icebox and emptied them in the sink. They were worth three cents each. We began to take sweets as well, and once we found a vase full of pennies. Sometimes, as we tiptoed around the kitchen, the family would be sitting in the living room listening to the radio.

Clearly this was an exercise of real power over the remote adult world and I found it exciting. I liked it. I don't believe we're born with an instinctive sense of property, we're trained to this, and at a certain age most boys steal. Most also stop. I didn't. I've logged months of anxious introspection as to why I didn't, and it is only now, some forty years later, that I begin to see how stealing cast me in my first successful role. I was more driven, hence less fearful, than my friends, and this was sweet to a boy who had often been the butt. I would take reckless and large chances and when my buddies, figuring the odds, refused to follow, I mocked them as yellow and went on alone.

I loved secret and forbidden places, for it was here I would transcend my common life and rejoin my true identity. The boy standing transfixed in the strange kitchen — hearing first a chair shifting, brief footsteps, then the muffled flutter of sound as the radio is retuned — is not I. I could never be standing here where I so surely do not belong. This is someone quite different. This is the Black Cat.

Zounds, the Chief Inspector murmured in awe, How does he do it! This one is not human. He comes and goes like the wind and wears a thousand faces. Mark me well, we'll never catch him . . .

I was caught one night in a grocery store. I wasn't stealing for food, though I stuffed my pockets with candy, and of the fifty or sixty dollars in the till I took only a handful of change because that was as much money as I could imagine having. The owner of this store, weary of Depression burglaries, was sleeping in the storeroom and when I blundered on him he rose from his cot, an apparition in long white underwear, and nearly shot me with the .22 rifle he had been sleeping with. I was not the burglar he had expected, that dangerous sneak who wears a striped sweater, a golf cap and a domino, and he was, at first, more startled and frightened than I. While he called the police I took the candy and change from my pocket and hid everything behind some canned goods.

The police, finding nothing on me, toyed with the notion I was a cat's-paw for a gang of larger boys who had set me to make the entry and then open the door for them, a gang I was now protecting with my silence. The police explained how these boys were using me, corrupting me, and how I owed them nothing. It's been my experience the police usually see more in a situation than is actually there. Whether motivated by ambition or boredom, they become conditional paranoids who find conspiracy in everything. It seemed they had given me an out, a safe way off their hook, but if I had gone along with their fantasy I would finally have had to produce this gang. I believe I told them I had fallen asleep in the back of the market to wake up after it was closed. It was a story I used more than once. They smiled at it.

When they booked me into the detention home I gave a false name — Malcolm Brown — an alias my father had little difficulty penetrating, and when he came for me in the morning he told me the one thing always to remember whenever I got into trouble was to be sure to give my right name. A nice irony, coming from him, because we had been calling ourselves Branning for the last year, an alias about as clever as my own. He was ducking the embezzlement, and when he was caught, because he was trying the same old thing in a new place, we were once more uprooted. I could probably recall and trace all these moves. It hardly seems worth it. I was arrested again. In someone's home. This time I questioned the detectives about Sherlock Holmes, asking if they solved their cases as he had, and they told me Holmes worked under the influence of cocaine.

FALSE STARTS

I had taken some condoms and I still recall one detective's snickering allusion to this. He called them "white elephants" — an expression I have never heard again. I thought they were balloons. They fed me sandwiches and locked me in a tank, and I climbed the steam pipe to write my name, very large, on the ceiling. When the jailer saw this, he said, "You little shit, I ought to make you scrub that off."

High School

My FAMILY DISINTEGRATED when I was fourteen. My father, like myself, disappeared from time to time. I simply ran away; my father went off with other women, leaving my stepmother to manage with his children, and after a while she decided it was a poor show. There was little between her and me. I was a liar, a sneak, a thief, and, unlike my sister, I had been too old when she had come to us for her to touch me in any intimate way. Still, when my father was gone, we drew closer, and while she looked for work, I tried to help around the house.

This all happened one last time in San Jose. My father was gone for weeks and when we finally heard from him it was only by phone. He called to say he had been in an automobile accident. He was better, but still confined to the county hospital in Redding, California. He promised to send money for our fares and, a few days later, we were once again on a bus heading for a new life.

My stepmother allowed herself to be picked up on the bus by a man even I could tell wasn't much, and it's some measure of her desperation that she appeared to consider him. I can see the two of us, me and this drifter, neither quite able to meet the other's eye, standing side by side using the urinals at some rest stop while he asked me if I thought I'd like to have him for a father? I nodded without enthusiasm. Why should I care? None of these people cared for me. I no longer had any hope this kind of change could help me. It would only be more of the same.

My stepmother probably used this man to restore some of her confidence and liven a dull ride. He vanished, and we settled on the outskirts of Redding. My father came by occasionally, out of the hospital for an afternoon or an evening. *Yes, nothing much shows, but the doc thinks my spine may have been implicated, and he wants to observe me for a while longer. You know how careful doctors are.*

I didn't care. I had spent most of my life trying to avoid him. It was my sister who was being chopped up now, but I didn't understand that either. And my father was so careless — or uncaring — he allowed my stepmother to observe he always drove off in a direction opposite from where the hospital was, and soon she understood he was living on the other side of town with another woman. She gave up.

Her first gesture toward freedom was to take me down to the courthouse and turn me over to the county probation officer, a brisk, blunt, but essentially generous middle-aged woman. Her name was Edna Saygrover. My stepmother explained how she had been abandoned by my father, how she wanted to go to San Francisco where she felt she might have a better chance to find work, how she felt she could manage with my sister, but couldn't afford to feed me. She would send for me when she could.

Mrs. Saygrover had no reason to doubt this, but I had been palmed off, dumped on anyone who would put up with me, before, and I quietly accepted the end of one part of my life without quite understanding it was necessarily the beginning of another. When a child is left by his parents, first one, then the other, it can seldom occur to the kid that the fault might not be entirely his own. At that juncture, beyond getting along day to day, I had no vision of my future.

However, the rejection was mutual, and in a curious denouement I was given my own chance to underwrite it. Mrs. Saygrover placed me with people who were picking up some extra money in the orphan trade. They were decent, warm-hearted, and, at my request, the lady of the house drove me by my former home to see if I could find my puppy, who ran away a few days before the bomb fell.

As we drove by the house for the last time, my father was standing in the front yard. He was holding one of my sister's toys, staring at it, and beside him was the other woman, obviously in her last months of pregnancy. If I had said anything to the woman driving, she would have stopped, and maybe he would have taken me with him and my whole life would have been different. But I said nothing. I sat quietly, looking away, as we drove past.

That late summer afternoon in 1939 when my stepmother gave me to the State of California, County of Shasta, marks a major boundary. On the one hand, though it didn't become official until a year later, I was now a ward of the state, and had joined the slender ranks of the state-raised. But on the other hand, I began to warm and wake up, thawing from a frozen paralysis, a process which has never quite stopped. And when I entered Shasta Union High School as a freshman that first fall I discovered my second successful role. I became an artist.

I had some slight claim to it. My grandfather, on my father's side, had been an amateur taxidermist, ornithologist, lapidarian and flutist, while my mother's father was an amateur painter and frame maker. My mother herself turned out such *objets* as cameo silhouettes, block-printed bridge lamps and elaborate crepe-paper flowers, and my father had sketched the Draw-This-Face on the back of the envelope. And I drew, as children draw, racing cars speeding off in a plume of putt-putt-putts, and traced the women's underwear ads in the newspapers, leaving off the underwear.

I came to try the artist role by chance. I started high school in a serious frame of mind. In only four years, at eighteen, I had to be ready to support myself and I loaded my schedule with such solids as business math, Latin, general science and mechanical drawing. Too heavy. I decided to drop mechanical drawing, and my class counselor talked me into substituting something lighter — freehand drawing.

It took. I learned quickly, and mostly what I learned was that while it was inconceivable I could solicit love for my own poor and rejected person, I could openly court admiration for my work. Armored behind this slender pretext I became relatively aggressive in my pursuit of approval, and this led directly to my friendship with Howard Clark Ross.

Howard was unique in my experience. An art student, already an artist manqué at thirty, and a graduate of U.C., he was marking time in Redding teaching social living, a freshman requirement, while waiting for an appointment to teach art at the University of Maine. He was a genuine representative of the great world of Culture which everyone, in those green days, respected without question.

I was in his class and managed to engage his special interest by asking him to criticize my drawing. It's fair to say he fell in love with me. If I were to meet him today, his soft russet eyes and slight stoop, his hesitant but clever conversation, his graceful manners, his diffidence in the face of the obvious interest of the young female teachers, as well as his obsession with that inversion of taste we have come to call Camp, would all hint to me something of his nature. At the time I had no idea, and it wasn't until some years later that what I had observed and unconsciously recorded suddenly crystallized. Then I knew I had always understood.

Some underscore is necessary. Often I have found myself in real situations which appear to mimic dramatic cliché, and I have seldom found the common expectation, the language of newspaper accounts and police reports, to hold the truth. A friendship between a homosexual teacher and a lonely, uncertain kid could seemingly only go one way, with scandal and psychic damage looming in the wings, but while I stayed with Howard in his small apartment many times he never made the slightest move. He treated me as a friend, a person of value, and I'm grateful to him.

He was genuine. He gave me a real model of someone I might be like and even in the hard eye of retrospection he tests out with a very low level of bullshit. He encouraged my drawing, but he didn't slobber over it and he gave me good advice. He spoke to me as if I were an adult, which I surely wasn't, but everything went into the computer and eventually, when I was ready to hear, it played back. One example. I soon learned to play orphan, skimming the rich cream of automatic sympathy, but Howard refused me this. He said there might be many ways I would find the situation a blessing, and when he considered the dark pattern of antipathy and obligation marring his relations with his own family he thought an orphanage might well have proved a better deal. Who can know? But for me, he was dead on. I was much better off.

Edna Saygrover took me to live on the County Ranch, which was far less grim than the title implies. I lived, along with a shifting handful of other strays, thirty miles north of Redding with a failed farmer and his wife. They still kept a few cows, some pigs and chickens and in the summer there was a garden, but there were many hands to turn to chores, and the lady, used to cooking for harvest crews, fed us so well I still marvel at the meals I can remember.

We rode a bus back and forth to Redding to attend the district high school, and I began to have some success. I did well in subjects that engaged me, but ignored those that didn't, and I still refused to prepare myself and I seldom turned in my homework, even in courses I liked. Another example. Biology excited me. I was eager to know these things and I read not only the text assigned but several which were supplementary, but I didn't copy the material we were expected to keep in our notebook. I'd like to say I rejected the drudgery of rote, I didn't need to copy to learn, which was true enough, but I would be copping an attitude which never occurred to me. If somehow my notebook had recorded itself automatically, full of sections, sub-sections and neat drawings of mitosis, I would have gladly turned it in for the credit. As it was I had to tell the teacher, who liked me, I had no notebook and she looked at me with a pinched smile and said, "You used to be halfway decent."

She marked me *Incomplete*, and on those records, now a part of my prison file, it stands so today.

Having played the role of retard, now, sadly obedient to the law of compensation, I tried the part of prodigy. Some of my energy unblocked and I began to reproduce the literary and artistic clichés of the 1930s. Without any intuition of the interaction between the art and politics of those years just before the war, I produced proletarian works — paintings of hungry children and peasant soldiers dying in the trenches of World War I. Soldiers named Raoul, who died staring up at the Christmas star. I would have mimicked any style then in fashion. I did it well enough to see my stories printed in the school newspaper, and I also had some success with light verse. The snatches I can recall are a limping (occasionally a verse rocked home) version of "Casey at the Bat."

My paintings of the local landscapes were largely my own. I learned to *see* the countryside. The deep red earth, and a great range of greens, from the lightest tint not yet yellow to a dark poisoned (I thought of arsenic) blue-green, and the worn red brick, aging toward pink, with the corrugated metal roofs shimmering brilliant as mercury in the one-hundred-degree heat. The hills thatched with manzanita, whose glossy branches were the precise color marketed as Indian Red and whose leaves, the size and shape of silver dollars, were a dark green on one side and a light silvery green on the other and when the wind stirred the whole hillside seemed to dance with light.

The prodigy act played okay at school (every school has one) but at the orphan ranch I was written off as a freak and a bore. The couple who boarded us, much like the couple satirized by Grant Wood in American Gothic, except nowhere near so defensively uncertain, put me down in the devastating country expression "highfalutin'." They said I gave myself "tony airs." It was the same frontier mockery that caused every traveling charlatan to be called "Professor."

I still tried to work them, and I can recall the farmer looking at one of my portrait drawings. Here was a man who worked hard. He was up at four o'clock for the milking, at it most of the day and in bed by eight. After supper he sat for an hour, yawning with increasing frequency, before he went to bed. It was at this time I would hit him with the drawings. He always stared at them carefully and he always said, "There's something not quite right around the eyes."

At the end of my freshman year Howard drove off in a Model A Ford called Louisa and became the person who wrote me fond and chatty letters at greater and greater intervals. My sophomore year passed quietly if you can ignore the condition, which I largely did, that this was the winter the war started.

The following summer I went to work as a Civil Service fire fighter. When Edna Saygrover gave me formal permission to leave the ranch to take this job, she looked at me with a brisk pity (she dealt with many unfortunates) and said, "It doesn't look like your mother's going to send for you."

I nodded gravely, "No, I guess not."

"Well, you're almost grown-up now, aren't you?"

I was sixteen and I didn't feel grown-up — maturity is a clear threat to pseudo-precocity — but I nodded again and said, "Yes." She gave me money for a haircut, and wished me good luck.

The fire camp was much like the ranch, and the summer slipped by. We fought only one major fire, where we slept out for several days, and a boy from another camp was killed by a bear. The bear had been fleeing in blind panic and the boy had been unable to get out of its way. We saw the canvas-wrapped body at the mobile mess hall where we hiked in for a hot meal. It meant little to me. I couldn't be killed here.

We also saw a convict fire crew from one of the San Quentin conservation camps. They were given their own area where they were isolated and we were warned not to try to talk to them. They were high-spirited, eating hugely, shouting jokes and mock provocations among themselves. One young convict strutted and clowned continuously, audaciously making fun of everyone, and I found him disturbing. I saw all the convicts as incredible aliens, separated from us across the distance of a different species.

Just before the end of summer, a friend who had graduated in the spring and was now going off to college managed to pass me his job on the local newspaper. The friend, both bright and bitter, hated Redding for its small-town smugness (he'd probably been reading Sinclair Lewis), and I suspect he picked me to inherit simply because I wasn't an ordinary member of the community. The job was 80 percent office boy and 20 percent reporter, but, naturally, I thought only of being a reporter.

But I could hardly live on the thirty-five cents an hour I would earn before and after school and I appealed to Edna Saygrover. She worked out an arrangement where the county would guarantee my room and board, but I would supply all my other needs from my wages. This was more than I had hoped, and there was still more. The judge of the superior court (technically I was his ward) made private arrangements with his lodge to send me to college. I stress these things because playing orphan, even after all these years, is still a seductive habit, but I was obviously, just then, in an excellent position. And how could they, these county officials, imagine I would fail to grasp what they were able to offer? How could I imagine it? I had shown myself to be ambitious and eager to please, a decent boy, and I believed myself to be the person they thought I was.

But I had had little opportunity not to be. For two years I had functioned within a narrow schedule. I arrived on the bus minutes before first bell, and left as soon as school was out. The orphan ranch was isolated, miles from any settlement, as was the fire camp. Now, suddenly, I was free, living by myself, and I began to go wild.

Even when I had lived on the ranch, the orphan part had held a few sour lines. Style at school found its highest expression in filthy cords — they were never washed — but Edna Green, the ranch lady, wasn't going to send her "boys" out dirty, and she washed and bleached our cords until they were white. Clean cords were bad; bleached white they were hopeless and we might as well have gone to school in bib overalls. Other small graces were beyond us.

I was never able to buy the school yearbook. The yearbook was particularly important to me because it was here in these pages that my accomplishments were recorded. Like a miser fondling his stash, I would count the number of times I could expect my photo to appear, because this would be the concrete proof I was an outstanding student.

But on that last school day, when most were copying

canned sentiments, which still reflect real emotion, I was left out. And then I sensed it. The first year I hid in the toilet until the bus left. The second year someone handed me their album to hold while they ran an errand. When a girl I worked with on the school paper came by, thought it mine, and asked to sign it, I wasn't able to tell her it belonged to someone else. Beneath her picture she wrote: "To a really fine writer."

My slight success spoiled me. As long as I was living in quarantine on the ranch, thinking how I would suffer for my art as van Gogh had, I could go to school in my poor, pale cords, denim shirts and round-toed offish hightop shoes. This was clear masquerade, a malignant enchantment, which everyone knew was beyond my choice, and I could always dream of revealing my true self. *Gad, Sir, you're the Pimpernel!* That's right, and I can whistle the themes of six classical pieces, if you count Liszt's *Hungarian Rhapsody*, and recite most of "Ode on a Grecian Urn" and all of "Gunga Din."

My classmates described themselves by their clothes, and I was alert to this language. The boy who began the school year with twenty new sweaters — he rotated them through that first month and I could scarcely note when he began to duplicate — was telling us how favored he was, and we responded by making him one of the most popular boys in the class. We had regular features in the school paper which were simply descriptions of who had worn what where.

As long as I was clearly a ward of the court, living up in the hills, cut off from all social life, I was okay, but when I came down to live in town things changed swiftly. I was invited to parties (I wrote them up in the paper) where I socialized with Twentysweaters and kids like him. Here we competed openly for popularity and that meant girls.

We knew we weren't supposed to be obsessed with clothes. We were at war and already pants cuffs and jacket collars had been designed away and sent to fight, and for years we had been shown the example of the English princesses wearing uniforms which looked as if they were made from blankets. We knew beauty was only skin deep and the best thing to wear was a nice smile, but how much easier it would be to smile if I had several cashmere sweaters, a dark-blue jacket to wear with my gray slacks, and a pair of saddle shoes.

I spent the money I had earned during the summer, as well as the six or seven dollars a week, even with a padded time sheet, I earned at the newspaper, all on clothes, and, once again obedient to the law of compensation, it wasn't enough. After five or six weeks of living alone in Redding, I began to steal.

Burglary is an elemental act and the emotions it generates are profound. It's a treasure hunt as well as The Lady or the Tiger, a complete and separate experience outside whatever ordinary life you may be pretending to live. It's another way to reach the *now*.

When I stood on the rooftops, the secret spectator, looking over the scattered lights of Redding, the town lost its capacity to change or diminish me. Here I came to power. This I, here on this dangerous height, hugging himself with excitement, was not the same adolescent who walked these streets in the daylight. He was, I knew, both more and less.

I had marked a large laundry and cleaners on a dark and quiet side street, and circled it looking for a possible entry, very like a mouse looking to chew its way into a pantry. The back door and windows were bolted and barred and I had gained the roof by climbing a drainpipe. The skylight stood like a small triangular house on the graveled tarpaper, and the glass windows were open, raised like wings. They were open because the work below was often hot, and unbarred because Redding was a small quiet town and this business hadn't yet been hit so often that the investment in stronger security seemed worth the money.

I stretched out on the tarpaper to peer into the laundry below. The rising air was warm, heavy with soap and cleaning fluid, and the tarpaper still retained some of the sun's heat. The building was the equivalent of a two-story structure and I was looking down at a drop of approximately twenty feet. Below on the floor I could make out some hampers that appeared to be full, and if I could hit one it would break my fall, but the risk seemed too great. I slid back down the drainpipe and took a clothesline from a nearby backyard. As a rope it was weathered and frayed, but I planned to double it.

I climbed back to the roof and fastened the rope to a ventilation pipe. There's an odd moment when you first lower yourself. You are leading with your most tender parts and several large questions are not yet answered. Will the rope hold? Is there anyone below? Someone who has been asleep, but is now awake and aiming up at you? Your legs tingle, your stomach is hollow, and the emptiness draws at you.

I remember slipping down, tightening and relaxing my grip to slow my descent without burning my palms. I landed in a large hamper, full of damp sheets, and lay still a moment listening intently. It's never completely quiet. All around the concrete, the metal, the wood *tings* and *clicks* as the building slowly cools. It's possible to hear the electricity humming in the wires, and gross machines, thermostatically controlled, *whir* suddenly to life.

As soon as I climbed out of the hamper, even before I was certain no one was in here with me, I had to take a crap. My bowels were electric with it. I rushed to the back door to unbar it so I would have some way out, and then found the toilet, a windowless box, and shit with great excitement. I closed the door and turned on the light. My hands were black from the tarpaper and still red from rope burn. I felt secure here.

When I was finished, I looked the place over carefully to make sure I was alone. Then I went and opened the cash register. There was nothing there but the "bank" left to make change the next morning, between fifteen and twenty dollars, but to me this was a lot of money, and, more, the racks were loaded with clothes. It's impossible to pick clothes in the dark, but if something seemed to fit, I took it back into the toilet where I could use the light. Most things turned out to be the kind of suits sixty-year-old men were then wearing to church, but I found a few things, including a nice gabardine topcoat which fit me perfectly.

My life has handed me a number of ironies and I have collected them for the instruction they contain. From time to time I intend to pass them on to you, and here is the first.

A regular part of my job at the newspaper was to stop by

the police station and the sheriff's office to collect the crime news, and I was routinely given the details of my own burglaries, which I subsequently wrote up for the paper. At first it puzzled me to find my victims exaggerated the amounts I had stolen, but I soon came to realize these false claims were made with an eye to the insurance settlement. They, too, made money on the burglaries.

I bought the saddle shoes, which I found impossible to keep clean, and began to appear at school dances wearing a suit and tie. I asked a popular girl out and, amazing, she accepted, and after the dance I tried to screw her on her parents' front lawn. Kissing was okay, but when I made the critical move to her tit, she pushed me away easily (too easily, I decided in my many recapitulations) and asked, "What if I have a baby?" I knew some of the answers to this familiar question, but none seemed adequate. I walked her to the door and just before she went in, she kissed me hard, then drew back to ask, "Would you really have gone the whole hog?" Her expression held the kind of eagerness I have learned to associate with the exchange of particularly succulent gossip. I nodded and drew her close so she could feel exactly how ready I was. We kissed deeply and I thought: *this is it.* And wondered what I would do now that I was finally here. But it was too much for both of us, and again she slipped from my arms, which opened automatically to release her, and paused a moment in the door to blow me a kiss from the tips of her fingers. How often I replayed this to all the endings implicit, and how seldom I remembered, as now, how it really happened.

These were sweet days and I can, sometimes for long moments, sense my other and distant self just as if I were still

there. I can feel myself standing on the stage of the high
school auditorium, saying, with what I imagine to be an
English accent, "You rang, sir?" We are practicing the Junior Play. Naturally, my emergent ego urged me to hope for
the lead, but a lively and outgoing friend has won this prize.
Our vehicle is *Charlie's Aunt*, and I've been pieced off with
the part of Brassett, the butler, who neither "swells a scene"
nor "mounts a progress," and is the perfect vice for my vanity because playing Brassett proves I will do anything to be
on this magic stage. I clown a lot, tease the girls and miss my
cues.

Or I am walking with my English teacher, a tall, pale man
with a blue chin, who is married to an unsuccessful writer of
children's books. We are walking down Eureka Street into
the center of town, across the bridge that spans the Sacramento River. He is reading a poem I have written for the
girl who refused me on the lawn, trying not to laugh at my
near-comic misspellings. He explains why I must learn to
spell. It's hard to read my work for sense because the mis-
spelled words are like tiny rocks in a bowl of mush, distract-
ing to the pleasure of the eater. I listen. This is an adult
talking.

The river below the bridge is a deep warm tan. Sometimes I cut school with one friend or another to swim along
its banks. I remember a day spent there with Yardstick
Rhodes just before he enlisted. Yardstick was named for the
size of his tool and he liked to organize circle jerks so he
could display this prize. My own tool was not far in his
shadow and a third friend said between us we could measure more cock than the entire football team. Yardstick carried his burden with aggressive pride, but my own made me
uneasy. I tried to imagine putting it into a girl without

splitting her wide open, and it was in wild variance with my image of myself as the new Shelley, the reincarnate Keats, as was my avid interest in the small books Yardstick passed around, where Popeye is hosing Olive Oil (Slurp! Slurp!) with a priapismic majesty which makes even Yardstick look as if he's hung like Cupid, and Wimpey, in nothing but polka-dot shorts and the eternal derby, waits his turn.

Across the bridge I part from my English teacher, he to his home where his heavyset wife is writing sonnets on the redemptive quality of Jesus' love, and I walk on into the center of town to the newspaper office. The editor, his assistant and I make the entire staff. Both men wear green Celluloid visors and the assistant editor shelters a bad eye behind a tinted lens. They are both typing as I enter and the AP wire hammers in a corner, while out in the composing room the linos click and pound and the old web press cranks out the evening paper. My desk is stacked with things I am supposed to file, and my clerical neglect is beginning to spill onto the floor. I'm not unaware that the editor is beginning to give me a few long looks. I'm not the find I appeared to be. But I still can't cope with the filing. All this will come back to me. The time will come when just such dull clerical chores will be the precise labor by which I might win my freedom.

But today I sit hunting and pecking a poem I have written during study hour, and the two editors, who sit facing each other, begin to discuss *Time* magazine, criticizing its snotty tone and strained neologisms. On the AP wire the war is coming to us from all over the world.

Some nights I spend playing pool at the Pastime Pool Hall. I have a wobbly bridge and a slow eye. And other nights I sit with my high school clique in Eaton's Pharmacy drinking chocolate cokes. And walking home I sometimes slip out of this life to pull another burglary. I am content. But I also know this cannot go on.

I was failing in school. My job was almost lost. And once or twice a month I was placing myself in great danger. I didn't think — I was counting the number of times my picture would appear in the yearbook — but I was nevertheless hearing a definite, if wordless, warning. The solution I hit on was not so dumb. I decided to join the Navy.

I was seventeen. No one any longer expected the war to end quickly and at eighteen I was not only eligible for the draft, but would lose the option of choosing the branch of the service in which I wished to fight. No one wanted to be a dogface. The uniforms looked shitty and nice girls didn't want to go out with soldiers. The Navy seemed like a safe, clean place to wait until I grew older and could handle myself.

I announced my decision to my favorite teacher, the one who was directing us in *Charlie's Aunt*, and she looked at me in consternation. "But why go before you have to?"

"I'm not getting anyplace. You see how I do in school."

She replied firmly, "I know what you could do."

"But I don't. I need to be somewhere where I am made to do things."

She looked at me oddly. "What a strange thing for a boy your age to say."

This comment registered only in my vanity.

I quit the newspaper moments before I was due to be fired. When the editor called me aside, I sensed what was coming and immediately told him I had decided to join the Navy. He looked at me with what I recognize now as a decent, but distant pity. "You won't find the Navy very flexible. You can't act there as you have here."

I nodded brightly. "I know. I want that."

He didn't comment on my maturity.

A lot of us were going into the service and my enlistment caused no particular stir. It was expected we would enlist. It was our duty. And when a dance was organized in our honor I was quick enough to pretend it was duty that had called me. The art class drew pleasant caricatures of all of us who were leaving, and we were framed in paper laurels and posted around the gym walls. The dance was attended by Twentysweaters, already home on leave, and I recall the figure he cut with his high-laced paratrooper's boots and his overseas cap neatly folded under the shoulder strap of his uniform shirt. When I danced, finally a little bolder, I held the girls tightly, feeling their young tits against my chest, and because they could imagine I was going away to die, they too were touched with a bittersweet urgency, and I received several lingering and frankly sexual kisses.

I traveled with two other recruits on the night train to San Francisco for induction. I read all night in the dimly lighted coach and when my eyes were examined the next morning my usual 20-20 had dropped to 20-40 in one eye and 20-60 in the other. This wasn't quite enough to disqualify me, but when the Navy doctors looked in my mouth my military career was finished. I had a malocclusion so severe they feared the shock of Naval bombardment might cause me to bite the roof of my mouth.

When I returned to Redding it was as an apparition. I had marched off to war and there was no way to return three days later as the same person who had left. Edna Saygrover put me up in a downtown hotel and supplied me with meal tickets, but while she didn't say so, I knew this couldn't last. I thought of going to work as a logger, a romantic notion even then, but I made no move toward this employment.

I went back to school, but the emblematic photos in the yearbook were sharply diminished. My job was finished and the social invitations dried up. I had vacated my presidency of the art league and with it my seat on the student council. I even tried to reclaim my role as Brassett, which now seemed valuable, but the teacher-director told me tactfully, but with honest point, this wouldn't be fair to the boy who had stepped into the part, who was, anyway, doing a better job. I waited for something to happen.

It was raining the night it ended and I walked the two blocks from my hotel to the pool hall wearing the gabardine topcoat I had stolen on my first burglary. When it was my turn to play, I dumped the coat on a bench where it was discovered by the boy who owned it. He was also a student, a remote senior, a gifted athlete, and a natural antagonist to the crowd I usually ran with. He held up the coat to ask the room at large who had left it there.

My opponent said casually, "Isn't that yours?"

The senior turned to stare at me and I was immediately aware of his distaste. For a moment I wondered if I could deny the coat, but in my confusion it didn't seem possible. From this moment on I had no confidence in my ability to change what was obviously happening.

"It's mine," I said, and sealed it.

He showed me a cigarette burn on the hem I had never noticed, to prove the coat was his, and told everyone who was listening the coat had been lost in a burglary of the Nelson Cleaners.

I invented a lie. I had bought the coat from a man in the lobby of the hotel where I was staying, but if it was his, and the burn proved it, then he should have it back and I would take the loss.

But this wasn't enough. He followed the rules and he insisted we report this to the police. Four or five boys had gathered to listen and there seemed no way out of it. The station was two blocks away and we ran there through the rain. I entered not expecting to come out again.

The night officer took my statement and appeared to believe what I told him. I didn't invent anyone, but described a real character I had talked to in the lobby a few nights before. He'd been drunk, so drunk he would have talked to anyone, and when he found I was going to high school, he dredged up a few tatters of his own education to try to impress me with his knowledge of Latin. I described this in minute detail, inventing only the sale of the coat which I claimed I had paid five dollars for.

The night officer dismissed us and the senior said Good Night coldly and went home wearing his own coat. I went back to the hotel. My suitcases were full of stolen clothes, some still in the laundry wrappers. I considered getting rid of them. I considered leaving town, heading north into the woods and the logging camps. Right then. Instead I went to sleep.

The Preston School
of Industry

▰▰▰▰▰▰▰▰▰▰▰▰▰▰▰▰▰▰▰▰▰▰▰▰▰▰▰▰

THE SHERIFF WOKE ME in the morning. He thought my story of a man who sat in hotel lobbies and spoke Latin was ridiculous, and while this man, however unlikely, was real enough, when the sheriff turned out my suitcases the point became academic. He had his burglar.

I sat on the side of the bed in my skivvies and watched. A young deputy stood significantly next to the door. The sheriff looked at me with obvious distaste and said, "Now let's have the *real* story."

The real story didn't please him. The police, as I remarked before, have their own fantasies and the sheriff apparently hadn't put hands on a genuine, confessing burglar in some time because he was able to convince himself I was responsible for every crime committed in the county during the past several years.

I could have admitted everything he asked of me, copped

out and cleaned his books, but I wouldn't and we had several tense and angry sessions. First there in the hotel room, later in the county jail. He was a young outdoorsman, the other model I had of myself which made me yearn for the logging camps and the clean life I imagined there, but he saw nothing of this in me and he made no effort to disguise his contempt. He clearly thought me an affected fool.

He told me, never quite losing his air of moral superiority, I was going to reform school anyway and I wouldn't do a day longer for twenty burglaries than I would for ten. I can't explain my resistance satisfactorily; it was tied into my distorted, but still acute, moral sense. Mostly I was just what the sheriff thought me to be, but I owned a few narrow areas of strength, and to violate them, to compromise in this, would have been to lose any hope I still had of a normal life. Also, it wasn't lost on me that the merchants I had robbed had actually gained through exaggerated claims on their insurance companies, and now this honorable sheriff was willing to charge me with crimes I was almost certain he knew I hadn't committed. I didn't use these considerations to excuse myself — my bitter and lonely misery was the loudest thing I heard — but I did note them.

The paper I had so recently worked for bannered the headline: POET BURGLAR CAUGHT! And Edna Saygrover came to see me, angry and hurt, but I was also aware I had made her look like a fool. What was I to her? A house plant she had tended which now had gray mold. A chipmunk she had been feeding from her kitchen window now turned rabid. She accused me of having been a gentleman by day and a thief by night. I didn't understand then how I seemed to mimic the Jekyll-Hyde myth, with its implications of the potential for violence and anarchy boiling in each of us, but I did know there weren't two sides to my nature. Despite my fantasies of another self, other than the boy I appeared to be, I knew that what I had done, all I had done, I had done entirely.

I was soon forced to see myself in even harsher light — how others now saw me. The mother of one of my schoolmates called the sheriff to ask him if I had stolen her son's jacket from his locker at school. At the news of my arrest she had assumed I was the logical thief. The sheriff questioned me routinely and he too assumed I'd taken the jacket. A thief was a thief. They saw no difference between the darings raids I made on business establishments and this petty theft. The difference to me was the distinction between a spy and a paid informer, but, finally, what is that difference to those betrayed? Unfortunately the clarity of these harsh realizations faded after a few days.

Of my friends at school, only one came to see me, and I can't guess what motivated her, beyond simple kindness, because we didn't know each other that well. She was in a wheelchair with a broken leg, and her boyfriend helped her into the sheriff's office and stood silently behind her chair while we talked. We had shared journalism class and we talked about the novel she was writing, and I told her about the novel I was going to write, and the sheriff, busy with his papers, smiled occasionally with amused contempt. Neither of us mentioned the trouble I was in. We talked as if I would be back in school soon.

The judge I came to face was the same judge who had arranged for my education and he too was angry and disappointed. I asked him if I could join the Army rather than go to reform school and he replied tightly that the Army had no use for young men like myself. If I couldn't be depended on to simply go to school and stay out of trouble how could I be depended upon to obey orders and fight when I was told? He committed me to the Preston School of Industry, a commitment which held the power to bind me until I turned twenty-one.

After a brief advance into the warmth and light, I now began a long retreat. It happened, it happened to me, but I feel I also allowed it to happen. Beyond the obvious truth that it was I who committed the burglaries, did them in the euphoric assumption I couldn't be caught, I also had the subtle but definite sense I had stood aside and allowed my arrest. In some almost hidden hall of my own house I stood before myself as polar opposites, both accuser and accused, and the boy who claimed his raincoat was only an agent of my own destiny. Despite my posturing, I was a bright boy, and from this distant vantage it's difficult to see how I thought I could wear stolen clothes in a town as small as Redding. Perhaps I wanted them so badly I could dismiss what should have been obvious. But darker and more complex, perhaps my father was the authority who had not loved me and I could not and would not abandon this bitter disappointment until I could draw to myself an authority — the sheriff! — who would love me.

We cannot lose ourselves in this psychological labyrinth, where we can wander circuitously forever and catch no more of the Minotaur than his smell, but I would not be true to my charge here, to see this all clearly in your eyes, if I didn't suggest there was more to my arrest than its description in the records of the Shasta County Sheriff's Office. However, neither will truth be served by glossing the simple fact that I did break into stores and take things that weren't mine.

That cold clear morning in the last days of 1943 when the sheriff drove me south to Preston I had no idea I was about to enter another world where the few virtues I did own would be routinely dismissed as defects. The extent to which I had succeeded in Redding, compared to the absolute failure I had known before, led me to believe I could do well in any situation. My path led up, I could think of nothing grander than fame and fortune, and what I was involved with here was a slight misstep.

All I carried from my life in Redding was the Oxford Book of English Verse, a gift from Howard (his translation of the *Canterbury Tales* was neatly printed between the lines of the text) and folded into this book was a short story I had started in the county jail, naturally the story of my fall, and a list of rules I had formulated to govern my conduct. I remember only two. Don't speak to the other inmates. Learn to play either the violin or the piano.

The sheriff didn't warn me I could have worn a dress and it would have been no less damaging and dangerous than to enter Preston carrying a list of rules and a book of poetry. Preston already had more than enough rules, and, as in any institution, not all of them were official.

These journeys into the unknown are mostly beyond ordinary experience, though a trip to the dentist gives a hint of the flavor, and, though they seem to start slowly, they wind up with dismaying swiftness. One moment we were leaving Redding, on familiar roads, with over a hundred miles to drive and the next we turned a corner and through some trees I saw a turreted red-brick tower which could only be Preston. They have a look, these institutions, even the modern ones. However they are formed, that form takes on some aura of their function, and Preston was neither modern, nor designed to be reassuring to liberal sensitivities. It looked grim.

I was handed over as briskly, with a similar exchange of initialed papers, as a jeep returned to a moter pool. The sheriff returned his copy of the commitment to the inside pocket of his forest-green jacket and looked down at me. "Good luck," he said briefly and walked off. He was "Last Touch" with all my former life and it wrenched me to see him walking down the wide front steps. I turned immediately to the civil servant behind the admissions desk. He said, "You'll have to leave that book here."

A man came to take me down and dress me in. All officials were simply The Man. This one was a short, heavyset, middle-aged Indian who wore a gray cowboy hat and khakis. He signaled me with one finger, and started off without looking back, certain I had no choice but to follow. We walked down a long hallway floored with brown linoleum, buffed until it glistened, and through the office doors I saw other inmates, clerks at typewriters, dressed in olive-drab uniforms. One of them asked me, "Where you from, man?"

When I said, "Redding," he lost interest.

I was the only boy to come in from Redding in some years and my gang had but one member. I followed the Indian around an ell of the corridor and out a door. The ad building was taller than any other. In addition it was built on the hill so I caught a sweep of the school — stucco buildings, dry lawns, a few bare trees — before we descended a flight of steep stone steps down to the detail ground, a cement apron caged in cyclone fencing. A few boys, wearing red brassards, loitered around the detail shack. They were nothing but errand boys, but they were also the toughest and fastest cadets in the school. They affected a knowing look and moved with serpentine glide, and their attitude of hard coolness was already something like the persona which would come together in the life-style of the hipster.

As I walked by, obediently following the Indian, they looked me over without a flicker of interest. Unlike the office boy who had asked where I was from, they knew just by looking at the way I moved, the way I was dressed, I couldn't possibly know anyone or anything they would be interested in hearing about.

The Indian led me to the distribution center where he outfitted me from a large pile of Army surplus left over from World War I. He threw me a tunic, pants, underwear, shoes and socks. The tunic was the style worn by the doughboy, with the collar to which Nehru later gave his name, and I quickly learned this tunic was considered hopelessly square and worn only by fish and rums. The officer's style with the lapels was favored, and if the Indian had accidentally thrown me one of these someone would have taken it away from me before the day was over because, as I also learned, I was both a fish and a rum.

The Indian watched me dress. He was the school's tracking expert, who led the search parties after those escapees, few in number, who managed to get off the grounds before they were caught by other inmates. The hightop shoes I was lacing were notched on the inside of the heel to leave a distinctive footprint, one it hardly took an expert to identify.

I smiled up at the Indian, letting him see how I was cheerful and cooperative, and said, "I think I'll like it here."

Nothing large happened in his solid face, but the small shift of his expression from impassive calm to a flicker of distant and weary humor dismayed me. At that moment I began to realize the kind of trouble I was now in.

Preston was organized like the military into companies, and these companies were used to divide the races as well as to divide the more troublesome boys from the comparatively docile. We marched everywhere, and were always on "Silence." We could speak freely only on our training programs, our jobs, or during a brief period of Grounds after lunch. There was a command provided in the rulebook that did permit us to talk at other times, but this command was never given. We were easier to manage on Silence. This same rulebook told us we were all to be addressed as Cadet, and that we should never attempt to address a freeman unless we were at attention. Each company was in the charge of a freeman, but the actual work of management was performed by cadet officers, a captain and two lieutenants, and, usually, a striker or batboy, who ran errands for the Man, cleaned the state locker, where the cadet officers took their ease, and performed sexual services for the hornier officers and their friends. Usually these boys were fruits, but not always. Sometimes they were punks. The hard definition between a fruit and a punk was that the fruit wanted to where the punk didn't. A definition that pretty much held through most of my institutional experience, and I spent a number of years denying the one while trying to avoid the other.

The Indian took me back to detail, where we were told off to our jobs each morning, where we reassembled each evening, and handed me over to the detail officer, whom we called Mister T, a massive, severe old man, who dressed in huge double-breasted gray suits. Mister T took one look at me, and sent me across detail to the barber shop where I left most of my hair. We wore the same haircut as Marine boots, a chopped-off stubble which began two inches above the ears. Everyone tried to avoid the hook to the barber shop, at least long enough to grow the beginning of a duck-ass, and Mister T was constantly alert for the slightest hint of this degenerate style. We called it the Hollywood because it was modeled after Johnny Weissmuller's Tarzan, and I can remember cadets who sat all evening in the company room brushing their freshly chopped hair in the Hollywood against the day they'd be free to grow it back. This haircut was a long time breaking into the mainstream. It was still ten years before Elvis would come to wear it, and even then it was the very thing most people held against him.

I spent the rest of the afternoon sitting on a wooden bench beside the detail shack. At one point, a Mexican, with the face of an Aztec and the red armband of a detail boy, stopped to ask me, "Hey, rum, did you bring in a book of poems?"

"Yeah," I said uncertainly.

He smiled and walked away.

Before the afternoon was over, Mister T handed me my book. The short story was still in it, but the list of rules I had formulated were missing. Some kind heart in the ad building had tried to mitigate my offense, but the story circulated anyway and I heard about it. Preston wasn't the place to come if you had been trying to look and act like Percy Shelley, but I don't mean to create a false suspense. I was scared shitless most of the time I spent there, but except for a Sunday or two, and a few fights that didn't amount to much, I was never savaged, nor screwed. I walked a very narrow line, but there was always a victim around just a little softer than I seemed to be. I am, I know, in their debt. Because someone was going to get it and if it hadn't been them it might well have been me.

When the companies formed at the end of the day, I was assigned to I Company, the orientation unit, and marched off at the end of their ranks. This was a common sight — new fish, awkward in uniforms that seldom fit, oversized overseas caps perched in the middle of their heads, stumbling along in the rear of I Company, trying to keep in step, their fear and confusion obvious to all. It was a rare fish able to carry this off with any style, a big duke from L.A. or Frisco, who knew he was bad and ready to get it on with anyone who pushed him. These boys seemed to learn to march immediately, or they were so confident they simply strolled along hoping someone wouldn't like it so they could start building their reps.

I had spent a semester in R.O.T.C., and I was able to march a little, but it wasn't an activity I'd ever enjoyed, and, to this day, I have trouble telling my left from my right without taking a moment to remember which hand I write with. I always marched with my fingers crossed on my left hand for instant reference, which is, I suppose, slightly more sophisticated than carrying a small rock, or stuffing hay in one shoe and straw in the other.

We were marched by the cadet officers, who were not selected for leadership potential, but for their ability to fight and their willingness to savage anyone who stepped out of line. They were rewarded with shorter sentences, extra privileges and the freedom to brutalize the weaker boys. They made it possible to control a thousand boys with a very small official staff, and doubtless this saved a lot in salaries. When I remember these cadet officers I think of the slave drivers in period movies, who, hearing the command to move it out, immediately begin to curse and whip the slaves. If this common scene represented any reality the drivers would have whipped themselves into exhaustion and beaten most of the slaves to death before they could have traveled a mile. The cadet officers showed the same galvanic enthusiasm for their work and they were constantly shouting and strutting about to prove what a wonderful job they were doing.

It was as corrupt and cynical a system as I have ever encountered and it was practiced entirely without honor. If a boy showed any pride or distinction of bearing he was routinely beaten to humble him and train him to at least act as if he were frightened, and usually the first he knew he was in a fight was when someone copped a Sunday. The cadet officer slipped up behind, usually while you were somewhere at attention, and hit you as hard as he could just to insure his advantage. If one officer couldn't whip you, the others jumped on, and, if all this failed, the Man carried a lead-tipped cane. Sometimes, if one gave a good account, you might be promoted to cadet officer yourself, if you wanted to play that game. And I did see officers demoted while their successful opponents were brevetted on the spot. The Man didn't care who was shouting and who was listening, who was beating or who got beaten as long as it didn't get on him.

We marched to the company and I was assigned a position at one of the dayroom tables. This was my spot, this and no other. When we broke ranks in the dayroom we immediately went to our assigned seats and maintained silence. We were then released, a table at a time, to wash up and use the bathroom. Even here we were never left alone. A cadet officer leaned in the doorway and shouted "Shake it up!" Over and over like the cry of some large bird. "Shake it up! Shake it up!" We were allowed only six sheets of single-ply toilet paper. I learned to use it, and use it gingerly, two sheets at a time.

Afterward we were marched to the mess hall, and commanded in by single file, and we continued to stand on line to eat cafeteria style. We passed by a steam table to pick up our food on a metal tray and then carried it to our seats. If you were cool and confident you carried your tray negligently with one hand, not caring if you slopped a little on the tile floor, but if you were not cool, if you were anxious, stiff and frightened, you carried your tray with both hands. You were judged by your style in these matters.

Absolute silence was the rule here. Other places some whispering might be overlooked (we talked from the side of our mouth without moving our lips, like caricatures of old-time convicts) but in the mess hall even such whispering was a certain beef. There's always some way, however, and a large number of cadets took the trouble to learn the deaf-and-dumb alphabet, formed on the fingers of one hand, and rapped over dinner without making a sound.

The food wasn't bad, but if there was anything choice like a hamburger, a piece of pie or cake, the cadet officers were apt to demand tribute from the nearby rums, and there were boys in the company who almost never ate their own dessert unless it was something of as little value as tapioca pudding. I waited in dread for the time when some officer would signal me to hand over my dessert. Not that I would lose the cake, but that I would have to surrender it in front of the entire company, and have it finally demonstrated I was a coward, or that I would refuse and get the shit stomped out of me.

However, when it finally did happen and the captain pointed at my cake, chocolate with vanilla icing, and indicated his own tray, I looked down and shook my head. I heard someone snicker and looked up to see one of the captain's toadies make a stomping gesture and the captain smiled, and I spent the rest of the evening in an agony of dread. But I didn't get stomped. I gained the impression the captain didn't think it worth his trouble, like adjusting his step to crush a cockroach, but I don't know. We're all raised on the same myths — maybe he respected my stand. I met him some years later in Quentin, where he was just another con like myself, and he had become a mellow dude who played tenor sax.

After dinner, we marched back to the company to take our seats in the dayroom. Now we were released, a table at a time, to select a magazine. These magazines were donated by the free people, and passed from company to company and were often years old and falling apart. The first table released had the best choice, and the last table frequently found nothing but a few loose pages and some of the journals published by religious organizations. But the magazines were not rotated often and the tables were released in different patterns so eventually one read everything and often more than once.

We sat reading in silence for several hours, then they ran another latrine line and we were ready to march into the dorm to bed. This was the worst time. Now transgressions marked during the day would be settled. They hit when we were most vulnerable. First we were formed into ranks of two down the center corridor of the dayroom. For some reason they caused us to close ranks tightly, until we were touching, and when one was hit three might fall. This was where I was popped the first night. We were required to stand absolutely still, and I remember adjusting the set of my neck. Almost instantly my head exploded from behind and someone said, "Keep still, rum." I never moved again.

We were marched into the dorm and into a dressing room, where we took off our clothes, hung them up, and took down our nightgowns. We didn't yet put these on. We were required to come out of the dressing room one at a time. The Man, the cadet officers and the batboy all stood around the door. As we came out, we snapped our nightgowns to show there was nothing concealed in it, and then raised our hands, our gown hooked on one thumb, strained to our tiptoes and opened our mouths as wide as we could. Nothing hidden anywhere. We marched out like this, arms high, and if we were marked for it that night we first knew it when we were hit in the stomach.

One night I saw a small cadet fight an officer twice his size, getting up again and again, until he lay on the brown linoleum sobbing with exhaustion, still trying to get up to fight some more, and it was clear the officer had had the best of it simply because he was larger. If his smaller opponent had had even ten more pounds his greater spirit and skill would have put the other boy where he was now lying. But I saw no acknowledgment of this apparent truth. I was one of those children who were told that after the Battle of Little Bighorn the Indians had honored Custer for his bravery. Now I saw the officer smile and walk off, satisfied to have won however he could, simply so he wouldn't lose his few privileges, and, even worse, the smaller boy was a bully and a loudmouth who would have behaved the same.

I went to my bunk that first night, my ears still ringing, crawled between the rough sheets, covered my head, and there in the darkness began to cry. This was my one safe place. Here, until I slept, I could be without fear.

However, in a few weeks I was lying there trying to figure some way to jerk off without being caught. The nightman prowled the aisles in slippers watching our covers for any suspicious agitation, while we squeezed ourselves like a farmer milks a cow to come with hardly a sigh.

The "Industrial" in the school's title was justified by the trade-training programs, and while, as usual, a number of cadets were assigned to work as servants, cleaning and cooking, some of us were trained. It's hard to imagine the program was very effective because the far more elaborate programs I was to encounter later in San Quentin were not effective, but if you had a burning desire to learn, the information was there. And I believe it's important to remember that schools like this, if any remain, were originally seen as reform measures. Not many years before I was in Preston it had been a common practice to lease boys to contractors, who overworked and underfed them and grew prosperous on their enforced labor, and this, too, was a reform if you considered it was still better than being strung up on a gibbet.

I was assigned to the print shop and it was a good assignment. I liked the work and I liked the tradesman in charge. I learned composition and typography, and how to operate a linotype. I took pleasure in typographical design and, after a few months, became the editor of the school newspaper, a job no one else really wanted, and this precarious prominence brought mostly negative notice, such as the graffito

I discovered above the company urinal: *The editor of the Preston Review is a punk*.

I didn't exactly abandon my Percy persona — I knew there was another world out there where this part might still play — but my function was to accumulate attention against the hope some of it might be love, and to the extent that function must influence form I began to tinker with my image. Something of Percy began to give way to Pretty Boy Floyd.

The most serious and persistent charge leveled against institutions like Preston is that they function as crime schools where young naive boys are tutored in criminal techniques by the more experienced. I want to discuss this, but first let me explain why I have taken the decision not to describe Preston in any greater detail than necessary to suggest its effect on me. It's hard to imagine schools like Preston, seen as the accumulation of its grossest abuses, exist anymore, and while I'm sure some do, I don't know where they are, and it's difficult to imagine my abstract indignation could light the way to any practical reform. I am, in addition, ambivalent toward reform, on the general principle that my experience has shown each answered question to propose two more that remain unanswered.

The "crime school" charge, however, bears some examination. It isn't, I think, information one gets here. I heard many accounts of how to hotwire cars to bypass the ignition so they could be stolen without the key, but this technique never became clear to me, and I've never used it. And today anyone with the price of a movie ticket or access to a television can see the most elaborate criminal techniques worked out in accurate detail and presented as entertainment.

What one learns to want in a "crime school" is the respect of one's peers. This is the danger. The naive will be drawn into competing for status in a system of values that honors and glorifies antisocial behavior. We're none of us total strangers to the desire to simplify the restraints under which we live, and the yearning for freedom is never entirely unmixed with the yearning to set aside for oneself those finical considerations that bind the lives of others. This unraveling process goes swiftly in an atmosphere like Preston, where the ideal of criminal freedom was the common ambition, and there is one more aspect, even more insidious: it was all talk, all mouth, all part of the façade we supported as we ignored the most obvious condition of our lives — we were caught. The baddest duke on the hill had been caught and when the Man said, "Get to bed," he went to bed.

This has all been to try to explain why, though I got by in Preston and learned a few things of value, not the least of which was endurance, I escaped. When I had less than three months left to serve I ran away.

I didn't go alone. I made friends with three other boys, marginal types like myself, and we clung together like those orphans in a storm, making our world in this other world, where we still had hope of acceptance. We were neither the most powerful boys in the school nor the most hopeless, and we took comfort from the latter while trying to ignore the former. We called ourselves The Four Wolves and kept between us a scrapbook filled with cheesecake — Betty Grable, Rita Hayworth and dozens of other girls whose names are now forgotten. Of the four of us I was most marginal, most rumlike, closest in style to the dingalings and fruiters who marched alone in O Company, and occasionally the boy who was most like the ruling elite, my polar opposite in the narrow spectrum spanned by The Wolves, talked against me.

I ran into trouble by seeming to support some Mexican boys. We were issued red bandannas, and three or four Chicanos and myself took to wearing them flowing from our tunic pockets, and the cadet officers opposed this breach of the uniform code mostly, as I learned, because those who flew these flags were Chokes. The Chokes and I went to argue this in front of the Man and naturally lost because our argument was that it "made us feel good."

A few days later I was outside the mess hall with the other Wolves trying to score some food, and several detail boys who were loafing a few feet away called me over. I went, pleased to be noticed. One, lounging against the hood of a truck, asked me if I had anything to scarf, and while I shook my head the other moved around to the side and hit me.

The one who had spoken, still lounging, said, "You fuckin Choke lover, you better learn who your own people are."

I looked at the boy who had hit me. He was smiling. "Get out of here," he said.

I walked back to the other Wolves, holding my face, and Ray, the one in the pack I was closest to, asked me what had happened.

"Those guys popped me," I said.

Ray shook his head. "Poor Braly, you're always getting it."

But Jerry, who was afraid I was making them all look like punks, just stared at me, and I knew he would have more to say when I wasn't around. So I was clinging even to this slender chance to imagine I belonged, and it's not so surprising that when Ray, who had the most time left to serve, wanted to run away, it was I, who had the least time left, who went with him.

We earned release from Preston by acquiring credits. In many ways this was the best system I served under because you could make an additional effort from which you knew you would benefit. If you joined the choir in Preston this activity awarded you a hundred credits a month. No one speculated as to whether you were really interested in singing about Jesus or interested in the hundred credits, and even if you were only interested in winning an earlier release you still had to do the singing and maybe something would rub off. But in Quentin, joining the choir won you nothing but the suspicion you were trying to create a positive impression, and if you actually were won to religion and wanted to sing, you did so at some disadvantage. We'll return to these considerations.

Meanwhile, in some respects, the credit system was violently abused. Any cadet who caught another cadet in the process of an escape was awarded five hundred credits. In effect this meant the detail boys and the cadet officers were licensed to catch the rest of us and whenever someone broke ranks to run for it they were after him like hounds after a rabbit. One cadet captain caught five escapees, reducing his sentence by half, and the suspicion circulated he had forced the boys to run by promising to stomp them every night until they did.

To be surrounded day and night by a thousand vigilant and eager jailers made escape difficult, but Ray found a hole in the system. Most successful escapes are made through these holes, some flaw of design or routine tantamount to an open door no one has noticed, and the serious escape artist becomes a student of the fixed habits of his keepers.

Early one morning while everyone was washing up and using the bathroom we slipped out the front door with a possible five-minute lead. Three of us were supposed to go. Jerry was already at work in the mess hall, but Eddie had signed on with Ray and me. At the last moment Eddie punked out. Ray was ahead, already through the door, and I turned to see Eddie holding back. His expression was an odd mixture of fear and defiance. He was angry at us for having forced him to this foolish test of courage which he was now failing. It was a test I could not afford to fail. I turned and ran after Ray.

It was late spring, already quite light, and we raced around the back of the company building, up a short, steep hill and into the cover of the underbrush. We were barely hidden when we heard excited shouting behind us, and, moments later, the large escape horn began to bellow. Over my shoulder I caught a brief glimpse of the ad building tower. We had no plan for our former friend to give away and his fear only filled us with a glad sense of our own daring.

We ran until exhausted, threw ourselves down to rest, hearts pounding, breath ragged, and were up and off again almost immediately. Ray set the pace and I struggled along behind. The direction we had picked at random lay through country once ravaged by hydraulic mining. This was the center of the gold rush and in the final years of that adventure the gold had been torn from the earth with large jets of water, leaving scars which now, almost a hundred years later, were still raw. We moved through this ruined land-scape silently and as quickly as we could push ourselves.

We came to a ranch and found some clothes in the empty bunkhouse. We were able to change our uniform shirts and throw away our notched shoes. My stolen boots didn't fit and soon I was limping. Months later my toenails were still turning purple. By evening we came to a secondary road and, following it, we found a one-room schoolhouse and broke into it. We ate from the supplies provided for hot lunches — vegetable soup, cocoa and bread — and rested for a while.

We walked most of the night and while we continued to see farmhouses, none of them showed any signs of life. No dogs barked, and as dawn began to show there were no lights in the windows. We were baffled, and grew even more puzzled as daylight came and we passed still more quiet houses. Finally, we grew bold enough to enter one and an unusual calender on the wall told us these were the homes of the Japanese who had been arrested and taken away to con-centration camps. For a moment we remembered the great war smoldering on the other side of the world.

Late in the afternoon of this second day we came to a major highway, and decided, since we had walked farther and faster than anyone would expect, it was safe to hitch-hike. We got a ride easily and by evening were in Vallejo, over a hundred miles away. Later, checking a map, I found we had walked over thirty miles.

We spent the night at a construction project, homes for defense workers, sleeping on the floor of a half-finished house, and, in the morning, the carpenters kicked us out and told us to stay away or they'd call the police. We were tired, sore, dirty and hungry, but in good spirits. We spent the day resting in a small park and as soon as it was dark went hunting for something to steal.

We were in an alley looking for an entry into a store when the throat of this cul-de-sac suddenly filled with light and a car was drifting down on us. I was in the middle of the alley, Ray was nearer the edge, and when the spotlight bloomed, he ran a few feet, jumped a fence and was gone. I was left standing.

The car was manned by two plainclothes cops answering a call to investigate a report of prowlers in a nearby candy factory. When Ray bolted they knew they had found something. My bad luck was some other prowler's fortune and I'm sure he went home that night unaware of the freak chance that had left him free and put me back in jail.

Bad luck? Surely, but it's typical of the kind of situation fugitives walk into with monotonous regularity. As loosely woven as our communities seem to be, there are still dozens of ways we continue to check on strangers, and a penniless and wanted man who has no ID can't weather the most superficial examination. If I hadn't been caught that night, it would have been the next, or the next, though I was still years from realizing this. Simple logic suggests bad luck can turn, but those who persist in believing this go broke every day in Las Vegas.

Once again I was arrested, taken to jail, and urged to confess crimes I hadn't committed. I continued to say I was new in town, just taking a walk, but every time we went around the circle we came back to the question of why, if we were innocent, had my partner bolted. They knew, they smell it when you're wrong. Cops spend a working lifetime examining patterns of behavior, and no one legitimate, not even a young kid, goes drifting from town to town with absolutely nothing in his pocket. I made up a story — a family in the north, a job in Frisco — but they didn't buy it and locked me up to see what developed.

Ray was caught a few weeks later pulling an armed robbery, and because he was nineteen he was tried, convicted and sent to San Quentin. When I was back in Preston, I had a letter from him. He said Q wasn't that bad. You didn't have to work unless you wanted, and you could wear your hair long. He enclosed a photo, taken in what looked like a garden. His hair was combed into the Hollywood, and he wore a pressed white shirt. He said he was being trained as a cook and baker and that he hoped to be paroled into the Merchant Marine. He never wrote again.

I was identified and returned to Preston to start my time again. I had lost all my credits and for the first three months I was confined to G Company, the disciplinary unit. Here we were locked up alone and for me this was an improvement. I had the use of the library. We ordered from a catalogue, and the books came to us like precious goods, in chests. I read Hugo, Dumas, Dickens, not so much for their merit but for the length at which they wrote. I could order but five books a month, and I wanted to make sure they would last.

In fair weather we were kept busy at make-work. We tore down one small hill only to rebuild it fifty feet away. Then we tore down the second hill and rebuilt the first. We worked near the ruin of the brick kiln, where earlier cadets had labored to make money for the Man, and somewhere out there in the Army disciplinary barracks other boys, not much older, were digging holes and filling them again. Fortunately, it rained a lot during my three months and I spent the time in my cell where I used it to write and draw.

I began to submit poems to the *National Scholastic* magazine, a periodical limited to high school students, and they printed one or two. These poems were automatically entered in their annual contest, judged, at that time, by an awesome panel of three-name writers. I won a certificate and a five dollar cash award.

Months later, after I had been released from G Company and reassigned to the print shop, my certificate and check arrived. I spent the five dollars on candy and a pair of plastic sunglasses. I shared the candy around. It was gone in an hour, and one of the cadet officers borrowed the sunglasses and never returned them. However, I still have the certificate. And the poem.

Before I once again "go home" from Preston, I have an observation to make. When I was returned from G Company into the regular life of the school I was assigned to A Company. A Company was also a disciplinary unit, reserved for hardheads and stone fuck-ups. We were not affected during the day on our jobs or school assignments, but company life itself was designed to be stern.

We went everywhere at quick-step march, double the usual tempo. We were never given At Ease. We stood everywhere at rigid attention. We maintained constant silence. For the slightest infraction we "stood the line." While other cadets were trying to read magazines they had already looked at several times, or training their hair, or trying to sneak a smoke, the fuck-ups were standing in front of the Man's desk with their arms held out parallel to the floor.

Try this for fifteen minutes. We stood for hours. If you slumped, or let your arms down, you were popped.

I liked A Company. I liked knowing it was as bad as it could get and nothing was being held back to be awarded if you were quiet and cooperative. Sucking the Man's ass bought you nothing. We were denied the hope of small mitigations and I discovered I didn't care. I realize something of what I gained by managing to stand firm with the hard asses, and this was dear to the rum, the suspect punk, but I also learned there were things more important than the hope of comfort.

Preston, viewed as a machine, was designed to confine, control, and, finally waste our youthful energies, since they couldn't be channeled into useful social priorities such as fighting the war, and the cadet who spent his days trying to score an extra piece of cake was only playing into their game. I learned this, only to forget it again.

I walked off another nine months. Then they returned half my lost credits and paroled me in late 1944. I had decided not to go back to Redding. It wasn't my home either. When someone asked me if I thought I'd like to live in Sacramento, I said, "Sure."

Sacramento and Austin, Nevada

===

THERE WAS PLENTY of work during the war and I was paroled to a job in a defense plant. Parole was casual and the condition that I was a parolee had little influence on my life over the next few months. The P.O. drove me to Sacramento, checked me into the Y, advised me to keep my nose clean, and left. I never saw him again.

Whenever I was confined I always used the common phrase "Going home" to describe my release, but I seldom had a home to go to, and this was never more true than this first time. I don't remember if I was happy to be free, and how free was I, alone and confused in this strange city? But I was excited by the opportunities I sensed around me. Everywhere I looked I saw things I wanted to paint. I hoped for recognition. I yearned for fame. And I wanted a girl. Most of all I wanted a girl. In my imagination I saw her constantly, but saw her as a vision, a vision that evolved over the years of confinement. There in Sacramento she was the Lily Maid, great-eyed and slender in a flowing dress, appearing from the forest, standing at the edge of a moon-lit lake; she was cool, quiet, and though she smiled a great deal she seldom laughed, and the point I never rationalized was how I was going to fuck this ideal creature. In the reality I would have been grateful for any girl who wasn't clearly deformed.

I went to work on the swing shift in a plant where air-plane engines were being rebuilt. My job was to examine the valves of the pistons for cracks and set aside those that were damaged to be rebored. Most defense contracts were cost-plus and despite repeated appeals to our patriotism, there was no real pressure to move the work ahead. I was lazy, but didn't know how to loaf successfully, and when there were no valves to examine I became uneasy. I looked to my foreman for some authority to worry about, but he was drifting like the rest. It's absurd, but I saw this as a moral problem. I didn't like to work, it was all too slow and not exciting enough, and I was afraid for what this might imply for my future. I didn't understand how I could be lazy when I didn't want to be and I believed the problem to be surgical. I knew I had had an operation as a child, I carry the scar, where they had snipped a piece of my thyroid. I tremble to imagine what blind arrogance caused those doctors to cut into my throat, and I was sure they had sliced off too much of this energy-producing gland, condemning me to a life of laziness. I resented them and I resented my foreman for not making me work. I didn't envy the pilots who would fly the planes powered by the engines we had rebuilt.

In my free time I sat in the lobby of the Y and wondered how I could make friends. I had always been on the outside and I had no way to imagine how much I was missing, but I knew my life was empty. The friends who might have helped me I had never met.

I sat in the lobby and picked out poetry on a typewriter that operated with a coin slot, ten cents for half an hour, or I sketched the old men who sat there reading the free newspapers and magazines. I was a pleasant-looking boy and often others mistook my shyness for aloofness. I didn't know how to get started.

One result of growing up in a nation without a fixed tradition was that I had tended to raise myself on how-to manuals — how to make friends, money, even love — which list certain absolute standards for success, but the penalty for failing to grasp or properly apply these standards would be rejection. I would fail. At a time in my life when the most ordinary encounter glistened with mystery, I hesitated for fear my responses would be inappropriate, and the other, any other, who probably felt much the same, would think me foolish. Perhaps we never should have abandoned tribal traditions, since we seem to yearn for such certainties, and that at least would spare us the contradictory pronouncements of this legion of self-styled experts.

This is, in any event, all part of the crisis of authority, and that is the crunch I was feeling, without, however, understanding it at all. I floundered on at the defense plant for a month and then quit abruptly to take a job as a display man in a large downtown furniture store. I was little more than a glorified furniture mover, but, as before at the newspaper, I imagined I was an interior decorator. My evenings were now free and I signed up for several adult education courses — short story writing and oil painting. I was taken up by two women I met in these classes. They were, I imagine now, in their early thirties, married, and not particularly happy. They took my ambitions seriously, as I took theirs, and they encouraged me to join the Sacramento Art League, a group of largely amateur painters. If I had known how to press the point I might have had an adventure with one or both of them.

The more aggressive of the two invited me to dinner, and I spent an incredible half hour trying to make conversation with her husband, who worked as an engineer. He asked me how far I had gone in school, and I lied and told him I had studied non-degree at U.C. Then he asked me what non-degree was? I had heard someone use the expression, but had only the slenderest notion as to what it actually meant. Then he asked me why I wasn't in the service, and, having just finished *The Magic Mountain*, I told him I had tuberculosis. His mouth writhed.

The meal was dreadful. The husband picked at his plate, I picked at mine, and she talked with nervous brightness. She had told me if she couldn't have some interest outside her home she would kill herself. The closest she came to inviting intimacy was to tell me my eyes were Byronesque. I didn't question how she was in a position to make this comparison.

I was called for the draft. When I appeared for examination, my folder was tagged. From this point on in life my folder was always tagged. At the conclusion of the physical exam, where the overbite which had prevented my escape into the Navy was not even noticed, I was shunted to an Army psych, who immediately signaled his failure to understand his own trade by asking me if I thought I'd go AWOL.

I looked vague and told him I never knew what I was going to do. He grunted significantly and handed me a list of books to read (what could have been on that list?) and told me I'd be called back in six months. I left thinking I had fooled him, but actually I had told the simple truth. I didn't know what I was going to do.

If I could have been patient I might have made a life for myself (I felt this was always true) but I was bursting with urgency and the world was filled with things I wanted. Clothes again. I was crazy about clothes and soon my obsession led me back to the rooftops. Whenever I began to steal it was always with the rationale I wouldn't make the mistakes I had made before. Sacramento was a large town, I reasoned seriously, and it would take the wildest of coincidences to present me with someone on the day I happened to be wearing the clothes I had stolen from him. It didn't occur to me there were literally thousands of ways I could get caught. I was sustained by the confidence nothing truly awful could happen to me.

Still I recall a moment late one night in the back alleys of Sacramento, when I was half through a long climb to the roof of a particular building, resting briefly before going on, and the same quiet voice, which had formerly urged me to join the Navy, whispered: *If you keep this up you'll find yourself in San Quentin.*

I realized a moment of despair because I knew I had just told myself the obvious truth. Perhaps the mad have similar moments of such clarity, when the hard truth of their life is briefly apparent, and then they, as I did, drown again in fantasy.

I soon had a large stolen wardrobe. I was eighteen and

I used to go out at night wearing a dark blue suit and a gray homberg, wearing this uniform of the banker and the diplomat like Balzac strutting the streets of Paris unsuccessfully disguised as an aristocrat. But the new clothes still didn't help me with girls; the few I did meet weren't interested.

I began to wander again, drifting like Huck on the existential river, but I never worried as to where the current was taking me, nor did I entertain moral considerations along the way. I gave no thought to my father or mother. I doubt if I would have walked ten blocks to see either one of them, and if I had it would have only been to have them admire my dark blue suit and my homberg. I felt differently about my sister. I haven't conveyed it in these pages, but we were close as children, and I always hoped to see her again.

I fell away from my job at the furniture store. I was always late — five minutes, ten minutes, half an hour — and the shame I felt for this, rather than prompting me to be on time, had the contrary effect. I didn't go in at all. I invented illnesses no one believed, and still there was no danger I might be fired because help was so hard to get. So, in a sense, I judged and fired myself.

I left the Y to take a room in a boardinghouse where I could use the basement as a studio, and I began to paint. Even here I was so impatient I tried to frame my work before it was dry. Everything had to be immediate. Incidentally, no one, except my two hungry ladies, was particularly impressed with my painting. The oil painting teacher at the night school told me tactfully the writing teacher thought I had talent.

The writing teacher told me the same thing. He was a friendly man who affected a tough, cynical newspaperman's style, and talked knowingly of "slicks" and "pulps." He encouraged me warmly, but I didn't particularly like writing. It was hard work. I painted in a dreamy reverie, almost without conscious thought, which, doubtless, is why I didn't paint that well, but writing had to be chiseled out word by word, which required constant and intelligent attention.

I wrote some poetry, but my apprehension of this art was almost magical. I wasn't trying to write poetry as much as I was straining to write the *one* poem, more charm than poem, through which I would explain everything to myself.

Sometimes several lines would lock in my head and I would find myself silently repeating them over and over, a monk throwing a prayer wheel, as if these few words contained a spell potent enough to lift me above myself. At this time they were:

> *She walks in beauty, like the night*
> *of cloudless climes and starry skies;*

I didn't select these lines, they were simply those that stuck to me, and I didn't repeat them deliberately. They sounded in my head, below the level of my thoughts. This was another of my charms:

> *The Assyrian came down like the wolf on the fold,*
> *And his cohorts were gleaming in purple and gold;*

I must have been repeating this last the afternoon I ran into Bob Grossbart. Bob was a boy I had known slightly in Preston and hadn't particularly liked. I had thought him a braggart who talked constantly of the girls he had screwed and since I had screwed nothing but my hand he left me with little to say. Of course, I lied to him and everyone else, repeating the experiences of others as my own. His parole date had been close to mine and he, too, was being sent to Sacramento, even though he had been raised in Los Angeles, or Hollywood, a distinction he was always careful to make, and he suggested we might get together on the bricks in Sacramento. I shrugged and said, "Sure," without much enthusiasm. I never considered the possibility seriously.

Then one afternoon I ran into him on K Street and found, to my surprise, I was glad to see him. I had been routinely lying about my past, inventing stories, and here, at least, was someone who knew and didn't care where I had been.

For his part, Bob was out of work, going broke, drifting himself, while waiting for some direction to clarify. I appeared to him as that direction. I don't think he was stealing on his own. He wasn't very brave, nor particularly bright, but he had a certain confidence and he was shrewd. I allowed him to get close enough to realize I was in action — I had clothes, some money, and, doubtless, I dropped a few hints — and he hung on until I agreed to take him as my crime partner. I neither wanted nor needed a crime partner — whatever I was working through out there in the night was essentially a solitary matter — but neither was I a loner. I needed the company. And maybe it's fair to say I was trapped in an adventure, and the adventure itself demanded a partner. Legend and history are full of such pairings, shipmates forever, but however it was, my effectiveness as a burglar was diminished, not augmented, by this instant accomplice, and my gains were cut in half.

Still, Bob had something to trade with. He was good-looking and confident with girls. Since he was from Hollywood he thought Sacramento small spuds, and he was able to use lines he had learned years before in the south. It seemed fair to have him blunder along behind me on burglaries if I could blunder along behind him on his sexual adventures, and it worked out for a while. I helped him steal enough to live on and he helped me get laid.

I was, as noted, an idealist, but I wasn't a fool and I didn't think all my encounters would take place by moonlight to the accompaniment of strings. The poet who went around dreaming of the girl who "walked in beauty" was powerfully balanced by the tummy-belly man who would, literally, screw a chicken.

The men were off fighting and the girls were around. The men left were, as the song of the day had it, either too young or too old, and 4F, the terminal draft classification, was wryly spelled out as Fat, Flabby, Forty and Four-eyed, and in this atmosphere Bob was a catch and even I was acceptable. Though we were both eighteen, Bob looked a few years older and I looked a few years younger, which made him the natural leader except when we were actually on a job, and he soon proved the value of his appearance by buying a quart of Southern Comfort and taking it and me out to see some girls who lived alone on the edge of town. Not only had I never been laid, I also had never been drunk.

The girls were possibly a year or two older but, of course, in the special differential between the sexes, a decade beyond us, and one had a husband serving in Alaska, and the other was writing to several servicemen, planning to marry whichever one survived. They took our appearance calmly, without excitement, but immediately brought out ice and glasses so we could go to work on the bottle. Beth, the married one, was pleasant and quick-tongued, and she was naturally the one Bob went after, leaving me with Alice who had buck teeth and a good start on a pot belly. I remember nothing of what was said. I know I sat like a stump and was almost immediately drunk. Soon we all were.

Bob drew Beth into another room, and I thought how easy it would be if I had her, because she seemed nice, and Alice just sipped her drink and looked around at the ceiling, at the floor, at the ceramic plaques on the wall. In the other room, a bedroom I imagined, Beth began to moan, and Alice said, "There she goes again."

"What do you mean?" I asked.

She looked at me a moment and said, "Nothing."

Bob came in wearing only his shorts. He smiled and said, "Don't you know how to get started?" And he tipped Alice's head back, kissed her, and began to fondle her tit. When he finished the kiss, he slipped off her sweater and unfastened her bra. Her secret skin was very white. She smiled at Bob.

"Come on," he said, and led her by the hand. I followed into another bedroom, where Bob invited her to lie down. She did, and for a moment I thought he was going to fuck her too, but he winked at me and left.

Alice looked up, finally meeting my eyes, and said, "Well, come on, honey."

I stripped quickly and got in bed with her and fumbled off her skirt and pants. I tried to remember all I had been told. I kissed her a few times and rubbed her cunt and then heaved myself on her and somehow found the mark.

"Oh, honey, it hurts," she said.

I came very quickly, but went on pumping, thinking soon the tingling would stop and the real feeling begin. I felt her close around me in a drawing spasm, and then she said, "I'm dead. How about you?"

I knew what she meant, and I said, "Yes," and pulled out of her. She went into the toilet and was there about fifteen minutes. When she came back Bob was with her, and he pulled the blankets to reveal the hard-on I had been nursing against her return, and said, "Look what's waiting for you."

She came back into the bed and we began to kiss, and now I thought it would really begin, but she freed herself, turned her back on me, and went to sleep. I lay there absorbing the quality of my failure. Here she was a girl who fucked servicemen, almost a whore, as I saw such matters then, who took whatever came along, and I had hurt her. If I had hurt this girl how could I ever hope to love the Lily Maid? I stared at her back and wondered if she could be asleep already. I tried to plan some way to get her to accept me again, but I couldn't find the courage. How could I ask her to suffer pain against the hope of my pleasure? Suddenly the Southern Comfort turned in my stomach and I was violently sick. I found the bathroom and knelt on the worn linoleum to vomit into the toilet.

Bob talked me into going to Hollywood. He was homesick, wanted to see old friends, and he said we could make much better scores there. We were picking up a hundred here, two hundred there, and he said he knew places, rich private homes, where we could hope to find thousands. Then we could buy a car and we would be completely free.

We rode down on a Greyhound, took a room in a cheap hotel, and I followed Bob around while he tried to find the pieces of his former life. They were scattered. Girls had moved or married or were engaged to boys in the service. Before long I realized Bob hadn't been as popular as he had led me to imagine. He, like myself, had no one and this drew us closer for a while.

One bright afternoon we took the trolley down Santa Monica Boulevard to Ocean Beach and Venice to visit the amusement parks. This was the first time I was less than entranced, the first time I saw these enchanted places as shabbier than I remembered them. I registered the unconscious contempt of the barkers for the Alvins and the Clydes who strolled the midway, fat silly sheep who thought it fun to be fleeced, and I remember standing in the abysmal darkness of a mystery maze where someone had just taken a leak. But I still loved the roller coaster, the magic machine, where we were pulled up and up until the whole pier spread out beneath us, and we saw the deep blue of the Pacific where it met the sky, and I experienced a curious ringing calm, a trembling sense of perilous beauty, so swiftly passing, as the car reached the top of the first big dip and hurled us screaming into the darkness.

Bob's big score was the home of a wealthy Hollywood producer, a former friend of Bob's mother, and all we had to do was walk in and fill our pockets. We approached at night, and the house was dark except for a single low-watt bulb burning in the hallway.

We entered, without difficulty, through a bedroom window, and it was soon apparent this man's fortunes had diminished. There was nothing to eat in the kitchen except a few cans of tomato soup, and a thorough search turned up little of value except some jewelry and an old watch.

An easel, set up in the middle of the living room, held a half-finished oil painting of a sailing vessel, and in the bale of a portable typewriter there was the beginning of a short story. A large vase was stuffed with paintbrushes — I had never seen so many — and the paint was still wet on a large palette, filling the room with the soft, fat smell of linseed.

"Let's get out of here," I told Bob.

"No, let's wait until he comes home. I know he has money."

"There's nothing to eat in the kitchen."

"He eats out. Believe me, he's loaded. And he's old. He can't do anything."

"Okay," I said.

"He'll recognize me," Bob said. "You'll have to do it."

We had two guns we had taken in burglaries, a .38 police positive and a .32 automatic, certainly enough fire power to quiet one old man. Bob hid in the kitchen, and I was left to spring the ambush. I didn't like it, but this was my part of our partnership. From the beginning I had taken the risks.

After an hour or so, I heard a car pull to the curb. The door slammed. Then there were footsteps on the walk and I heard the car pulling away. When I heard a key at the lock I stepped forward holding my gun where it could be seen, and when the door opened, I said, "Come in and don't make any noise."

He was old as Bob had promised, and he was also small. He collapsed immediately, dropping a sixpack of beer he had been carrying to clutch his chest with both hands. "Please," he whispered.

His obvious distress quieted my own fear and confusion, and I immediately put away the gun to help him into the living room and settle him on the couch. He was terrified, but it was clear he was far more frightened of what might be happening in his chest than he was of me. He asked for water.

I ran into the kitchen. Bob was there holding his gun. "He's sick," I whispered.

"Did you get the money?"

"No."

I took him a glass of water and helped him drink it. He thanked me by touching me lightly on the arm. He had recovered enough to look at me and I smiled, hoping to relieve his fear, but it didn't seem to help.

"I have nothing," he said.

"May I see?"

He turned out his pockets. He had thirty-five cents and the beer he had been carrying. "I'm broke," he said. "You have to believe me. A friend just took me to dinner so I could eat."

"Pete," I called to Bob using the name we'd agreed on, "he says he's broke."

Bob called back, deepening his voice in an effort to disguise it, "Ask him where the money's hidden."

The man was trembling again, now that he knew there was still another man in his house. "Please, there's no money, I've been sick, I haven't worked for months." Almost absently he unstrapped his wristwatch and held it out to me. "Please go. I won't call the police. I won't even report this."

I took the wristwatch and the thirty-five cents. I touched his brushes and said, "I paint myself."

"Yes, yes, please leave. I have to call my doctor."

I went out through the back door, signaling Bob on the way, and we both ran a few blocks to put some distance behind us. When we slowed down, I handed the loot to Bob.

"That's what he had. That and a bad heart." Bob, for once, had nothing to say.

The next night we managed to steal a little over a hundred dollars from a garden supply store and nursery, and I insisted we return to Sacramento where I still had my room and most of my things. I considered breaking the partnership, but I didn't know how. It was like a bad marriage. I wasn't happy with Bob, but I couldn't let go because I was afraid of being alone. And doubtless he felt much the same.

Back in Sacramento we picked up a third partner. He was standing in a doorway on K Street as we passed by and we recognized him as still another Preston graduate. Neither Bob nor I had known him, but that meant little here. I remembered he had worked in the butcher shop, and once, during a free period in the gym where he had been stretched on a bench trying to sleep, I had hit him in the head with a basketball. Now, a year later, we fell on each other like lost relatives.

Norman Kelly, who called himself Mick, had been raised in Oakland, and liked to characterize himself as a hard-drinking, hard-fighting, hard-fucking Irishman, who could, as he often told it, chugalug a fifth of Old Bushmill as if it were tap water. I now imagine some weak and garrulous uncle, drinking and talking out the fierce drama of The Trouble until Mick was soaked in the romance of his difficult blood. He, too, was eighteen, cut off, alone, his father dead, his mother gone bad, and all he had was his butchering tools and his fake dream of Irish courage. He was a pale, slender, near-handsome boy with grass-green eyes and a nervous stammer, except when he was excited or angry. Then his voice thickened into a distinct brogue.

So Mick stepped out of the doorway on K street and joined us. He was more intelligent and more decisive than Bob and of some real use on a burglary. We made several decent scores, and now that we were flush, we rented a car and drove back to Preston to show off.

It was an odd thing to do, but the strangeness was lost on me at the time. Preston was the only past we shared and it was the only past we could all return to. We wandered around the school more or less freely, sporting our new clothes, and inmates who wouldn't have even spoken to us when we were cadets ourselves, pressed around to bum cigarettes, anxious to claim they knew us.

Back in Sacramento, we decided to go east. I can't remember why we picked this direction. We just wanted to go. We were on what the police call a "run," and the "run" provided its own internal sense and energy. We would steal a car and finance the trip with robberies. We also tried to be clever.

We knew a car stolen off the streets could be hot moments after we had taken it. So we broke into a garage on Saturday night and took a car from the working floor. They wouldn't work Sunday, and it would be Monday morning before the car could be missed. If we drove all night Saturday night, all day Sunday and Sunday night, by Monday morning we would be outside the circle covered in a tri-state alarm. We knew — and we never questioned the expertise we had picked up in Preston — that the local and tri-state alarm would hold for seven days, and only then would the car go out on a nationwide APB.

Bob, who was our automotive expert — his last job was in an auto parts house — guaranteed the car, a green Ford sedan, and we drove to my place and loaded my things, my paints, my typewriter, my writing, my stolen clothes, into the trunk. Neither Mick nor Bob had anything they thought worth bringing.

We drove to Lake Tahoe, and immediately our plan began to break down. Only Bob could drive. So when he announced he was tired and afraid he'd fall asleep at the wheel there was no way to go on. We were miles from Sacramento and it was impossible to worry. We took a motel room, slept soundly and started off again in the morning. By nine o'clock it was hot.

On impulse we decided to rob a roadside grocery. Mick and I went in, while Bob waited at the wheel with the motor running. We found the interior dark and small. Streamers of curled yellow flypaper, embossed with dead flies, hung from the ceiling, and baskets of potatoes, squash and onions sat about on the worn linoleum. A large middle-aged woman was behind the counter, holding her face into the air stream of a small electric fan.

"What can I do for you boys?" she asked.

Mick took the .38 from under his shirt. "You can be after givin' me your money."

I had never heard Mick's Irish act, and I smiled automatically, thinking it an odd time to be playing around. The woman's eyes flared, and, ignoring the gun as if it didn't exist, she began to throw cans from the shelf behind her, while she abused us in a harsh strident voice, calling us dirty little draft dodgers, and lazy scum. A huge old man pushed through a curtain leading from a back room and began to come over the counter after us.

I ran without thought, through the door and into the car. Mick was a step behind me. Bob stuttered the Ford into gear and pulled out. As we drove off the woman and her husband came running out. She threw a last can after us. I heard it thud solidly against the trunk.

"What the fuck happened?" Bob asked.

Mick had just discovered a cut on his cheek. "Jesus," he said, staring at the blood on his fingertips.

"They went crazy," I told Bob. "We would have had to kill them."

"Let's go back. I will kill them," Mick said.

I stared at Mick with some anxiety and Bob reacted by driving even faster.

"We should shoot up the store," Mick said. "Teach them a lesson they won't be after forgetting."

"They've probably already called the cops," I said quickly.

Bob pushed the Ford still faster. Now I was glad he was chickenshit. His anxiety to get far away was the mirror of my own. We were rolling out into the desert, into Nevada, at ninety mph, traveling straight into the sun. Mick wiped his cheek with his handkerchief and rummaged in the glove compartment for a first-aid kit. There was none. He wasn't so much cut as bruised and soon the bleeding stopped, but left him with a swollen egg high on his cheekbone. Finally, he touched Bob on the shoulder and said, "You better slow down. They'll pull us over for speeding."

I found myself saying, "I don't want any more of that."

Mick was in front with Bob and he turned around to stare at me. "What do you mean?"

"This gun shit. I don't know. I don't like it."

"Most people are easy. You show them a gun and they shit their pants."

"I don't like that any better."

"That's okay. Bob and I will do it. Right, Bob?"

Bob nodded, but without much conviction, and I knew him well enough by now to know he might do it, but he wouldn't like it.

"What's the matter with burglary?" I asked. "We've been doing that okay. Let's stop in some town and see what we can find."

"Maybe," Mick said easily. "We'll see what comes up."

I realized I was losing control. My power had been based on my skill as a burglar. If we became armed robbers I was going to be of little use. My position in the back seat suddenly seemed symbolic.

It was a clear, hot morning and it became steadily hotter. We stripped to T-shirts and rolled down all the windows. The sides of the car were too hot to touch. I sat quietly watching the barren countryside while Mick fooled with the radio trying to bring in a Reno station. I had never been in country so empty. Monochrome flats, baked dry, spotted with a dull gray-green vegetation, rising into small stands of round and rocky hills. Behind us the snow-streaked Sierra Nevadas barred half of the vivid sky.

We were on a highway traveling due east, straight across Nevada, and we had the road almost entirely to ourselves. Gasoline was strictly rationed and few were driving these days. But we had no worry. We had stolen a number of ration books from the garage when we took the car and didn't have to worry about gas as long as we had money. However, we had little money left.

Mick had been playing with the .38 ever since we had been chased out of the store, and now, suddenly, he aimed and fired twice out the window. The wind sucked the sound of the shot and I couldn't see that he had hit anything.

Bob said, "I've been wanting to try that."

He pulled to the side of the road where a sign told us we were forty miles from Austin and seventy miles from Eureka, towns we had never heard of. We scratched a line and began to shoot at the road sign. I had had these guns for months but had never fired them. I was a fair shot with a .22 rifle and I expected to be able to hit something with a pistol, but found I couldn't. Neither could Mick. Bob, however, was a pretty good shot. He liked this and began to make cowboy moves, firing under his leg, over his shoulder, and practicing a draw from his belt. When we tired and started off again, Bob had somehow won the right to carry my gun. Now Mick had one and he had the other, and I was unarmed.

When I complained, Mick gave me one of his butcher knives. It seemed I was being shuffled to the side, just as I had been in Preston. The guns were mine and they had just taken them. I didn't remember at that moment how I had come to have them but I did remember I had still another. An antique Colt .44, a huge old pistol that fired a slug the size of a marble, and had once been used to bring down buffalo. It was little more than a novelty. I had no shells and didn't even know if it would fire. Further, it was too large to carry in my belt and I had it in a zipper bag.

We had decided to keep going until we reached Salt Lake City, which was fine with me because I had heard one of the world's largest amusement parks was located there, and I knew once we were back in a large city I could find places to burglarize. Until then all we needed was food and gas, and we could sleep in the car. I let the miles drift away dreaming of Salt Lake.

Abruptly, with a sharp explosion, the car broke down.

Bob managed to steer it onto the shoulder of the road and cut the engine. Smoke poured from under the hood. We got out to look, but we all knew it was finished.

For years when I told this story I always said Bob was so dumb he'd stolen a car without an oil pan, which betrayed how little I still knew because it wouldn't have gone a mile without a pan, but it now seems obvious it was low on oil and we simply burned up the motor. Bob was the car expert the way I was the burglary expert — only slightly less ignorant than the other two.

We started to hitchhike and got a ride quickly. It was blazing and the desert was actually dangerous, so no one who was at all conscientious would have been willing to leave us stranded out there, but the man who picked us up was clearly uneasy. We must have been radiating strangely. He was a salesman and I tried to talk to him, saying too much in my effort to be friendly. He dropped us off in Austin, a small, one-street town, and drove off quickly.

We ate lunch at the only café and talked about what we should do. I insisted we had to go after the car because I could be identified by the things I had in the trunk. So we hired the local mechanic to go out with the wrecker and tow in the Ford. This went without incident until it came time to pay. The bill was ten dollars for towing, plus the first month's storage, and we could muster between us only seven dollars. The mechanic took the money, but it was clear he was troubled.

I took as much of my things as I could carry, and we walked through town out to the highway. It was midafternoon, still very hot, and the streets were empty. A few old people sat in the shade of their porches and stared openly as we walked by. We were wildly out of place in our California sports clothes, aliens from the outside world, and I still find it odd, knowing what I did about small towns, that I didn't realize the impression we were making. Three strange boys, not one of them in uniform, who stored a burned-out Ford in Ansel's garage, and underpaid him three dollars before going out on the road to hitchhike. A dozen theories would be advanced to explain our presence.

We stood on the side of the road, kicking the soft dust, waiting for a ride. Bob began to tease me about the poetry I had rescued from the trunk. He thought if we had to wait here long the poetry might prove useful as toilet paper. Mick studied me with his strange green eyes, now oddly complimented by the purple bruise on his cheek, and smiled at Bob's jokes. They both carried the guns in their belts, under their shirts, and touched them from time to time as if they could draw strength from them. I had my comic Colt .44 in the ditty bag.

Traffic was slight. The few cars coming by didn't even slow down, but we weren't worried. We had just eaten and it was still some hours before dark. I gave no thought to where we might be going, no thought to where we had come from. I was simply there on the side of the road, and in some ways I've never again been as free as I was that afternoon on the highway outside Austin, Nevada.

Finally, a car slowed, braked and came to a stop twenty-five yards beyond us. We ran to catch up to an old black sedan driven by a middle-aged man wearing blues and a sweat-stained white cowboy hat. He sat solidly, looking back at us, and when we reached him, he asked, "Are you the boys who stored the car?"

One of us said, "Yes."

He looked us over deliberately, but with no particular keenness. His eyes were the same faded blue of his worn denim shirt, and his two-day stubble was white as frost against the warm reddish-brown of his cheeks. "Well," he said slowly, almost irresolutely, "I'm the sheriff here, and I'm going to have to ask you some questions about that car."

"Why?" I asked. "Something wrong?"

He stared at me for a full ten seconds. "It don't seem reasonable you boys would just go off and leave that car." He leaned across and opened the door. "Now I'm going to have to ask you to get in."

We stood looking at him, unable to believe the turn this had taken. Then Bob got in the front seat with the sheriff and Mick and I took the back. We were silent on the short ride into town. The same old people still sat on their porches and it didn't seem to surprise them to see us with the sheriff. He parked and we followed him up a short flight of stairs. I was just behind him but I couldn't see whether he carried a gun. We entered a small office which held a large oak desk, a single file cabinet, a gun rack with two rifles, and a deputy.

The sheriff called the deputy Percy. He was ten years younger than the sheriff and fifty pounds heavier, but he had the same faded blue eyes and when he smiled, which he did a lot, his teeth were speckled with light brown spots. He had large red hands.

The sheriff took his seat behind the desk, pushed his hat to the back of his head and played his ace. "I got a wire from Frisco on that car — they claim it's stolen."

It was a sad ploy and doubtless he had first seen it used in the movies. I smiled. And Percy smiled too, apparently glad we weren't worried.

"We've never been to San Francisco," Bob said.

"We're driving across from Reno," I said. "We have to get to Salt Lake City."

The sheriff considered this without apparent interest. Percy, speaking for the first time, asked, "Whose car is it?"

No one answered for a moment, then I said, "It's my father's. He'll send someone for it."

Percy took a slip of paper from his shirt pocket and slowly unfolded it. He stared at it a moment, lips moving, then asked, "What's your father's name."

I realized he had the information from the registration, and I had no choice but to go on lying. "Branning, but he's a used car dealer and this is just one of the cars off his lot. That's why we weren't real worried about it. He has hundreds of cars." I was going now and couldn't stop. "He let me use the car to get to Salt Lake to see my mother, who's sick. They're separated, you see, and I've been staying with my father, but now that my mother's sick she needs me at home."

The sheriff looked at Mick and Bob who were standing against the wall trying to appear calm. "And these boys?" he asked.

I waited for either Mick or Bob to say something, but they continued to stand quietly. I could see the gun butt where it angled slightly under Mick's shirt. "They're friends," I went on. "We all have to report for induction next week and this is our last chance to get out and look around."

I watched the sheriff earnestly trying to project concern for a sick mother on the part of a decent boy who would soon be going off to fight and maybe die just to save his leathery old ass. The sheriff turned to Percy. "What do you think?"

Percy smiled and looked at the paper again as if the right answer to the sheriff's question might be written there. "I don't know," he said.

The sheriff shifted in his chair, sitting up straighter, and I knew he had made a decision. "Well, I hope for your sake you've told me the truth, but I'm going to have to hold you boys until I can check on that car. If it's like you say you can be back on the road in the morning."

There was a long empty pause, while no one found anything to say. Neither Mick nor Bob made any move. We couldn't just go back to jail. Percy put the slip of paper back in his shirt pocket and stood up. "I better see if you got any guns on you," he said, grinning at the absurdity of his own caution.

"I've got a gun," I said. "It's here." I went on one knee to unzip my bag and bring out the Colt buffalo gun. Percy's grin broadened and he stepped forward to take the gun, obviously to examine it as a curiosity, but I stood, took a half step back, raised the gun and cocked it. "Stay back," I said. "I'll shoot you."

Percy's grin faded slowly and his hands half rose. I could follow his thoughts in his eyes as his easy expectations crashed into this frightening reality and he began to look like a man who had just been hit in the belly. He never noticed the large cylinders in the Colt were empty.

Mick exploded now and jerked his own gun from his waistband and began to stomp around, eyes blazing, shouting in that crazy fake Irish brogue, and even Bob produced his gun and stood holding it pointed at the floor. The sheriff seemed to sink behind his desk, slowly collapsing, suddenly old.

We handcuffed them both and took them back into their own jail, four primitive cells along a single cement corridor, and locked them up. I caught Percy's eye and was briefly distressed by the confusion of emotion I saw there. "We'll probably be back," I said. He stared at me numbly.

We took one of the rifles, thirty-five dollars we found in petty cash, a box of shells and the keys to the sheriff's car. Then we ran back downstairs, into the old black sedan to drive through town out onto the highway once again heading in the direction of Utah.

The old thieves would have called this part of the state one-gutted — there was only the one road, and no way off it. The occasional feeder roads we passed were little more than rutted wagon tracks and there was no way to tell where, if anywhere, they might lead. We were headed straight for Eureka, now about thirty miles away, and there seemed no way to avoid it. Beyond Eureka was another and larger town called Eli, and a few miles beyond that lay the Utah border.

There was no way to guess how long it would be before the sheriff and Percy were discovered. It could be hours, but somehow none of us thought so, and we immediately had another problem when we discovered the gas gauge trembling just above empty. The road lay straight across the flats, and Bob gunned the old car until it developed a high-speed shimmy so furious it seemed on the point of tearing itself apart. Again I was in the back, holding the rifle across my chest, watching for any road we might try. We were — we all sensed it — riding a greased chute.

Just before we reached Eureka I spotted a car parked on a

siding below the road. A brown coupé with two old people sitting quietly in the front seat. The woman wore a large hat. I saw an immediate picture of how we might commandeer the car. One of us could wear the hat, and the other lie on the floor while Bob drove safely into Utah. I shouted this to Bob, but he ignored me. He was doing one of the few things he did well, in control for the moment, and we sped on at ninety mph.

He slowed as we came into Eureka, another small town exactly like Austin, and stopped at the first gas station. No one seemed to be around. A car with the back wheels off sat on the grease rack, and a few bottles of some soft drink stood in a galvanized tub, cooled by a half-melted block of ice. Bob honked. No one came.

Mick said, "I'll fill it," and stepped out to try the pump. I put the rifle aside and started to get a cold drink. My eye was caught by a car speeding down the single street. It pulled to a sharp halt about thirty feet behind us. Two men, armed with rifles, jumped out. One dropped to his knee to brace his gun. The other took aim standing. Neither said a word.

I was half out of the car but immediately fell back, slammed the door, and dropped to the floor. Mick had to run around the front of the car, and before he was in his seat they opened fire. Bob was so frightened he put the car in second and we started off jerking and half-stalling until the car gained enough speed to match the gear ratio. This moment seemed curiously extended and I endured it in an eerie calm where my mind was empty of any thought of consequence and the hollow booming of the rifles seemed far away.

As soon as we pulled out, the firing stopped and I sat up.

Bob was hunched over the wheel, and I could just see the crest of Mick's blond hair. The rear window was shattered and except for a few ragged holes the starred glass was completely opaque. I used the rifle to knock out the glass with the butt. The other car was coming after us, a few hundred feet behind, and the man on the passenger side was firing from the window with a pistol. I tried to shoot back, but the rifle was awkward to manage and impossible to aim.

The air in our car was full of cotton waste shot out of the upholstery, and there was a hole in the dashboard so large I could have stuck my hand into it. Mick was grimly excited. He shouted at me to duck and I hit the floor again while he pumped six shots into the back seat. My bare arms were covered with bits of cotton. I sat up and tried to use the rifle again, but as I was attempting to aim the car behind us suddenly stopped. I watched as they made a three-corner turn to head back to Eureka.

"We scared them off," Mick said with satisfaction.

Suddenly I was shaken. The fear I hadn't felt when the bullets were pounding into the car came to me now, and I began to tremble. I pointed to the hole in the dash. "Look at that," I said, noting how pinched my voice seemed.

Mick examined the hole. "They're using dum-dums," he said quietly.

I thought of that large ragged lump of metal tearing through the air inches away. "I don't want any more shooting," I said.

Mick turned to stare at me. "We're not choosing."

"We have to get off this road. They're going to box us in and kill us."

"We'll have to walk out, then."

"We're out of gas anyway. We better get off the road."

"All right."

Mick seemed sustained by his anger. It was an emotion I had not experienced. At the next set of wagon tracks we told Bob to pull off, and he managed to make several miles up this rudimentary road before we hit a washout and plowed nose down into the sand. The back wheels were off the ground, spinning without traction. Bob sat silently at the wheel as if reluctant to admit the car was finished.

It was late afternoon, it would be dark soon, and our first problem was to put distance between ourselves and the wreck of the sheriff's car. The two men who had almost killed us in Eureka had freed us of the idea we were dealing with timid fools. I had no trouble imagining them tracking us across a sheet of glass. We decided to walk all night against the chance this would put us clear of the area they were most likely to search tomorrow. I remember the escape from Preston where I had made a similar long walk and I thought it still possible we might get away, but the country here was far more forbidding, and it was hard to imagine what we could find to eat.

At first we made easy jokes. We were alive and it was hard to worry. We would find a sheep, slaughter it with Mick's knives, and roast it over an open fire. But as we walked along we saw nothing living, not even a snake or a lizard, and, as the sun began to set, it rapidly turned cooler.

The desert appeared to have a regular and definite conformation. A series of broad flats, glistening with alkali, spotted with outcroppings, broken by small stands of round barren hills. If we crossed the flats at night, we could hide in the hills during the day, and then our only pressing problem would be to find water. So we reasoned with some care, but the desert was no more real to us than the crazy ride in the sheriff's car. Still our plan might have worked if it had been just been Mick and I, but Bob collapsed almost immediately.

As soon as it was fully dark, the desert became very cold, as cold by night as it was hot by day, and Bob began to limp badly. His feet were large and flat and he had never liked to walk, not even a few blocks, and his shoes were no good for this work. Doubtless, also, the desert night frightened him. It was suddenly awesome, so dark we couldn't see where we were stepping. There was no moon and the stars were tiny points of fierce light.

Bob stopped and said, "I can't walk anymore."

"We just started," Mick said.

"I can't help it. My feet hurt."

He sat down. I could just make out the pale blue oval of his face. Mick sat down beside him.

"This isn't getting us to Utah," I said.

"What's in Utah?" Mick asked.

Bob answered him with a weary sarcasm, "The world's largest amusement park."

My own feet hurt. I was wearing loafers and the slipping heel had worn a blister. I remembered the time I had walked thirty miles in boots several sizes too small. I sat down myself. We were all shivering.

"Why not try to go back to California?" Bob said.

"What's in California?" Mick asked.

"We're not," I said.

Bob liked his idea and a small enthusiasm stirred in his voice. "No one would expect us to double back the way we came. We could hit the road and hitchhike. We could be home in a few days and this would be behind us."

There was some sense in what he was saying, but I wouldn't admit it.

"I'm not going back to California," Mick said flatly. "All I ever got in that state was shit on. California's the asshole of the universe."

We huddled together for warmth and I slept fitfully, rising to uneasy consciousness a dozen times, shivering and miserable, turning on the hard ground in a futile search for some comfort. Mick talked incoherently in his sleep and I heard Bob moaning with the cold. I woke the last time, just before dawn, and knew with some clarity that whatever happened we were in serious trouble.

I watched the day begin. At first I couldn't be certain it was growing lighter, and then, very gradually, the scrub brush around us took form, and then the sky began to grow pale.

Soon it was warmer.

Mick woke up, smiled at me and pushed Bob, "Wake up, morning glory. Rise and shine."

Bob groaned and buried his head in his arms. Mick punched him in the leg. "Come on. Get the fuck up."

Bob sat up and looked around. There was nothing to see. "I'm hungry," he said.

"That makes you unique," Mick said with some asperity. "You ready to hit it?"

"If I have to," Bob said.

As soon as we started out the slight optimism I had gained from the light and the warmth faded. My feet hurt, and Bob was limping painfully. The air was soon so dry I had trouble swallowing. We needed water. The going wasn't particularly difficult, but the featurelessness of the terrain was depressing. Even when we had been walking several hours the mountains ahead seemed as far away as they had when we started. They might be twenty miles distant, but they could as easily be fifty. We knew only that our path lay directly into the sun. I slogged along thinking mostly of my sore heel. Already I was sweating.

Then we topped a slight rise and there, no more than five hundred yards away, was a parked truck. Either we had unconsciously angled back to the highway, or it had curved across the desert to intersect our line of march. And here was a truck.

"Let's take it," Mick said.

"Why is it just sitting there?" I asked.

"It's early. The driver probably pulled over to take a nap."

Mick was right. None of us had a watch, but it probably wasn't eight o'clock yet, and the driver curled on the seat seemed real to me.

"One of us should stay back with the rifle."

We flipped odd man with three pennies and Bob won — or lost — the toss and I handed him the rifle and took the automatic he had been carrying. Bob hadn't fired yesterday and the clip was full. I hoped the truck driver would just quietly surrender and not faint or go crazy. Bob sat down with the rifle cradled in his arms. He managed a smile. "Honk when it's okay," he said.

Mick and I approached at a low run. For some reason we decided to circle half around the truck and take it from the passenger side, but before we could even see the road, a line of men stood up from behind a small rise, and began to fire at us.

We never considered surrender. I'm not sure we could

have. They seemed determined to kill us. I wheeled away from this enormous danger and ran straight out into the desert, and threw myself into the first gully that offered hope of cover. I heard Mick land beside me.

"Now we're in it," he said.

"They're trying to kill us."

We looked at each other and for an instant I saw how Mick must have looked when he was a child. His face was streaked, his lips cracked, but his eyes were the same clear green. The scab had torn from his bruise, and a drop of bright blood clung to his cheek.

"Take it easy," he said.

The firing was no longer in a volley, but individual shots still rang out. We inched up to look. I saw between fifteen and twenty men, mostly in denims, wearing the same large white hats I had first seen on the sheriff. They were armed with rifles, firing deliberately, and the sunlight flashed from the lenses of their telescopic sights. I saw a puff of rust-colored dust ten feet in front, but this was my only indication, other than the sounds of firing, their guns were even loaded.

It didn't seem possible anyone could have survived the first volley, but we were unhurt. Mick was firing the service revolver, but when it was empty he didn't bother to reload. "If we shoot them," he said bitterly, "we're just as dead as if they had shot us."

Abruptly all firing stopped, and we watched Bob walk in with his hands over his head. "Don't shoot." he called, "I don't have a gun." Four men ran out to grab him, anxious to lay hands on this exciting prize.

"Let's go in," I said to Mick.

"If we can last here until night, we can slip away."

"Slip away where?"

He gestured behind us. That way lay south and suggested even barer and harsher terrain. "What about water?"

"We can make it."

I didn't think so. My lips were dry, my throat sore. The sun was beginning to look like brass. But we lay where we were, face down in the hot sand. The men opposite us settled down as well. Occasionally someone got off a shot. I heard them arguing about how to set their scopes. One thought we were two hundred yards out. Another thought it closer to three hundred. A few times I heard the metallic ring of radio transmission. It grew steadily hotter.

"I think we better give up," I said.

"Do you know the kind of time they'll give us?"

"We're not in that much trouble."

"*Shit!* They'll bury us. They'll have to pump in daylight."

Our eyes met. Mick's were hard and angry, but, after a moment, he looked away. "Give up if you want. I'm waiting for dark."

"Don't you think they'll try to light this up? Someone over there's thinking. They decoyed us with the truck."

"Bullshit, we stumbled into them. If that fucking clown you buddy around with hadn't froze last night we'd be miles from here."

The morning wore away. Whenever either of us lifted our heads, if for no other reason than to ease our anxiety, shots sounded. I didn't so much control my fear as learn to ignore it. It was important to be brave, but I was afraid I wasn't and I sensed I could drift into a kind of mindless and beating panic where I might run screaming across the desert. I felt if I proved myself a coward my life could never be valuable.

The sun was high above us when we began to hear a sound, a distant mechanical beating that gradually grew louder, and, then, coming toward us from the east we saw the black silhouette of a small plane. I knew immediately it was coming because of us. I took a look toward the road and several men were standing, waving their arms, obviously directing the plane.

Mick began to load the .38. "I wish we had the rifle," he said.

"You can't hit that."

"I can try."

"Jesus Christ, neither one of us can hit shit."

Mick lay on his back, using the gun with both hands, and as the plane began to circle over us he fired until the gun was empty. I could see someone up there looking over the side of the plane. Then something was falling. A gray cannister, turning end over end. It hit ten feet away and white smoke gushed from it. Another followed. Then a third.

The smoke flowed over us and my eyes began to burn. I gagged helplessly, but had nothing in my stomach to vomit. This was agony, and I acted to save myself. I threw the automatic toward the road and stood up with my hands on my head. I began to run. The line of riflemen stood up and aimed at me. I don't think I cared at that moment if they shot me.

As soon as it was clear I was harmless, a number of the riflemen ran out to grab me, hauling at my arms, and some ran past me, which was the first I knew Mick was coming in as well. Through my tears I saw the faces around me and realized this posse was either middle-aged or no older than we were. This was their war too. Simulated conflict in the American desert. Later, I would wonder how we all might have acted differently if we had never watched a movie.

"Well," one weathered man said slowly, "they don't look like much, do they?"

This brought laughter.

"May I have some water?" I asked.

A boy my own age offered me his canteen. I swallowed carefully. My throat seemed raw. I handed the canteen to Mick, and he rinsed his mouth twice spitting the water into the sand. I still expected to be handled roughly, even slapped around, but we were simply searched and handcuffed. The sheriff from Austin came up to look us over. He smiled with satisfaction. "We'll see if we can't make it a little harder for you to get away."

Again the men around us laughed. It came to me they were enjoying this. Nothing so exciting had happened in years. We were the bad guys so they must be the good guys and how often is anything so clearly drawn? One man was pacing off the distance to the gully where we had been pinned down. "Two hundred and sixty paces," he shouted, and the boy who had handed me his canteen shouted back, "You pace like an old lady, Harry," then caught my eye and smiled.

We were taken back to Austin in separate cars. I was transported by the sheriff from Eureka, who had almost shot us the day before in front of the service station. The alarm, he told me, had been given almost immediately. Someone had spotted us in the sheriff's car — I remembered the people on their porches — and had gone over to see what had happened. The sheriff was unlocked and on the phone in minutes, but the Eureka sheriff had been on another call and hadn't got the message until moments before we hit his town. "It's a wonder," he said gravely, "one of you boys wasn't killed right there. Maybe all of you."

I asked him why he had stopped following us and he said they were low on gas, but more cars had been on the way from Eli, and he had seen no way we could get away with the whole countryside aroused against us. The truck we had hoped to take to Utah had been used to bring out some of the posse, and when they had seen Mick and me running across the desert toward them they had been just as surprised as we were.

Back in Austin they locked us in the same jail where we had left them the day before. It was Percy who turned the key. He smiled at me, showing his speckled teeth, and shook his head with some sympathy.

"Well, you said you'd be back."

The Nevada State Prison

===

THE FIRST THING we heard when the corridor door closed behind Percy was Bob's voice.

"I thought you guys were dead," he whispered. He was in the cell next to me.

"We might as well be," Mick said.

I looked at my cell. It was an iron box with an old ten-gallon paint can for a shit bucket. The bunk was an Army cot, legs welded to the metal floor.

"What do you think we'll get?" Bob asked.

"The book," Mick said.

I didn't know. I couldn't think about this. I walked to the small barred Judas window and whispered, "We'll get another chance to escape."

"Shit," Bob said, with some grievance, "we wouldn't be here if we hadn't gone back for that fucking poetry of yours."

"Or *if* you hadn't fallen down out there last night," Mick added, "and *if* the dog hadn't stopped to shit, he might of caught the rabbit."

I thought about what Bob had said. It was true. Also I had pulled the first gun.

"The trouble with these jails," Mick was saying, "is I never can figure whether I'm sleeping in the can, or shitting in the bedroom."

A procession of investigators came to question us, and we admitted everything — the burglaries in Sacramento, even the robbery in Los Angeles. It didn't seem to matter. Soon we would escape again. The sheriff brought in his buddies and got us to tell them how scared Percy was and Percy brought in his friends so we could tell them how scared the sheriff was. The sheriff was apparently trying to cover his own tracks by claiming Percy made them. Percy brought us a pint of rum, and walked back and forth between our cells pouring into our cups, and his wife sent me some books. Three novels by James M. Cain. A fair way to pass the time.

One morning we were taken out to plead guilty to armed robbery and receive a sentence of not less than five years and not more than twenty-five years in the Nevada State Prison at Carson City. Percy told us we'd only do a few years. The night before the gray goose flew he came back with some more rum, and I got drunk and lay with my head wrapped in my arms dreaming of all I still hoped to do in my life.

The next morning we were unlocked and taken out one at a time. I was last and when I came into the office I found the others already cuffed. Mick's hands had been cuffed and then Bob had been cuffed to him as if they were paper clips linked together. "What this?" I asked brightly. "A daisy chain?"

A large old man with a great sagging belly and sour red eyes looked down at me. "Save your jokes," he said. I was cuffed to Bob and we were led, necessarily walking sideways like a trio of crabs, out into the bright sunlight where an old gray panel truck was parked. A few idlers watched from across the street. We were put in back where we were free to arrange ourselves as comfortably as we could on the bare metal floor. The back door was closed, locked and bolted. We were cut off from the driver's compartment by welded metal bars. Essentially the truck was a wheeled metal cage.

While the transportation officer walked from the back to the front, I asked Mick, "What do you think?"

He winked. His bruise had almost faded. "We've got a lot of time," he said.

The transportation officer settled behind the wheel, grunting softly as he arranged his stomach. Then he gave us a long hard look to make sure we were still where he had left us a moment ago. He touched the barrel of a rifle leaning against the vacant seat.

"Don't give me any trouble," he said.

Originally the Nevada State Prison was a cavalry post, and it looked very much like a movie fort — high, sand-colored walls, broken by a huge wooden gate, commanded by a Gatling gun mounted directly above it. This gun, we learned, was a genuine relic.

I tried to watch closely as we unloaded, but there was little to see. The prison stood by itself in the desert, and the few houses clustered around it were probably the homes of the officials and the guards. The road stretched as far one way as it did the other. Carson City was somewhere nearby, but nothing indicated where. Reno wasn't far, and beyond Reno lay the Sierra Nevada mountains and Lake Tahoe. It was Tahoe I dreamed of that morning.

We were hustled through a sally port, directly into receiving. At that time the Nevada Prison didn't go in for a lot of form. We were logged in and dressed out quickly by one of those small, meticulous clerks who everywhere keep things moving, and we hit the main line just at lunch. The other prisoners, over two hundred, had just started eating when we were brought into the mess hall, and for a moment we were the cynosure. They knew who we were and what we had done. The three gunsels who had shot up one of the central counties and locked the sheriff in his own jail.

The mess hall was another cafeteria setup, with long benches, and we were assigned places by an inmate waiter. Mick and Bob were seated together, but I was put next to an older man.

He nodded at me and said with some approval, "You kids tore ass out there."

I flushed with pleasure even though I was pretty sure the ass we tore was our own.

"My handle's Whitey," he continued.

Whitey was one step away from middle age. He wore pressed blues, leather sandals, and a visor of dark-green Celluloid. The hair which had once earned him his common nickname had faded to a smoked tan. There was something about his expression that made me uneasy. I learned some time later he had bribed the inmate waiter to seat the "best-looking of those three gunsels" next to him.

Lunch was watery red beans, canned spinach and a few slices of white bread, but Whitey was eating a can of Spam. He offered me enough to make a sandwich, but, instinctively, I refused.

After lunch we filed into the yard and were free to do what we liked for the rest of the afternoon. The yard was simply that space enclosed by the square of the walls, the ad building and the cell block, approximately an acre, and while little beyond planting some grass had been done to make it pleasant, nothing had been done to make it unpleasant either. The yard was surrounded, framed, by various facilities, those vital organs of prison life — a bathhouse, a laundry, the mess hall, the library, the bull pen, a tailor shop, a barber shop, and the ground level custodial office known as Four Box. Just behind all this was an area enclosed with cyclone fencing where, on rare occasions such as the Fourth of July, we were allowed to play softball. Adjacent to the ball diamond and just behind the library was a small stone building containing two cells and the gas chamber.

This was it. Here we would lead our lives, walking from the cell block into the mess hall, from the mess hall to the yard and back to the cell block. We were not assigned a job. All workers were volunteers, and most men passed the days gambling over cards in the bull pen, or manufacturing handicraft to sell to visitors. That first afternoon we met one prisoner, the librarian, who had been confined in this narrow routine for thirty-one years.

We were celebrities that first afternoon. The accounts of our brief rebellion in the Reno papers had made it all seem much larger than it had been — the description of a government plane flying from Eli to gas us into surrender was somehow far more than the actual plane circling above us — and they saw our caper as a brief but gallant charge in the war they imagined between the over- and underworld. It was fantasy, of course, but one we were pleased to play along with and in the airless life of this small prison we were briefly a major event. Big John Grimes, the king of the bullpen, came over to hear our story. He was a Midwesterner, six-six, no longer young, but still with every show of vigor. He listened, an amused glint playing in his smoke-blue eyes, and when we finished our account, he stood up and squeezed Mick's shoulder. "You'll do a five spot," he said. "Two-and-a-half here and two-and-a-half in California, and that's the fastest you'll ever do two jolts."

We dismissed this. We were going to escape. But we immediately learned one stunning fact. Three men, under sentence of death, shared this yard with us. In weeks, or months, if the courts ruled against their automatic appeals, they would be taken to the gas house, and put to death. If these most desperate of men were confined just as we were, and they had found no way to escape, how could we hope to?

Subsequently, I came to the conclusion they never considered escape. Surely they fantasized, but in this real world they pinned their hopes on the courts, and one, at least, cheerfully accepted his position as hopeless. He was passing time working in the barber shop, and he sometimes cut my hair. Once he told me, "You've just been shaved by a dead man."

"Your appeal will come through," I said uneasily.

But he shook his head and smiled. "No, I'm dead. I'm just waiting for them to get around to it." And he was right. A few months later, they took him out and pulled the plug. Another kid looked like the peasant soldiers I wrote about in high school, but his name wasn't Raoul, it was Billy, and I often played chess with him. He wasn't the brightest in the joint, but he was far away the best chess player. He crushed you with the coordinated savagery of his attack. We sat in the sun, facing each other, pushing wood, and I never saw any emotion I could read as the apprehension of his death. It seemed I was far more aware than he of his terminal appointment. He was nineteen and I never knew whom he had killed or why. They gassed him early one Friday, because this was the morning Jesus was killed, and one of the guards told me Billy had tried to hold his breath. They go two ways, he went on, either they suck it up or they try to hold their breath.

Those first days we studied the prison as the men who had built and modified it must have studied it. We tried to see that second prison known mostly to the guards. The only post at ground level was Four Box and the desk there was manned by an unarmed sergeant. Directly behind this office and separated from it by bullet-proof glass was a small barred cage called the armory. An armed guard sat here and contolled the solenoid that operated the gate that led out to the ad building and, beyond it, to the outside. There was no shot through here. This prison had never endured major trouble and it was quietly run. The duty sergeant walked around the yard several times a day, checking the bull pen, the kitchen and the bathhouse, filtering and noting the endless stream of small complaints, exchanging gossip with one man or another. He was protected only by the wall towers.

There were only two of these towers, located at either end of the yard. Either gun bull could see most of the yard and the little that one couldn't supervise was overlooked by the other. The guards were armed with rifles, and there was no way to know how well they shot them. Tower duty's a dull turn. You can't read or rest comfortably. They stood twenty feet above us, rifles at port, counting the days until they would be automatically rotated.

While we thought of escape, we could think of nothing else, and we spent most of our time trying to put together a plan. At first we had five plans and we shifted from one to the other, working variations until we were back to the first. They had celled Mick and me together so we were able to conduct this exciting exercise both day and night.

Bob began to pull away from us immediately. He drifted into the orbit of Big John Grimes, who was behind most of the poker games in the bull pen and had plenty of brass, as we called the metal coinage they gave us in place of money, to buy extra food. Within a week Bob was celling with Big John. The implications of this move were clear to everyone, and Mick felt shamed by them. Bob had become a commissary punk, a boy literally bought by a wealthy convict for the extra food and few luxuries he's able to provide. The commissary punk is not a homosexual and doesn't necessarily enjoy his work. It's not unlike the bargain many women are forced to make in patriarchal societies.

"Now I know we got to get out of this fucking place," Mick said. "They'll figure we're birds of a feather."

Mick and I were subjected to the same pressures. Whitey continued to ply me with extra food, which I usually refused, and a friend of Big John's propositioned Mick. This touches one of the dominant myths of prison life which holds

that young prisoners are routinely screwed by older convicts. This comes up again and again. Always as I have heard
the story the kid is caught in the bathhouse and offered the
narrow choice of putting shit on someone's dick or blood on
his knife. I'm sure this has happened, I'm sure it is happening
somewhere today, but in my own experience, it was always like the similar stories you heard in high school about
the girl, crazed on Spanish fly, who ruptured herself on a
gearshift, or had a Coke bottle removed from her quim — it
always happened somewhere else in another town, and it
seems clear these stories describe more of our sexual ambivalence than they do any common reality.

What Mick and I encountered was far closer to seduction
than to rape. We were casually courted, almost never
pressed, and like nice girls of the time, we said No, and that
was more or less that. Our foolish stand in the desert had
earned us some respect and the men after us weren't monsters. They had all been locked up most of their adult lives
and what they were looking for was simulated romance, an
attachment that mimicked the other life they might have led,
and I was never convinced they were only after sex. Of
course, if we'd been willing, I'm sure they would have
fucked us.

Within a week someone handed us an escape plan. I had
naturally gravitated to the library. In the old prison flicks
the nice old con or the innocent kid, railroaded on a bum
beef, always works in the library as servant of whatever
slender culture is available, but in real prisons the library is
seldom a good place to work and those who do work there
are often either weaklings or degenerates. Nevada was no
exception. Two inmates ran the library without civilian

supervision, and one was a patricide and the other was a pedophile. It was the patricide who had served the thirty-one years, far longer than any other man in the prison. As a kid he had ambushed his father and killed him with a rifle. He never said why.

His assistant, the pedophile, was called Holdum and Fuckum. He and his lady of the moment had been convicted of the rape of a nine-year-old girl in a Reno hotel room. The girl friend had restrained the child's head and arms while Holdum and Fuckum had enjoyed the lower half. He was the most despised prisoner in the institution. Thieves hold themselves to be superior to sex offenders and baby rapers were the absolute bottom of the pile.

The plan was originated by the patricide. He had had a great many years to study the prison and dream of escape, but he didn't have, when push came to shove, the balls to try it. We thought we did. It was simple, as most good plans are, and it required the help of two other men who would not be able to escape with us. We were still naive enough to believe this requirement presented no obstacle.

If you see the prison yard as a simple square, we planned to leave by the lower right-hand corner. Here, just at the end of the cell block, there is a spiked fence approximately seven feet high. Beyond this fence on the one side sits the gashouse, but on the other it is possible to go around the far corner of the cell block, where we will be completely hidden while we try to figure out someway to scale the twelve-foot wall. One tower is directly above the spiked fence where we will make our jump so the area is blind to the guard posted there. This left only the other tower, and Four Box. The patricide volunteered to handle Four Box. The sergeant posted there was also the censor and patricide had only to go over with a number of letters and stand respectfully in front of the desk while the sergeant went through them. This would effectively limit his view of the fence.

We talked another man, an Indian, into handling the other tower. It wasn't unusual for the tower guards to carry on shouted conversations with the inmates on the ground below. The bulls were bored and grateful for the slightest distraction. It had been years since anyone had even attempted an escape from within the prison and the tower guards must have sometimes viewed their positions as more symbolic than real. The Indian was buddies with the guard on duty in the critical tower. They were both artists at leather tooling, and had much to say to each other. All Mick and I needed was thirty seconds, and the chance of this seemed excellent.

These difficult arrangements were made easily and it remained only for us to prepare ourselves. We had learned something about escaping over desert and we began to horde bread. We picked up a few cans of tinned meat and some bottles of apple juice. Mick, who was handy, sewed up some small knapsacks out of sheeting, designed to be worn under our shirts.

We had to frame our break within the regular head counts — morning, noon and night — but as soon as we were over the wall and into some cover, then the sooner it grew dark the better for us. We could travel in the cover of darkness and rest by day. This meant we had to break in the afternoon and must carry our supplies until then and their significance would be immediately apparent to anyone who saw them. The little knapsacks worked well.

We packed up on our last night. I still had my poetry and once again I planned to take it, along with the bread and meat and apple juice and a gift-bound copy of the *Rubaiyat of Omar Khayyam*. I still had the loafers I had worn on the desert outside Eureka and now would have to wear them again. We hoped the going would be easier. We would cross back into California and try to reach Lake Tahoe, where we dreamed we would find an empty cabin with some canned goods, where we could rest and swim and lie around in the sun.

I lay awake for a while wondering if I would disgrace myself, wondering why we were once again throwing ourselves into the unknown. It's a singular situation. We were safe in the prison. We would be fed, clothed, kept warm, provided with an opportunity to work and make a little money. We could read, study, wear out the time; no one thought we would do more than a few years. We were young. I would turn nineteen in a few days. Now I imagine our dream of escape was instinctual. Every prisoner must dream of escape and always a few will act on that dream.

We drew a hot clear day in early July and spent an anxious morning making sure the patricide and the Indian knew exactly what to do and were still willing to do it. Tension turned my lunch even more tasteless than usual, but I forced myself to eat it, and, after lunch, we sat quietly in the library waiting, our knapsacks in place under our shirts, while Holdum and Fuckum, sucking wetly on the stem of a dead pipe, advised us to go to Des Moines where we could make new lives for ourselves. He described a clean, quiet and prosperous city where we would never be found. For a moment he brought to life the broad streets, arched by overhanging trees, where on long summer afternoons the asphalt softens and men wash their cars beside their white homes.

We decided to jump at two o'clock. The next count would be at four and it was then, we hoped, they would first realize we were gone. Two hours to make tracks in and then possibly three more to hide out until it grew dark. The country out there was a blank slate, but we were confident we could improvise whatever was necessary. The Indian wandered down to talk to the tower guard and the patricide gathered his letters — he looked tense — and walked to Four Box. The Indian was drawing a design refinement in the soft earth and the tower guard was watching closely. As soon as the patricide was in front of the sergeant's desk, we ducked out and ran the few feet to the fence. Suddenly I sat down on the narrow border of grass. I felt like a hunchback with the pack. I felt anyone who glanced at us would see what we were up to and raise an alarm.

"Let's go," Mick said.

I couldn't move. The sun was warm on my face and arms but inside I was cold, too cold to move. I looked down to where the Indian still held the tower guard, but it seemed he might look up at any moment, must look up soon.

"Come on," Mick said. "If we're going it has to be now."

I stood up, still half hunched over, and I felt feeble. It didn't seem I had the strength to climb the fence. At that moment the tower guard did look up and glance around idly before going back to his conversation, and though this is what I thought I had been waiting for I still couldn't go. I was poised like one who has charged himself to make a long dive into dangerous water.

I met Mick's eyes and saw him pleading there. "I can't do this alone."

I moved, and once I began to climb the fence my energy

flared like a fire shot with oxygen, and I was suddenly going. I cleared easily, but Mick spiked himself and tore the soft flesh between his thumb and his forefinger.

Long after it occurred to me we could have made a jig to cover the spikes. If we had measured the distance between them we could have made corresponding holes in a piece of two-by-four, stuck it on top and vaulted the fence as easily as those I vaulted so often in schoolyards, and then taken the two-by-four with us. I mention this now to show how little thought we gave to this venture. Always before, when I have told this story, I have lied and added this telling detail to give the weight of some shrewdness to our break, but the truth is, we simply ripped into it, hoping to get lucky because we believed in ourselves and our right to that luck.

We made it to the comparative safety behind the cell blocks and, when we heard no shouts or sirens, concluded we now had the time we would need to scale the wall we found in front of us. Suddenly it seemed very high. We had no ladder, no rope, no tool of any kind. Even standing on Mick's shoulders I couldn't reach the top.

We began to search for something, anything we could use and we found a shovel. The ground was sandy and apparently some of it had been hauled off and this shovel accidentally left behind. Once again on Mick's shoulders, I was able to use the side of the blade as a crude grabbling hook and it held as I worked up the handle to pull myself to the top. The wall was thick and I was able to lie across the top and extend the shovel to Mick. My legs hanging over the far side were enough to counterbalance his weight and he managed to climb up beside me. His left hand was covered with blood. We hung full length down the free side, kicked off and dropped.

I remember running down a small dirt road and looking back over my shoulder to see a number of trusties walking back and forth taking their exercise in front of the main prison. They were staring at us in amazement. It didn't bother me to be spotted. I didn't think it possible another prisoner would betray us. Preston had taught me nothing I was prepared to realize at that time, and I assumed the convicts would all be for us. I was never so naive again.

We were desperately exposed. There was no cover, no place to hide, and we knew our only chance lay in covering as much distance as quickly as we could. We took our first risk when we crossed the highway because we thought it would help our odds and, once safely across, we headed straight into the desert. It was a different day and a different desert. The middle of the afternoon, the hottest time of day, in the middle of summer, the hottest time of year, and in moments we were both running sweat and close to exhaustion.

The dry desert air sucked the moisture from our mouths and soon it seemed I was trying to breathe clouds of hot white dust. The cover didn't improve. Most of the chaparral was less than a foot high and anything taller was too scattered and too skeletal to hide us. We skirted a small hill, just to put the weight of that earth between us and the prison, and when we reached the far side we had to stop to try to catch our breath. We sat down in the sand, which was hot enough to burn through our pants, and took a bottle of apple juice from our packs. We had made another mistake. The juice was hot and thick and seemed to cling to our throats.

"Let's dig in here," I said.

Mick looked around and shook his head. "We're still too close. They'll be over this area like a bad smell."

He was right. We started walking now, keeping a brisk pace. My heels were already sore. There was a larger hill directly in front of us and we decided to risk the energy necessary to climb it against the hope we could find someplace near the top where we might hide and still be able to keep some sort of lookout.

As I climbed I promised myself this would be the end of this life for me. As soon as I was able, I would slip away from Mick, go somewhere, anywhere, where I could work and earn my way. I would give up my crazy ambitions and settle for the quiet wholesome family life I imagined was the birthright of any American.

The hill took all we had and when we came to the top we both fell, too exhausted to even try to talk. I lay face down, struggling for breath, staring at the pale-red earth, sensing the sun like a circle of hot pressure against the back of my neck. When I could, I rolled over and sat up to look at my heels. I found angry red circles the size of quarters. Why had I ever bought these fucking shoes! I remembered how dear they had been to me. Penny loafers and saddle shoes.

"Look!" Mick said.

His voice was so charged I spun around into a half crouch, ready to run or duck, certain I would see a line of armed men running toward us. Instead, at the bottom of the far side of the hill, edged in a small blur of green, I saw a pool of bright blue water. Surrounded by a half circle of trees that looked like willows, it shimmered with reflected white light like a mirage.

"How about a swim?" Mick said and started down. With

a half thought to the safety of the hilltop, I rose to follow. I forgot my sore heels. Ahead of me Mick slipped, rolled, righted himself and ran on. I thought I could smell the water like a horse, and when we reached the edge I went right on running, splashing into it.

It was only inches deep. And almost as warm as the air around it. Still, we knelt in the soft mud and drank like animals. But, unlike animals, we had no instinct for the danger of water holes and we heard nothing.

"Stand up and turn around."

The voice buckled with obvious strain and we instinctively moved with cautious slowness. We found a guard standing there, still in uniform, with a rifle pointed somewhere between us. He had stepped from an ambush in the trees. His name was Meyer and he was the outside guard in the mess hall on the evening shift. I had never had occasion to say a word to him. His face was flushed and he was shaking so violently the small black hole in the end of his rifle seemed to dance before us.

"You rotten little bastards," he said unevenly. "I should kill you. I could shoot you right now and claim you tried to run."

We stood absolutely still. The warm water had left a taste in my mouth as if I had eaten garbage, but I didn't dare swallow. It was so still I could hear Meyer's breath, and it was only when the rhythm of his breathing slowed that I felt the muscles in my back begin to relax. It was only much later I realized Meyer was dealing with his own fear. He probably thought we might try to jump him. He, too, had seen movies.

He gestured with the rifle, an awkward crabbed gesture, because he didn't want the point off at least one of his targets too long, to indicate the direction to walk in. We started off, Meyer behind, and we came to some wagon tracks which we followed. Soon we met a larger party of guards led by the captain.

The captain, a white-haired man, who, in his uniform, looked like a failed airline pilot, shook his head over us. "You kids are crazy," he said. "Before you get out of this you'll have long white beards . . ." The other guards simply stared at us. Now they wouldn't miss supper. Mick's face was set. If he felt despair or regret it wasn't apparent. We didn't wonder how they had organized so quickly, and it was only months later we learned the patricide had ratted on us.

They herded us down the road where two official cars were parked, loaded us separately, drove us the quarter of a mile back to the prison, and locked us in the hole.

In many jails solitary is called the hole. In Nevada it was a hole. A rough cave under the prison, blasted from heart-rock, and used originally to quiet troublesome Indians and hold men waiting trial or transportation to the territorial prison. It hadn't changed.

The actual detention unit was a line of four iron cages. We were stripped, thrown suits of long underwear and locked in. We were supplied with a gunboat of water, a shit bucket sprinkled with lime, and a single blanket. There was no bed, no mattress, and when the guards left us there they turned out the light, and, except for a brief visit once a day to feed us and change our honey buckets, we were left in darkness.

At first our food was a loaf of bread each day and a can of fresh water. The guard and the convict orderly who serviced us had little to say. The guard seemed angry and the orderly had clearly been told to keep his mouth shut. He was black, and day after day he stepped into my cell to take my bucket and he never spoke, but sometimes he winked at me. Once he dropped a sack of Bull Durham, cigarette papers, and a small bundle of matches, which he had carefully broken in half to make less bulky. The hole was always warm, and we grew used to living on bread and sleeping on the iron floor, and if the guard wouldn't talk to us we spoke whole books to each other.

Time went swiftly. Soon we were sleeping over twelve hours a day and telling each other the stories of our lives. Mick remembered everything and soon his experiences came to seem as vivid as my own, and it seemed I almost knew his young mother, his lost father, always somewhere at sea, and I could sense the streets of Oakland with their poolhalls and sweetshops. I saw the stores where he traded adventure magazines, two for one, and the corridors of the high schools he had briefly attended.

I came to know so much about a girl, Artemis Pappas, that it seemed in my imagination I had loved her too. I knew the vacant house where they had hidden together. I saw the peeling wallpaper, the broken lathes, the gray coat of plaster dust on the floor, scored with their heelprints, and the broken cardboard box — a stove came in it — they had used for a bed. I climbed the tree they climbed to slip through the open second-story window and I argued with Artemis when she wouldn't, as she never did, take off all her clothes. Almost I could sense her there in the darkness with me and when I stroked myself and came, still listening to Mick's voice, the pleasure was sharply bittersweet. I jerked off a lot, as often as I thought I would lose myself in it, and I don't know if Mick did, over there in that other cell. We never spoke of it, the one thing we never spoke of, but I imagine he did.

At first we assumed we'd be here in the dark for thirty days. A standard sentence. But the thirtieth day passed and we immediately assumed we had lost count, even though this hardly seemed possible since the only important task either of us had was to keep track of the time, and we checked with each other constantly.

Then at the next feeding period, they added a can of hot soup to our ration and we knew we were going on. If we weren't doing thirty, we were doing sixty or ninety.

One morning we woke up to find a third man in one of the remaining empty cells. His name was Elmer White and he was one of the volunteers in the mess hall who had been busted for selling milk. This immediately marked him as a hard-luck case because everything in the kitchen was for sale and everyone who worked there sold food. The convict politicians bought control over most of the meat, butter, eggs, milk — the good stuff — and the mainline got whatever was left over.

Elmer was fucked from birth and nothing good had ever happened to him. He was thirty-nine, no one had ever given him a nickname, and he had never lived with a woman for more than a few days at a time. He had worked every faceless and grinding job our society reserves for those who are truly without a choice, and every time he tried to free himself by some bold act he had been caught. He had, he said, served seven years in California for stepping on board someone's yacht in the Balboa Yacht Harbor to take a shit.

Day after day as his sorry story unfolded it seemed I was relentlessly pinned in the empty center of his despair. Elmer had struck out in his genes long before he was ever presented with his equal chance to make trouble for himself, and had served over thirty years in one institution or another — orphanages, foster homes, asylums, city jails, county jails, work farms and prisons. He was the product of institutions, their creature, and I never doubted, though he still talked hopefully, he would serve thirty more. I came to know many like Elmer, but the time when I would compare them to myself was still far in the future.

I was alive, and even when the shots were crashing in front of the gas station in Eureka or when the trembling eye of Meyer's rifle drifted across my chest, I had never thought I could be killed. If he had shot me I'm sure my last feeling would have been amazement.

As the days in the hole wore by, the guard who brought our food began to loosen a little. Sometimes he asked us how we felt. Mick tried to talk to him, but I never did. Once Mick asked him how the weather was and he said it was boiling outside and we were lucky to be in the coolest place in the joint.

Then one morning he told us the war was over. We had dropped some dreadful bomb and the Japs had been forced to surrender. I had missed this war, but fought my own, and I, too, surrendered. I gave up covertly and didn't admit it, even to myself, for I sometimes continued to talk and, rarely, even act tough, but my open rebellion was over. I knew if I continued they would kill me and kill me routinely. I might try to stand outside our society, to mock its excess and scorn its reward, but I knew it was impossible to oppose it directly and live.

We were released from the hole at the end of sixty days. It was by modern standards a harsh punishment, but where was the punishment exactly? We were warm, fed enough, they never even slapped us, or indeed, appeared to take any satisfaction in our situation. We were simply left alone for a period of time.

In real terms the hole was only a jail within a jail, the literal end of the line, and once you have reached this terminus your only real choice is to stay, or begin the journey back. This decision to live is in no way automatic — others I knew then and after, Mick included, decided not to live, unless on their own terms, and found they had nothing left to bargain with.

Doing Time

===

I BEGAN TO SERVE my time and we did two and a half years in Nevada, exactly as Big John had predicted that first day, and the balance of his prediction was equally accurate. Nevada was a good-natured, old-fashioned prison where one never heard the word "rehabilitation." There were no official programs. No school, no trade training, no group counseling, and mostly what we learned there was not to draw to an inside straight and how to lay the note.

No one suggested we had become prisoners as simply a symptom of our psychological impairment, or for any reason other than the obvious one that we had broken the law and had been caught. If we followed the simple rules, locked up when we were told, ate when we were told, and didn't attempt to escape more than once or twice, or lead riots, most of us could hope to be set free in a few years. We were allowed to while away the days, the weeks, the months and the year doing absolutely nothing. We lay in the sun, walked the yard, played cards, told lies, worked hobby for spending money, and made plans for the one big caper that would make us rich and truly free.

I will sketch some of the ways I passed this time in Nevada, but, first, I want to take this opportunity to write a muted love letter to a class of men I met there, the last of their kind, whom I have always thought of as the Old Thieves. The man who now looks back is not the boy who first listened to the tale with such admiration, but we will hear evidence from both these witnesses, and try to learn the truth without losing respect.

Incidentally, I don't presume my understanding of sociology or the function of myth is either unique or particularly sophisticated, nor will I attempt to burden this narrative with the apparatus of scholarship. I remain typical of those prisoners forced into thoughtfulness by the effort to understand and perhaps reverse the apparent ruin of their own lives, and I make my observations only from the vantage of the special experience which entitles me to them.

For me the Old Thieves were the last of the western outlaws, idealists trapped in the closing frontier, and now the most famous of these men are gradually metamorphosing into heroes. With Frank and Jesse, with Butch and Sundance the process is complete, and as Dillinger the man begins to fade into history, Dillinger the legend begins to emerge. Why do we celebrate such men?

Heroes have always been free to function outside the law. Gilgamesh first lived as a beast in the field, and Herakles, while occasionally used to illustrate some point of custom, was more often pictured as an unprincipled adventurer. He was always riding in, saving the situation, savoring some reward, then tipping his white hat, like Hopalong Cassidy, before he took off for the next adventure. Theseus behaved much the same before he took up the king profession.

These myths, of course, are richer in implication that any simple and admittedly tendentious reading can suggest, but one of their most persistent themes is the freedom of the quest, and almost always the hero moves in the company of his companions. What yearning might we imagine on the part of the mythogenitors who blended Robin Goodfellow, the Celtic Pan, with Robin Hood and his happy band of noble bandits, who lived in the first forest, free of the tedious restraints of the agrarian life and of the women who had made agriculture their mystery. We see in Robin Hood and his Merry Men the hunting band, and the mythic element is the primal freedom of the hunt, the adventure of the constant unknown and the glory of the kill.

But if Robin took from the rich to give to the poor, the chances are large, as we often wisecracked, he found no one poorer than himself. The same was said of Jesse James. He and Frank also fought the powerful and endeared themselves to the unfortunate, and, to make the point even sharper, they set themselves against the railroads, the very instrument that was destined to destroy the wilderness. They were fiercely loyal to each other, their relatives, their immediate friends, and only disloyal to that larger and more abstract society that demands unquestioning loyalty in the form of patriotism, but often returns only the arrogance of bureaucracy and the insolence of privilege. Again Frank and Jesse form the hunting band. We seldom hear of their women and when we do they are either ornaments and diversions or impediments to their freedom.

DOING TIME

In the most recent retelling of Frank and Jesse's legend there is a scene where they are riding around gathering together their gang to ride off and have another go at the railroads. The wife of a middle-aged rancher is shown tearfully begging her husband not to go. She fears for the safety of the children and the harvest is not yet in. As the rancher rides off, leaving his wife in tears, he says casually to Jesse, "Women don't understand why we have to do this." Maybe, but maybe he didn't care that much about ranching.

The forests were gone, and the frontier had almost closed before Dillinger sketched his brief life of defiance, and everything in this country was tightened up and squared off before I met some of those men who had been his peers. They were not so classic and probably only one or two might have had those qualities of energy, intelligence and carefree daring which could have pushed them into major confrontation with the society they tried to live beyond. But they all assumed the style of outlaw, proudly referred to themselves as thieves, and held this calling to be clearly superior to the modest occupations available to them within the normal arrangement. They were loyal to their friends, concerned with honor, proud their word was good, and, of course, though I could not realize it at the time, they were failures and losers many times over.

Most of them were men approaching middle age, who had been born around the turn of the century, just a few years after Sir Francis Galton made the first practical classification of fingerprints and a few years before the invention of the vacuum tube. These two radical developments destroyed the Life. Before, an outlaw could usually outrun all but the most determined pursuit and change his identity as simply as changing his name.

My friends grew up riding the rails. What a marvel that must have been in those days before the airlines stitched the world together. To take a free train ride from one coast to the other. They weren't gunmen for the most part, but if the times were poor and opportunity limited they would try robbery before they would try work. Generally they were safe crackers, con men and weeders. They ranged mostly in the Middle West — the East was too built up — they avoided California which quickly became an extension of the East, and they stole mostly in the small towns and partied in cities such as Chicago, St. Louis and Kansas City, which they called Chi, St. Loo, and K.C. They were outcast, unattached, womanless, but free in the Life.

I don't know what writer first described the safe-man as the aristocrat of the criminal class, I'm only sure it was a writer and equally sure few safe burglars have ever denied themselves the distinction. From the first I heard the secret lore of this art. Everyone talked knowingly of punching and pulling and cutting and drilling and before long, without ever having once settled to the work, I thought I could crack a safe.

The yeggs were honored, if not quite as aristocrats, because they stole clean, with only the slightest potential for violence. They deplored violence and dismissed it scornfully as "rawjaw" — a classless and inartistic crime which needlessly frightened and stirred the ordinary people, which put pressure on the police who made the life of a quiet outlaw more difficult. They were also respected for their traditional knowledge and their craftsmanship. It was generally accepted that any master safe cracker could easily earn his bread in the straight world if his sense of honor were not too fine to permit him to disgrace himself by working for wages.

More realistically, they were respected because they had the skills necessary to steal very large amounts.

Just once did I work with an experienced safe cracker, and I tell the story here, out of narrative context, simply because it is such a splendid irony with which to backlight some of these romantic projections.

I was in the Frisco City Jail for suspicion of burglary and I fell in, walking and talking, with an older man and his younger partner. They seemed smart and they acted like sober and seasoned thieves working their way through a piece of modest trouble. The older man, call him Bill, floating somewhere in his fifties, liked to talk safe cracking, at which, he was willing to admit, he was an ace, and I was pleased to listen as he lectured on such refinements as day com.

Day com is used when the manager of a store, fearing robbery, wants to give the impression his safe is locked, and still not have to rework the entire combination every time something is needed. The combination is worked in the morning, the tills removed, then the safe is closed and the dial moved only a few numbers. It can be reset to the final digit and opened at any time, but, in case of robbery, a quick spin will scramble the combination, and throw the safe on total lock.

Sometimes the day com is overlooked when the store is closed in the evening, and when the safe burglar approaches any vault his first shot is to hope it's on day com. You apply steady tension to the handle and turn the dial slowly hoping to come on the magic number. There's just one catch. Do you turn the dial right or left? If you pick the wrong direction you'll break the com and lose the chance of an easy score.

The direction is determined by the number of tumblers, and there is no way to see this, you have to know. If the safe lock has four tumblers you end turning left. If it has five you turn right. So it's either/or, unless you are familiar with all the makes and models.

Bill was familiar. Through those slow days in jail I walked away the time with him reliving the years he had spent studying stolen manuals, the nights spent drinking with straight technicians as he slyly picked their brains, the hours of dry practice and the thrill of big scores beautifully taken. It sang to me. I was still climbing through broken windows to pry open filing cabinets. I suggested to Bill if we all hit the streets he might find a use for me. I was young, strong, a good entry man, and I knew San Francisco. He said, "Maybe." I took this to mean no.

We were all freed within a week of each other, and one afternoon not long after I ran into Bill's partner on the street. He was a man who had started life by trying to work but he had liked drinking and partying too much and had slid out of his community into the streets. He was broke, as I was, and he suggested we try something together. It was reasonable. Who is more likely to be trustworthy than someone you have just met in jail?

I asked him what was wrong with Bill? He said Bill was boozing a lot. He was getting old, his nerve was frayed, and he didn't seem able to settle down to form a working plan. Maybe he would come around, but, meanwhile, they needed walking money. That was okay with me. I knew I was being used, but I didn't care.

We decided to hit easy stuff and after looking around for a few hours we finally broke into one of the state licensing bureaus. We found a large vault and inside we imagined a big pile of cash. We studied this safe carefully, and recognized our only real hope was day com, and for this we needed Bill. It was early, not yet midnight.

We found Bill in the bar next to his hotel. He was drunk and talking loud to the bartender about some swindle he had been caught in at the racetrack. His partner managed to draw him aside, and he made a pretense of not recognizing me. Then when I had placed myself, he wasn't sure he trusted me. He was flushed and abusive.

He told us we didn't know shit, we were punks and amateurs who couldn't do shit without his help, and what kind of a baby's piggy did we need him to help us break into? His partner whispered earnestly, building a mounting pile of five dollar and ten dollar licensing fees until the possible total began to seem splendid. Enough for us all to get well. All he had to do was call the shots. We'd do the work.

He wanted another drink. Then he'd go. I watched his eyes. Something was wrong. His partner explained how the place was just hanging open, we'd smashed a large window, and we didn't have forever, but Bill insisted on the drink as the first price of his cooperation, and he called for a double and then invited one of us to pay for it. The partner was empty, so I came up with the money.

We hurried back to the alley and prepared to re-enter the building. Here we got the first shock. Bill wasn't coming in. "I can't stand another fall," he said. He was leaning against the wall, rolling slightly on his shoulders, head down, his shirt pulled half out of his pants. "One more bust and they'll bitch me."

"You don't have to come in," I said quickly. I didn't want

him blundering around inside. He said all he needed to know was the make of the vault, and I made the run, leaving them both outside.

The safe was tall and double-doored with a center lock. It was a Mosler. When I told this to Bill he seemed even drunker than he had moments before. "A Mosler two-door. Let me see . . ." He paused, frowning. "That's a four tumbler, no, I think it's five." He looked at us. "It's hard to remember."

"Do you remember anything?" his partner asked.

He decided this offended him and pulled away and began to sway back and forth in the center of the alley. "I remember a lot," he said.

He was beginning to raise his voice. "What do you think?" I asked.

"It's left," he said.

I crawled back into the darkened office and turned the knob left. Nothing. Naturally, I also tried it right, even though I knew this could no longer work, and then I ran back to the alley to see what our next move should be. The alley was empty. I wasn't particularly surprised.

This story has another story within it as an equally ironic footnote. Still more years later, when I had finally squared out and was working in an office, I used to try to amuse the secretaries with exaggerated accounts of some of my capers, and I talked about techniques I had heard of from Bill and others like him, implying I had once been the master of these hidden arts. Idle talk on a coffee break. The next day one of them brought me a small bank. She thought there might be a few dollars in it, but she had lost the key and didn't want to smash the bank to find out. She hoped I could open it. I worked on it for a while with a paper clip and then had to give up. I saw real disappointment in her eyes, not over the few dollars, but because I had exposed myself as another big mouth. She had believed me. I'd believed Bill, too.

I also never met a real con man, although I knew dozens of short con amateurs who talked wisely of "laying the note" and "playing the strap," but I did meet and admire a genuine weeder. Del York. For obvious reasons, to protect the guilty, I'm not using real names, but Del was seventy when I first met him in the Nevada prison thirty years ago and there's small chance he's above the ground.

He'd spent most of his adult life in one jail or another, but he was able to view his experience without bitterness. He had chosen, he said, knowing the risk. He thought those who lived on the other side had also chosen and he would never deny them the right, but it was clear he thought them fools.

I've been looking at a poem I wrote for Del. It's called "The Road" and it's dated June 5, 1946. It's an indulgence to slip in old poetry on you, but I've talked about it a lot and perhaps it's no more than just to flash a fragment. Further, these lines show more clearly how Del impressed me then than any of the complex retrospection I find in my head today. Starting in the middle then . . .

> So my shoes are shot
> My hair turned white
> Behind Waupon's walls and my hands
> were broken in Lancing's mine
> So my friends are dead or doing time
> and my life is gone

> *and I am left behind*
> *My life is gone*
> *and that is that*
> *A man can always find a place to sleep*
> *and hustle enough to eat.*
>
> *What do I know now,*
> *but what the walls could teach me,*
> *my life passed as a dream*
> *that never quite came true,*
> *and I never knew that other life,*
> *holding a job*
> *growing old with a wife,*
> *The saving, the spending*
> *The fear of it ending*
> *Would it have been better to scuffle and scheme*
> *or grow old chasing a dream*

I have to take some responsibility for the romanticism, but, reflected through me, this is largely how Del saw his life. It could be argued he had no option. His choices were largely made and if he couldn't have lived with the result, his only alternative would have been to live in despair. I'm sure he had his bad moments, we all do, but generally he was full of warmth, humor and serenity, and I believe these emotions are not only impossible to counterfeit, but beyond the power of casual choice. And since he had served seventeen years in a single stretch of solitary confinement (and how does that reflect my sixty days on bread and water?) his gentleness as well as his sanity must be seen as extraordinary.

I can't tell Del's tale, as pleasant as that would be, for though I listened to many of his stories, the details have faded and I am left with only a few fragments and a scene or two. I see him living on the Barbary Shore in San Francisco in the 1890s, the fancy man of a famous madam. I picture him riding the rails back and forth across the West, and stealing chickens to boil in tin cans at the hobo jungles, which were once everywhere. He told me the difference between hoboes and bums. Hoboes would work, bums wouldn't. He told me chickens were called gumps because they were as chinless as Andy Gump in the Sunday funnies, and he taught me how to steal them with a line and a hook baited with a bit of bread. I never have. A lot of men were moving around the country, riding the rails, looking for work and a better place to live, running from the union busters and running from the law, or just drifting. Drifting south in the winter, drifting down to St. Loo, and north in the summer, up to Chi. Thieves like Del blended with the general traffic. At this time, he was a weeder.

The prime, and perhaps only, requirement for life as a weeder was a working knowledge of locks. Locks were much easier to pick then, but some skill was still needed. The most common lock was the hogeye padlock, and it was as easy to open with a pick as it was with a key. If you knew how.

The weeder drifted into a small town and stayed with a friend, if he had one, or put up at some local hotel or rooming house and pretended to be looking for work, or traveling with some line, to cover his suitcases, or, if he preferred a grander style, looking for property to develop. Late at night, he slipped from his room, fed the local dogs with whom he'd already made friends, and picked the locks on the various stores. He carefully "weeded" their merchandise, never taking so much it would be missed the next morning, and even when inventory turned up the shortage it was never so great it couldn't be written off as shrinkage due to shoplifting. Weeders took the smallest and most expensive items — imported perfumes, silk stockings, watches, jewelry. When they were finished, they locked the doors behind them and went on to the next town.

They worked regular routes through a roughly established territory, just like the drummers they so closely resembled, and were careful never to show their faces too often. The thing they hated most was for someone to come through their territory going rawjaw. Some crude burglar (like me) ripping off doors, smashing windows, breaking locks, looting stores and generally smoking up the state. This brought heat, and caused the local merchants to invest in stronger and more sophisticated protection. It happened just this way. Gradually the hogeye gave way to the more complicated cylinder lock, and while this, too, could be picked, it was nowhere near so easy.

I liked to imagine these quiet weeders, working their way across the country so deftly no one can be certain a crime has been committed. Collecting a harvest to sell in one of the party cities and then playing for days, weeks or months, like a cowboy blowing his pay at the railhead, before they went broke and had to move into the field again. Sometimes, I imagine, they met men in these cities who talked them into other lines of work, playing on the long con, or setting up jobs for a safe man, or even driving for armed robbers.

But as weeders I see them as unlicensed tax collectors, even though I know they were parasites. Still, it was the difference between a bedbug, who can tap you so deftly you don't know you've been bitten, and the clumsy outrage of a mosquito. As has been observed of other criminal careers, the weeder probably worked as hard for smaller wages than the traveling salesman he so closely resembled. His choice then was made from other motives. He was in the Life, free of the schoolmarm and the ladies of the church, the same as the hookers he helped support and the gamblers to whom he lost his money.

I doubt there are weeders anymore and Frank and Jesse aren't robbing trains. Most men don't hunt for their lives, or steal golden apples for glory. The frontier is gone and the moon is a dead rock, but the dream of our old freedom dies hard. When I asked Del why he had chosen to go as he had, he said, "I wasn't interested in much else."

I'm compelled in my moderate service of truth to lay some stroke against this golden glow of nostalgia I've been laboring to produce. I'm sure some weeders were mean bastards who stole as they did only because they were too timid or too cowardly to attempt larger game, and Del, himself, didn't do seventeen years in the hole for simple breaking and entering. He robbed a train. And I never saw these pastoral weeders, these gentle rogues. I am only repeating what I was told, as I repeated the lore of the safecracker, and maybe none of it was true as I heard it. The point I did miss at my peril was that all these old thieves were in jail, and had all been in jail many times, and I certainly wouldn't have credited expertise on the banking industry I had gained from the idle conversations of those I met in the poorhouse.

Big John Grimes, Bob's protector and jocker, also told the tale. He was a safe-man, working on his fourth conviction, and to the extent that anyone led us he was our leader. A huge man and the softest touch in the joint. He was always making loans, canceling gambling debts, trying to get some free-world money to someone's sick wife. He made law, dispensed justice and fed the hungry. I tried to write about Big John for the *Reader's Digest*, as my most unforgettable character. I said he "had a smile as broad as a Jack O'Lantern and a heart as big as his head." I don't know what he was really like.

The day he went home he came on the yard wearing his street clothes. You left Nevada wearing whatever you had worn in, and John was in an old-fashioned three-piece suit, and he sported a high-crowned Stetson. He looked uncomfortable in these clothes, as if this suit were the strange uniform and not the blues he had just discarded. I couldn't imagine then how he must have been wondering what he would find to do in the alien world he was about to enter, but I could plainly see he was nervous. A few months later we heard he had been caught busting a safe in Colorado and they had bitched him, convicted him under a habitual criminal act, which was equivalent to Life. One by one, they all went out and failed.

Most of the quality of those years in Nevada is distant to me now, and when I think of prisons it is not this one I remember. As it comes back to me the day is always warm and Mick and I are turning flips on the lawn in front of the bull pen, and seated not far away is a young Indian, who every day without fail comes on the yard carrying an apple crate, which he places in a particular spot, and then sits there silently all day long. He cells alone, he speaks to no one and no one has ever seen him do anything except eat and sit on his apple crate. This is odd enough. Then someone told me one of the handful of older Indians in the joint is his father.

Maybe Steamboat, named for the shuffling quality of his locomotion, will come down the metal steps from the sick bay where he lives and take a short walk in the sun. Steamboat is the oldest prisoner, deep in his eighties, and was first sent here, rumor has it, for fucking his mule. Or maybe I will fall into conversation with a friend who wears a pair of French, Shriner and Urner shoes, and he will once again direct my attention to these marvelous shoes and explain to me they are the finest made and then wonder if I have enough brass for a cup of coffee in the inmate canteen.

Or I'm playing bridge in the bull pen, learning from a bright man I now recognize as an Easterner, or going broke in a poker game. Or I'm working leather, learning the art of Mexican saddle tooling. We walk and talk and the months pass. I seem neither to change nor to suffer very much. I am only waiting for my life to begin. But I am one of those who keep a tight lid, and underneath a lot is going on. I'm learning I'm mortal.

My mortality came to me in a terrifying siege of acute hypochondria which lasted well over a year and only released me when I had learned to accept my own death, not as a function of the remote future, but as an immediate and constant possibility. Not someday, but anyday. Not tomorrow, but tonight.

This is how it happened. I began to use Benzedrine, a trade name for amphetamine sulphate, one of the compounds now known as speed. It was simple to get just after the war, which had spurred its development. The Army supplied it to soldiers to charge them for desperate ventures and the drug supplied a massive thrust of confidence and energy. When they came home they recognized the active principle, compounded with several volatile oils, in the Benzedrine nasal inhaler.

At first, the bolder inmates, claiming colds or sinusitis, simply asked some friendly guard to bring them an inhaler, and the guard, usually unaware, would be happy to do this small favor. In time, when everyone was hep, even the dimmest of friendly guards, someone had to be paid to smuggle them in, and it was still the cheapest possible high. The inhaler cost less than a dollar, and another dollar for the guard bought enough benny to stay high for days.

The inhaler was cracked open, like removing the meat from a nut, and yielded an accordian-pleated square of absorbent paper, stained a vivid yellow-orange and so redolent of menthol it provoked an immediate reflex of nausea. Folded into the small yellow accordion was a slip of paper warning that improper use might cause irritability and restlessness. This bootless whisper of medical authority amused us because it carefully ignored one other effect — a small piece of this charged paper could get you off for hours.

Someone handed me one of these doses. I took it and I liked it. It was like an infusion of sunlight bringing a tide of optimism and energy. I enjoyed working, which I never quite did when I was straight, and this had continued to bother me. Suddenly I could write for hours. I lost my shyness. It seemed I could sing. Conversation became an event. However, the downs were ferocious. For every golden moment there was one of leaden aftermath. With dope I have always found the law of compensation both subtle and relentless.

After I had taken this drug a few times I happened on a copy of Coronet magazine with the banner: BENZEDRINE

CAN KILL YOU! You can imagine how that interested me. The article was far more temperate than the banner, but it still offers a fair example of how subjects of this kind were, and are, routinely slanted. Benzedrine could kill you if you took massive doses and drove for several days straight, as many truck drivers were said to be doing, because, unable to recognize your profound fatigue, you might drift into highway hypnosis. This slender premise was fleshed out with a more general warning. These stimulants were hard on the circulatory system and presented grave danger to those with unsound hearts.

I laughed at the article. But the next time I was high, sitting in my cell writing, I remembered and decided to take my pulse. My heart was going around a hundred and thirty. Since I had no idea what a normal heartbeat was, I asked my cell partner to take his. He was doing eighty. Immediately I plunged into panic. My heart was racing out of control. I had always enjoyed the kind of health where I was scarcely aware I had any organs. Now my heart pounded like some crude and almost disabled engine.

I raked the bars with my tin cup, the traditional call for help, and, after a long time when I thought I might die at any moment, I was taken to the infirmary. Nevada didn't afford a doctor and the sick bay was run by a convict nurse, a middle-aged homosexual who was living with his muscular young orderly. He looked me over, not without sympathy, told me I was simply upset. With the guard standing next to me I could hardly confess I was dying from the effects of a dangerous drug. The orderly gave me a few ounces of bromide, which had no effect, and sent me back to my cell where I passed a terrible night.

The box I opened so casually was Pandoric. My anxiety produced the symptoms and the appearance of the symptoms increased my anxiety. This cycle swiftly tightened to an almost unsupportable tension. And while I suspected — and hoped! — from the beginning I might be pumping this disaster out of nothing, there remained no method by which I could convince myself I wasn't really sick.

My fear raged that first night. I had been abandoned. No one cared. No one had ever cared and I would not live to see morning. If I had been free I might have broken my focus, but locked in a dark cell with another man sleeping a few feet away, I could find no way to help myself. I had passed the gunfight in Nevada without fear and stared calmly at the point of Meyer's rifle, but now, finally, I was frightened.

I wore the night away rubbing my feet together, and polishing my breastbone with my thumb. Instinctively I created a distraction, a counterirritant on which I could focus for those few moments I needed to slip away. Finally, a little before dawn I fell exhausted into sleep.

This problem came full-blown and that's how it persisted. I immediately stopped taking the Benzedrine, but it was too late and for months I was almost never free of my morbid anxiety and lived under a sentence of death I expected to be executed at any moment. Days were only slightly easier than night. I was free to move around, find distraction, wear myself out with exercise, but always dreading the end of the day when I would have to lock up and deal with my terror one to one. When the lights went out each night I was instantly back in the pit.

My symptoms were pervasive. My feet tingled, my skin

crawled, my eyelids twitched, my heart continued to lurch and pound, and my nerves everywhere trembled. I decided only one illness could account for all these symptoms — high blood pressure. I accepted this with some relief because I was much too young to die from hypertension. I had time. Time to free myself and find a doctor who would cure me. Then, again by chance, I noticed a small article in the Reno paper reporting the death of a local man. He had died of hypertension. He had been twenty-two. I was immediately back fighting the bear.

There was no one to talk to about this, no friendly figure of conventional authority and wisdom, no doctor, no minister, no psych, and if there had been I'm not sure I would have gone to them. I was too proud. I took the condemned man who had cut my hair and joked about his own death as my model. I remembered his cheerful resignation and I thought of him decomposing out behind the gas house. I struggled for a similar strength.

At the same time I pursued hope. I reasoned with myself. How could I fall to such an outside chance? How could I die at twenty of a disease of the old? But these things happened every day. People sitting quietly listening to the radio were killed by a plane crashing through the wall. What could be more unlikely? Yet the people were dead. What did it mean? I collected so many such stories the incredible began to seem the norm. Anything could happen at any moment. The art of logical prediction was bullshit. The true nature of reality was madness.

That was my trouble. Not my heart, not my blood pressure, but a full-blown, raging case of existential dread. Nabokov ends *Pale Fire* by suggesting somewhere, for each of us, an assassin is on the move, and it was those footsteps I was hearing.

Finally, I came to a point where I would rather be dead than continue to suffer. How could it matter so much? One day I would be dead and that day would surely come. How could I worry so? While I was alive, I would try to live.

When this reached a point of absolute conviction, when I lay exhausted, ready to die, the knot that racked me loosened, and my imaginary symptoms vanished. They have never returned.

All this time I went on walking and talking, but I never just pulled time. I always had projects, interests, hopes. I remained ambitious. I resented the passing time, but I didn't yet feel diminished by it. I was young. But it did bother me not to be able to finish the projects I set for myself. If I couldn't work, how could I live?

Mick and I remained close and we worked on a lot of ideas together. We tried to become cartoonists. We tried to write a novel, but gave up when we couldn't agree as to whose name would come first on the title page. Then I began an autobiographical novel with the unfortunate title: *As the Twig Is Bent*. An even dimmer project. It was abandoned after thirty pages. The first of many novels I never finished.

My poetry written at that time, which by the wildest chance I still have, takes brotherhood as its dominant theme, and contains laments for the soldiers and sailors who died in the war I ducked. I had begun to fantasize heavily. I dreamed of adjusting the atoms of my body so I could slip through the bars and the walls out into the night to walk to Carson City, where I would slip through the wall of some clothing store to dress carefully before walking through the wall of a bank. And at other times I dreamed of my poetry being published and an admiring world of poetry lovers would exclaim: Why is this sensitive boy in prison? Why is this full-hearted lover of mankind being punished?

Some marginal house offered to publish my poems in the slender volume I so dearly imagined if I could guarantee the sale of five hundred copies. I couldn't guarantee the sale of five copies, and there, for some years, the matter ended.

We spent the entire time in Nevada under detainer from California. They wanted to try us for the Sacramento burglaries and the robbery in Los Angeles. We often tried to imagine California would dismiss their charges and drop the holds against us. It wasn't unreasonable. Our crimes were routine, and often when the state placing the detainer is notified the men are now free to be taken, the D.A. will decide against the expense of further prosecution, particularly if the time served seems adequate punishment for the aggregate crimes. But not California. It was said California would enter Hell to pick you up on a charge of carrying a concealed sandwich. Being close to Reno didn't help. The detectives who drew the assignment would be free to spend a day or two gambling and playing before they drove down to Carson City to pick up the meat.

L. A. County Jail

IT WAS STRANGE to dress out knowing we were not being freed. I put on a stolen tweed suit, now a little too small, and my saddle shoes, and stared at the boy in the full-length mirror. I looked like anyone else. Bob and I were going to L.A. together. Since Mick had had no part in the robbery, he had been taken to Sacramento to answer the burglary charges. Bob and I had had little to say these last two years, but we weren't awkward with each other. Big John had passed Bob to one of his friends and Bob had spent the entire time playing cards and eating well, but it didn't seem to matter now. Bob maintained the fiction that John Grimes and Yonkers after him had simply been friends, and I had no reason not to go along with this.

We were picked up by two detectives working out of the Hollywood substation, and because I was such an escape artist they fit me with an Oregon boot, a large steel doughnut that locks around the ankle. It's awkward, heavy, and makes it impossible to run. The boot shamed me even more than the handcuffs and I sat in the train station trying to hide it behind my unencumbered leg.

We waited an hour for the train to L.A. and the scenes I saw there, the little flashes of ordinary life, touched me deeply. I watched an old man in a large black coat eat a bag of peanuts, dropping the shells on the marble floor, watched a child playing around its mother's feet, while she read a magazine, and I fell in love with a young girl who sat patiently, her legs framed by her luggage, next to a sailor who slept with his arms folded across his chest. Occasionally he began to snore, disturbed himself, almost woke, then settled back to sleep. The girl looked at the floor, when she wasn't staring off across the station at a large yellow clock. Here was the girl of my poetic fancies, the delicate child-woman, my friend, my playmate, my companion and inspiration. My lover. How could I imagine this and not see Alice. How many times now had I heard Alice groan and say, "It hurts, honey." Now I closed my eyes and heard this girl say, "Oh, I love it when you do that to me." But when I met her eyes briefly she looked down into my lap where my hands were cuffed. I carried her face in my mind for several years.

It was so strange to be here like this. In the prison the physical weight of it made it seem a sensible place, but here, almost free but for the cuffs and the boot, and the detectives, it seemed awful to be held, not to be free to get up and walk into a different future. It still never occurred to me I would be sent to San Quentin for a thirty-five cent robbery.

We traveled by compartment. We were shackled to our bunks with special chains long enough to reach the toilet, and then the porter was called in, given the keys, and told not to return them until we reached Los Angeles. He looked at our chains and looked away with what seemed to be embarrassment.

As the train started I began to imagine it would be wrecked, but wrecked in such a way I would be thrown free, suddenly unchained, to make my way to — to where? Then I began to worry about those who might be killed in the train wreck I had wished for. My fantasies were no longer limitless and gradually they were becoming circumscribed by a loose net of general rules. If I fantasized invisibility I also found myself wondering if a real invisible man would be able to see.

The train trip was pleasant. We enjoyed the different food and played cards with the detectives. One was a cold-eyed meaty man, who seemed contemptuous, but the other was young and pleasant. He told us he'd smoked marijuana, which neither of us had ever had the chance to try. He had decided, unofficially, he should try to understand what it was like in case he was ever called to deal with someone under the influence, and he'd taken a joint from a few ounces he held in evidence. First he warned his wife to stay away from him, then he went into the bedroom, sat on the edge of the bed, and smoked. He'd found the effect negligible and couldn't imagine why people would risk their freedom over such a thing. He didn't go on to wonder why it was against the law.

Big John didn't predict the six months we would spend in the L. A. County waiting trial on the robbery, and this jail was not Big John's territory. It was 1948 and the twenties and the thirties, John's era, were lost beyond the war and new styles were being evolved. I saw only the reflection, but once again began to alter myself as I sought acceptance on new terms. The flavor of Carson City had been rural, but here in L.A. County it was urban. The talk was always of fast cars and clothes. The zoot suit was still being worn. Of parties at Malibu beach houses and distant connections with various movie stars. However, neither dope nor music had yet become a dominant theme. We talked scores and whores, and I told the tale of those few hours in the Nevada desert over and over again.

The old man I had robbed of the thirty-five cents and frightened so badly came to court to testify against us at our preliminary hearing. Two unusual things happened. First, he identified Bob as the man who had robbed him, evidently confusing the incident where I had been along with an earlier incident where Bob had been alone, and, second, he suffered another heart attack while on the stand and had to be helped from the courtroom. Our confessions were sufficient cause to order us held for the superior court, but there was clearly some question whether our victim would live long enough to testify against us. Also, it was clear Bob was hooked here, but I wasn't. It was a common practice for those who couldn't beat a beef to cop out and free their crime partners, and as we left the courtroom I had a minute to put this proposition to Bob.

He looked at me calmly and said, "I'm not going up there alone."

He was going to take me along for company.

The feeling at L. A. County was different from Carson City in other ways. It seemed much closer to the free world. We knew it was there, just on the other side of the walls, and we all hoped to find our way out of this trouble. If prison is hell and the streets are heaven, then jails like L. A. County are limbo. You drift suspended, undefined, waiting for judgment and its definition.

It seems all I did was play bridge. My partner was a man who claimed to be a Polish prince, and he signed himself *Prince Bielsky*. Of course, no one believed him, certainly not me, and I played a sly game with him seeing how close I could come to calling him a liar without actually saying so. Maybe he was a prince, but we assumed anyone who claimed the slightest distinction to be a phony, and some of the others were pissed at him for thinking us so foolish as to swallow his story. They gave him a blanket party. While he was sitting tailor fashion on the floor, playing a hand (I was dummy) they slipped up behind him, threw a woolen blanket over his head, and anyone who felt mean jumped in and began to kick him. I didn't kick, but I identified with the kickers. I didn't get away with it either.

The next morning he joined me as I paced the narrow corridor in front of the cells. He had a dark bruise on the ridge of his pale forehead and his nose was slightly swollen. "You knew what they planned?" he asked. He had a slight accent.

"No," I lied.

"I think you did. I think from the way you acted you did."

"No, I didn't."

He looked at me closely. "You think I care about being beaten. Those sneaks! I am sad you could be involved in something so petty."

Bob and I were assigned a public defender. Los Angeles maintains a large staff of P.D.s and, unlike other smaller cities, this is the only legal work they do. They are paid from city funds and anyone with a practical knowledge of the world would immediately realize they must work closely with the D.A.'s office. Sometimes this can help you. If the P.D. is convinced of your innocence he can convey his conviction to the D.A. with far more force than a hired attorney who says only what he is paid to say. But more often they trade off clients with the prosecutors, giving up one to save another, and, obviously, they are neither the most vigorous nor intelligent lawyers in the area. It's a safe, quiet job and they like it that way.

Our P.D. was a kindly and fatherly man who approached us with apparent sympathy. Yes, he acknowledged, you might beat them in a trial, but why take the chance when you could lose? Then they'll jam it into you. Take the middle course. Cop out. Save time, theirs and yours, save money. Cop out and do it the way that's easiest for everyone. There was, he said, little chance, considering the time we had already served, we would be sent to San Quentin.

Bob was convinced, and, with some reluctance, I agreed. As soon as we entered our pleas of guilty, we were routinely processed and swiftly sentenced to the California Department of Corrections at San Quentin for a period of not less than one year and not more than life.

This official process was marked by another irony. We had been sentenced and returned to the crowded bull pen to await return to our tanks. Bob seemed stunned. "San Quentin isn't Carson City," he told me. I knew that. Everyone had heard horror stories set in San Quentin. But I had also heard they had a school there, and I was telling myself how hard I would study, how much I would learn, how hard I would try, and what was another year or two. I was still young.

The P.D. came in to say a few consoling words to us, but he happened to sit down next to two other kids, even younger, and began to father away at them, telling them of the opportunities to be found in Quentin, and one of the boys burst into tears. They were juveniles who had not yet been sentenced. They were sitting there waiting to go home and here was this strange man telling them they were being sent to San Quentin.

The P.D. rose in some confusion and finally recognizing his mistake began to look around for us. I turned away and rested my head on my arms. He had advised us badly, failed his promise, cost us several years of our lives, and now he didn't even remember what we looked like.

The night before I was scheduled to be transferred to Quentin, I had my head shaved. Prince Bielsky regarded my transformation with sly amusement, and said, "I know why you had that done."

I was embarrassed and annoyed. This strange man not only knew I was afraid, he knew exactly what I was afraid of. Again I lied. "It's good for your hair."

"And you have such trouble with your hair. I don't know why you try to act so tough."

I looked away. I could hardly say: I am tough.

The Guidance Center

==

THE TRIP I made this first time to Quentin is one I have
made more than several times since — not over the same
ground, I speak of the journey I realized in my head — but
this was the only time one of the more active components
of my misery was apprehension. I knew Carson City had
been a country club. San Quentin was the real thing. The
real prison.

We were carried by bus, an old Greyhound auctioned
to the state, and we rode as free as any passengers except
we wore white coveralls and our legs were shackled. There
were thirty of us on this chain and if we had acted together
we could have overpowered the two guards and seized the
bus, but they never worried we would act in disciplined
harmony, we would have been too busy deciding who was
going to be captains and lieutenants and sergeants and cor-
porals, and I never heard of an escape from a transportation
bus. You start at one jail and end in another and all this

works as smoothly as if every jail in the state were inter-connected by underground tunnels.

Bob wasn't on this chain. He had, as I learned later, en-tered Quentin several weeks before. I no longer blamed him. I no longer believed he could have saved me. I had done it to myself. I knew the first rule — never cop out! And I had copped out, taken the plea, simply because some time-serving old bastard had made it seem like the easy and agreeable thing to do and I had wanted to please him. I al-ways copped out, always for the same reason.

My seatmate, by an odd coincidence, was a writer. Years before, while doing time in a small midwestern prison, he had written and published a novel, a feat which astonished them into granting a parole, and he had followed his star to Hollywood, where it had flickered for some years before setting dramatically. "I couldn't stay off the sauce," he told me. He was a nervous and intelligent man with pale eyes and a red face. I took him to be around fifty. I had been standing next to him in the bull pen where we shaped up for the Quentin chain, and one of the transportation bulls had walked up to him to ask, "Are you the writer?"

And Gerry had turned with a smile, much as if he had been asked for his autograph, and said, "Yes, I've written twenty books."

Twenty books and thirty-five B pictures later, here he was on his way to Quentin for bad checks. It troubled me. It threatened my faith in the possibility of change. Despite the vast literature which feeds our hunger for positive growth, I had observed that many people did not appear to change. And if I could not change what would happen to me?

We took the central route, up U.S. 98, and I remember it

was early spring. In jails you starve for clean colors and good smells, and I watched out the windows trying to make the most of this brief trip. Everything looked so good. I could have lived in the towns, worked on the farms, swum in the ponds and slept in the shade of the trees. It was already a long time since my life had been my own.

I had traveled this route before, up through Bakersfield and Fresno, in those years just after the Depression. Moving on to a new town, just, in a sense, as I was now. My father had told me, "We're going to a new place where you can make a fresh start."

San Quentin occupies a small point of land with the same name along the shore of San Francisco Bay, and you pass through this lovely city to reach it, through San Francisco and across the Golden Gate Bridge, past Sausalito. A sign warns you are entering a prison reservation.

For years the walls at Quentin have been painted green, and while this has no bearing on their essential function it does make the prison seem less grim. You drive up as a tour bus approaches a hotel and unload into the first gate. You are stripped, searched and photographed. I remember Gerry, we were friends by now, sitting naked on a wooden bench. It's hard to sit naked like this in a strange and possibly hostile place without crossing your legs and folding your arms across your chest, and this is the posture Gerry had unconsciously assumed. When I sat down beside him, he said, "Wouldn't it be awful to die in here?" I knew exactly what he meant. It was like being lowered into the earth. How to imagine you would ever come out?

In the room where we had our mug shots taken, some wit had hand-lettered and posted several signs. The prediction attributed to Louis XV "*Après moi, le déluge.*" Gerry translated. And the motto said to be Eisenhower's: "*Illegitimus non carborundum.*" I thought this stuff classy, and it occurred to me I might meet smart and sophisticated men here.

Also we learned we had been granted a reprieve of sorts. For three months we would be assigned to a prison within the prison, an orientation unit called the Guidance Center, and we would not mix with the general population. To insure this we were dressed in Army fatigues rather than the usual blues. When we asked the attendant what we would do in the Guidance Center, he smiled scornfully. "Sit around and take a bunch of tests."

The point of these tests was to gather information for the Classification Committee and they would determine how and where we would serve our time. There was variety in California. At one end was Chino, the first of the wall-less prisons, good food, good visits and the Man wasn't staring down your throat all day. At the other end stood Folsom, stuffed with psychos, knife artists and other varieties of hopeless cases. Killing was unknown at Chino, rare on the Quentin yard, but a commonplace at Folsom. You could be shanked there and not even realize how you had offended. Or so it was said. I certainly believed it.

I sat and stared into the lens of an old view camera to have my mug shot taken. This photo is laminated into your identity card, as well as your privilege card (you must still have your identity even though you have lost your privileges) and you carry these cards constantly. After a few years the face under the plastic no longer looks like the face in the mirror.

When we first entered the main prison we found ourselves in a small garden, sarcastically scored as The Garden Beautiful, and I recognized it as the place where Ray had stood in the photo he had sent me at Preston. There was a lawn intersected with cement paths, and flower beds bright with pansies. A small birdbath played where the paths cross, but I never saw a bird in it.

We moved past Distribution and Household, past the cream stucco of the ed building, past Four Box, down to Four Gate and there was the big yard. All of the Nevada State Prison could have been set in this yard. At the time there were close to five thousand men in Quentin, enough for a good-sized town, and at various times of the day every swinging dick was on this yard. Five thousand men, four thousand of whom at any given moment are beating their gums, telling the Tale, laying the rap, pissing and moaning, walking and talking, and here, it sometimes seemed, it was easier to hear Freud and Jung than Dillinger and Floyd.

We crossed that first time just before evening lockup, marching Indian file, raw, awkward, intimidated, like the new fish shuffling along at the rear of I Company, and a thousand men came to stand and watch us pass as if we were a parade. "Wait for me, baby," someone shouted. "Don't hook up in the Guidance Center." There was no way to know who had been yelled at. I kept walking, looking at my feet.

Then I heard my name and Mick was running across the yard shouting at me. I was glad to see him. He had already pulled four months on a one-to-fourteen out of Sacramento. He fell in step beside me. "You've got three months of shit to wade through."

"I know."

Someone else shouted a wisecrack. "Don't pay any attention," Mick said.

"I don't," I lied.

"They do this every time fish hit the yard."

"What've they got you doing?"

He looked scornful. "Working in the jute mill."

Already I knew this to be the worst possible assignment. "Tough tit."

"It ain't shit." Later he told me when you listened to the looms working, you could hear them saying: *I-gotyou-fucked, I-gotyoufucked, I-gotyoufucked.*

We walked down the yard, parallel to the East Block, toward the South Block—The Largest Cell Block In the World! we were told. No one said who had gone around to measure. And out of the yard and into the South Block Rotunda, where I caught a glimpse into an enormous mess hall, toward the large iron door that led to the old West Block, once called Knife Alley, and now the temporary location of the Guidance Center.

Mick stopped and said, "See you in three months."

"Okay."

"Take it easy."

"You, too."

Mick smiled and said, "I'll take it anyway I can get it."

This was one of his stock remarks. He had several for every occasion. I said them too. They were meant to convey the impression we were wised up and the true masters of this situation.

Lockup was in process in the Guidance Center yard, and here a smaller population, dressed in green, was filing into the West Block. Gerry and I thought we might cell together, but a Quentin rule set the age difference between cell partners at seven years, to prevent the older prisoners from getting at the younger, and I ended in a cell with someone I've forgotten. We washed up and were released for dinner. Again we were served cafeteria style, lined up all the way around the walls of this huge mess hall — you could have stored zeppelins here — slouching toward the steam table and the food. Which wasn't bad. Chili Mac, salad, green beans, five slices of white bread, black coffee and spice cake. What you are aware of here is the noise. Thousands of spoons and forks thrashing away at thousands of metal trays, thousands of conversations, mixed with the banging of metal dippers against steel cauldrons at the serving line, while back in the kitchen the dishwashing machines roared like reapers. Across the mess hall we can see the blue Quentin population. There is every type. The kind of street bravos I had known in Preston, mixed with creeping old men and intellectual cons, spooning chili and reading books, and a lot of just plain prisoners. The blacks were segregated in the mess hall. The Chicanos weren't. High above us, on a narrow metal walk, two bulls walked around and around carrying rifles.

The cells were the same as the cells in Nevada, two men crammed into a space designed for one, but Q issued radio headsets and I hadn't heard the radio for several years. I settled down to listen. *"The Dickie Bird said, 'Haven't you heard? Spring is here, spring is here, spring is here.'"*

I read the Rules and Regulations of the California Department of Corrections. Nevada had ten rules, California over a hundred.

The next morning after a breakfast of hotcakes, I ran into Bob on the Guidance Center yard. He had been here two weeks, so compared to me he was an old-timer. He told me what to expect. Halfday we would spend at Orientation Class with a Guidance Center counselor. We would learn the institutional ropes and he would have the opportunity to take a long hard look at us, and weed out the worst of the nuts and fuckups. The other halfday would be spent testing. They had tests to measure our every aspect. I looked forward to them. I usually scored well on almost any test and I looked to them as a source of fresh confidence, a re-affirmation of my special qualities. After three years in Nevada and the L.A. County I felt shabby.

Bob was anxious to impress me and I was equally anxious to be unimpressed. In prison the slightest distinction is cherished and enlarged. I told my gun-battle stories and how I escaped from the Nevada prison after having been there only twenty-eight days, and Bob, since he had bad feet, had been allowed to keep his own shoes rather than wear the Santa Rosa hightops which were standard issue. He had polished these shoes until they glittered, and, as we spoke, he continued to rub one shoe and then the other against his pants leg. He also wore the watch Big John had given him, and he glanced at it frequently as if he had an important appointment and wasn't just standing around, as I was, killing time until lunch.

"What's Quentin like?" I asked him.

"It's okay, I hear. If you keep your nose clean and mind your own business."

"If they let you. I hear half the yard's packing either a shank or a pipe."

"I don't know," Bob said. "I'm going to push some iron."

He went over to the iron pile. We had two complete sets of York dumbbells and some horizontal bars along with courts for volley ball, basketball and handball. It's a rare con who doesn't at least think of hitting the iron. The cult of thinness is still in the future and we all want big shoulders and thick necks, particularly when in a couple of months we're going to be walking the big yard.

The word on the big yard was as Bob had given it to me — keep calm, walk slow, obey the important rules and appear as ordinary as possible — then you could drift through Quentin like a shadow, and the only way you might find trouble was if you had the bad luck to become cast in someone else's fantasy. Which is what happened to me.

I was assigned, by the luck of the draw, to a Guidance Center counselor named Harlan Peterson. He was drifting reluctantly into middle age, and, while the handsome young man he had been was still apparent, he was now running to a general soft plumpness that blurred the line of his jaw and swelled his waist. His hair was gray and he wore it a little longer than the fashion of the day. He was one of those men who begin to need a shave in the middle of the afternoon and the blue shadow of his beard contrasted strangely with his red lips. Overall there was something faintly suspect in the way he dressed and carried himself, and the yard, ever alert for such signs, had nicknamed him Penny Peterson. I had hoped my counselor would find me interesting. He did.

We quickly learned we were expected to view this journey through prison as a quest, and the object of our quest was to discover our problem. It was assumed we were here because of psychological problems, and our task now, by which we could expect to be judged, was to isolate and come to terms with them. Boys who had stolen cars were thought to be acting out a symbolic return to the womb and once they had been helped to understand their true motivation and recognize its utter futility they would be free of the compulsion. I mock this now, even if I didn't mock it then, but it's not the most basic notion at which I will invite you to laugh with me, but simply at the grotesque extensions which sometimes flourished here in the California Department of Corrections. And no matter what your private opinion, when the Adult Authority, the remote body authorized to grant parole, asked in tones of high seriousness if you had come to grips with your problem, you were willing to concede you might have a problem even if you had to invent one on the spot. Penny Peterson decided my problem was latent homosexuality.

I detested whatever aspect of my appearance invited these suggestions, and here on the edge of Quentin I worried about the trouble I might draw to myself with my blue eyes and fresh face. And latent homosexuality is one of those impossible charges to defend against, like the nutbusters Joe McCarthy was beginning to invent, and if you said, and how already damning to even have to say it, "I don't suck dicks," the response was, Yes, but how do you know you don't want to?

I was, by now, soaked in Freud, having read most of his basic work in Nevada, and under the duress of his potent authority, I was forced to accept the condition that my real nature might be hidden from me. Almost surely it was. Our real selves were hidden as elusively as the murderers in novels of detection and were only drawn painfully to light and judgment by a careful and expert examination of apparently unrelated clues. And unlike the mystery stories solved by amateurs, this work of detection could only be accomplished by remote professionals. Self-analysis was unthinkable. This suggests a tale of detection where the fugitive is the detective's schizophrenic other self, who would know precisely how to deceive its psychic twin.

The Old Man is under attack today and the vast dark continent he first glimpsed has been cut up by his heirs, but in the forties and fifties Freud was the prophet of the True Faith. Jung, Adler? They were terriers pissing on the spoor of the Great Bear. We were never allowed to doubt we were just as he had said we were. Our difficult search for self-realization has always been hampered by this tendency of specialists to associate themselves with fixed positions, and in prisons, tiny tributaries of the psychological mainstream, this yearning for certain solutions often proves dangerous. I mention, in passing, only the hundreds of men who were lobotomized.

Penny was certain, I was uncertain, and I was in a potentially destructive situation. What I wanted from Quentin was the opportunity to go to school, but if Penny's charge stuck my chance might be lost.

The department had recently started segregating obvious homosexuals. A few years before the queens had been free to swish around the yard and carry on open love affairs. We heard stories of the Jocker's Ball, a sort of Beggar's Holiday, when once a year the guards looked the other way and the queens sallied out in full drag to dance with their lovers to the music of the prison orchestra. But there were too few queens, too many potential lovers and there were some killings. The decision to isolate was taken.

At the time I was threatened with their lot the life of a

homosexual prisoner was even drearier than a mainliner's. They were strictly segregated and celled by themselves in the Old Spanish Prison, the first block constructed on the site, without toilets or running water, and they were marched everywhere, isolated in a strutting and giggling squad, and the only work to which they were assigned was in the prison laundry. An ironic footnote to the feminist movement — even these false females were put to woman's work.

Still, at first, this dubious battle with Penny seemed far from hopeless. I sensed his sympathy and his own nature, shadowed in his ambivalence, but like the Inquisitors, he sought confession. Drive the sulking little brute into the open. The ventilation would do me good. And I was left to say more than a few times: I don't feel like that. What do you want? Should I start swishing and putting out head? He had the grace to blush at this, and we might have gone on in this harmlessly jesuitical fashion if Bob hadn't decided he was too frightened to hack it in the Quentin yard, and opted out in the only way he could imagine. He told them he was homosexual and asked to be segregated. He served his sentence limping along at the end of Queen's Row.

This came close to tearing it, and it provides a pretty illustration of how the prison bureaucracy functioned. This is how they reasoned. Bob was queer. Bob and I were crime partners. Statistics indicated when one crime partner was homosexual the other usually was too. In their pursuit of small certainties, they overlooked the "usually," and overlooked the condition that the crime Bob and I had partnered on had taken place well over three years before.

And I doubt Bob was homosexual. I know Big John fucked him and he must have made some accommodation to the physical act, but in his dreaming self I believe he remained the same Hollywood Romeo I first met on the streets of Sacremento. He was simply chickenshit and preferred to live with the sissies than take the chance he might be killed on the Quentin yard.

My life was simple at this time. I read, listened to the radio, went to class, fenced with Penny, took tests, walked the yard with Gerry and waited for the weekend movies. I wasn't particularly unhappy. Compared to the Nevada Prison, San Quentin was interesting and offered far more opportunity. But sometimes at night, when the lights went out and the radio was silent, in those moments when I turned to compose myself for sleep, I would have a brief vision of the man I might have been rather than the boy I was.

Gerry was a good buddy, but someone soon put him to work. Not because he was a writer, but because he could type one hundred wpm. The prison was stitched together with paperwork and it sometimes seemed every guard needed two clerks if he was to continue to function. Gerry's agent had already hustled him a job and he was working on a film script. He sometimes carried it under his arm as we walked the yard and it excited me just to be close to someone who was close to this magical manuscript.

The orientation classes were interesting and useful for a while. We heard volumes as to how the prison *did* function from the cons. Penny told us how it was *supposed* to function, and we were in a position to adjust the disparity. Penny told us approximately how much time we should expect to do. How the Adult Authority would judge us during our parole hearings, and how we might hope to improve our chances. He laid out the various prison programs to which we might be assigned and attempted to clarify the philosophy behind them. He tried to answer our endless questions.

But each of us had only one motive here. How to get out as quickly as possible, and all this pressure in a single direction soon filled the air with special pleading. This is the real content of almost any exchange between inmate and staff. We were all in on bum beefs. Maybe we had held the gun, stolen the car, written the forged check, but beyond this trivial detail, in the higher sense, we were innocent, and California's focus on our "problems" didn't help, because if we had stolen because of some problem, acted out in a way beyond our immediate control, then we were without guilt, and why were some of us facing assignment to the jute mill, where we would work our asses off and still not eat as well as the captain's clerk?

We were all eager to point out to Penny those considerations that made our case special and those bolder and a little slyer were soon attempting to manipulate him. The classes were spoiled by grievance and calculation, and Penny, because there was nothing else to do, began to take us over to the lower yard, the athletic field, to play softball.

I had never focused on games. My father had tried to push me into sports, had insisted I play, and shown obvious disappointment when I wasn't much good. So I had dismissed ball games as mindless. I struck out twice, but the third time I got a soft bouncing single which I tried to stretch and was thrown out on second. I came back, pleased to have even hit the ball, and Penny motioned me over to where he was sitting a few feet away. He patted the bench beside him. I sat down. I have to tell you I didn't mind the attention.

"I'm sure now you need help," he said.

"Because I don't play ball well?"

"It's more than that." He looked around. "It's apparent to everyone."

This really bothered me. "No one says anything to me."

"You won't be here in the Guidance Center much longer."

"I've been around a while. Nothing's happened to me so far."

After this he began to threaten me with the MMPI, one of the battery of tests we were taking. If I were queer, no matter how deeply I might have repressed the tendency, the Minnesota Multiphasic Personality Inventory would rat on me. Further, this test was designed with such marvelous subtlety it couldn't be tampered with. Those who constructed the MMPI had reckoned with our natural desire to appear normal, whether we were or not, and had built in various alarm and detection systems. If you tried to outfox the test, horns blew, bells rang. Obviously, if I tilted the MMPI I would convict myself automatically.

This test is factored in a series of indices which measure a number of psychic conditions such as manic depression, paranoia, hypomania, schizophrenia as either more positive or more negative. The specific index with which Penny threatened me was the M/F file, simply masculinity-femininity. He indicated this file on someone else's chart, someone whose M/F was comfortably below the median line, and said, "You'll be quite high here."

There are over twelve hundred questions and it takes several hours to answer them all either Yes or No. I approached this with some apprehension. There were some rare queries: *I am a secret agent of God. I often have a lump in my throat. I sometimes think of things too terrible to talk about.*

/ 163

I began to notice a series of questions that appeared tauto-logical. *I would like to be a flower arranger.* That was easy to answer No. *If I were a reporter, I would like to cover the ballet.* This was on the edge, but I said No. *If I were a reporter, I would like to cover sporting events.* I told my first outright lie and said Yes. *I would enjoy the work of a forest ranger.* I could say Yes to this. *I would like to write poetry.* Here I abandoned myself and said No.

There were no more than six or seven questions whose apparent import was so clear and I was sure these obvious leads were simply one of the traps, and there was a subtle organization to the more obscure questions that would expose my attempted deception. I could imagine the inferential associations stretching through infinite levels of complexity.

I sometimes have black, tarry bowel movements. Here was a statement with the rich smell of bait. I once heard two psychs discussing the test of a man who had slipped this particular card into "I Don't Know" and it was their opinion he probably had a light in the well of his toilet. I also wondered at the fate of anyone innocent enough to answer *I am a secret agent of God* in the affirmative.

Most of the class were interested in the MMPI charts. We all wanted to stare into this psychic mirror. Popular magazines ran tests to determine if you had, say, an inferiority complex (an ephemera of the time) but these were toy tests. The MMPI was the certified real thing. In its clear, cold light we would stand stripped of all pretense.

"Well, let's see what this tells us," Penny said, unfolding my chart, where my deepest secrets would be exposed on a graph like the thirty-day Dow-Jones during a period of frantic trading. He shook his head, and shot me a puzzled glance.

I was firmly in the safe male zone of the M/F index, but not so firmly as to open the suggestion of overreaction. My whole psychic profile was utterly bland. It arced along the norm without significant peaks. If this test was as valuable as the claims made for it, I apparently didn't belong here.

But they didn't trust the tests either, the MMPI, or the whole imposing battery. They were rude maps, a few solid sightings pressed around by vast areas of *Terra Incognita*, and useful mainly to confirm conclusions already drawn. The pragmatic proof I belonged in jail was because I was there. This charge, put to me in various ways at different times, was always unanswerable. It remains so.

The other tests told me what I wanted to hear, though hardly as emphatically as I wished. I was verbally quick, numerically slow. The Kuder Preference Test, designed to determine the occupation for which you are temperamentally suited, did not, as I confidently expected, tell me I should be an artist. It told me I would enjoy being a mortician.

When I was classified this first time, at the end of orientation, Penny Peterson sat in on the committee. The Classification Committee was made up from representatives of the various prison departments. The real power was shared by two cooperative branches — Care and Treatment, and Custody. At this time Custody had the final clout. Care and Treatment endlessly proposed various "welfare" programs which Custody routinely attempted to wreck because they feared these programs might threaten their fundamental responsibility which was simply to keep us locked up until the Adult Authority said we could go. Roughly, Custody was the old way, Care and Treatment the new. Custody was usually represented by a captain or lieutenant of the guards, and Treatment sent an associate warden. One of the chaplains would be present, as well as a psych, or sociologist, or, later on, a correctional counselor, and, usually, some one from Education came in.

You always have to wait on the CC, sometimes for hours, as they grind through the men before you. Finally you are shown into the hearing room by a guard, and you find the committee seated around three sides of a large table. They all look you over, then go back to your folder. On the fourth and open side stands a single wooden folding chair. This chair always annoyed me. The committee is seated in comfortable leather swivel chairs, and even, as time passed, and the prison instrumentality had begun to call me Mr. Braly and attempt to present the illusion we were all equals here gathered to discuss the reasonable merits of a proposed cooperative venture, I still sat in the same straight, hard chair. If I were a set designer dressing a scene to show how positive and equalitarian the treatment of inmates had become, it would seem a small detail to provide the subject inmate with an equal chair. But I expect this won't happen until all the priests have discarded their mantles, and the judges have put aside their robes, and the last Royal Person descends from his throne.

I sat on the folding chair and they asked me about Typhoid Bob, and I explained how it had been over three years since we had been arrested together. He had gone his way. I had gone mine. They took this in with apparent skepticism. In the prison bureaucracy any scrap of hard data remains relevant. The ink never fades. They have so few real facts they are reluctant to see those they do have questioned. Hegel wrote that a man is always guilty of any crime he has ever committed. Fair enough, but hardly an appropriate position for those exploring the possibility of rehabilitation. However, they classified forty men a week, every week, and such a case load is impossible. If we depend on God for justice and mercy it is only because we know he has all of eternity to straighten out his files.

> CHRONO-103-A   6/7/48
>
> Subject Inmate, Braly, A-8814, was
> processed this date by the Int. Class.
> Com. Assignment: Print training.
> Custody: Close. No spec. rec.
>
> RECLASS: 6/7/49

At the conclusion of the hearing I attempted a small speech. I thanked them for fair treatment, and thanked them for assigning me to the print shop and not the jute mill. I promised not to fail their trust in me. They stared at me, unconvinced.

Penny caught me in the hall before I could start back to the center. He put his hand lightly on my arm. The only time he ever touched me. "They all agree with me," he said.

There was nothing to say.

"Be careful over there," he continued.

"I will."

The next morning I rolled my bedding, put my few things into the pillowcase for an easy carry, exchanged my green uniform for Quentin blue and hit the yard.

San Quentin

AFTER ALL THIS overture and my own natural apprehension, I found San Quentin an easy jail to do time in, and had soon worn myself a small routine. I celled in the South Block, the dirtiest and loudest of the blocks, which we called Skid Row, worked in the print shop as a trainee, and spent my spare time trying to learn to paint. We worked five days a week and spent weekends walking the upper or lower yards. There was a great variety of men in Quentin in those years just after the war, and I had soon made friends with others like myself.

George was a tall, slender, handsome boy, a few months younger than I, with an IQ that would have been considered high at Harvard and was phenomenal at Quentin. This potent abstraction brought him nothing but trouble. A member of the adult authority told him, "Do you know if I were as smart as you, I'd have a Ph.D. by now?" And another time they asked him a more ominous question: "How do we know you won't use your intelligence to become a criminal genius?" George, like myself, couldn't keep out of his own way, and he didn't want to be a criminal genius, he wanted to be a movie star. He had read things I had not yet encountered. He steered me to Malcolm Lowry's *Under the Volcano*, and Philip Wylie's *Finley Wren* and Huxley's *After Many a Summer*. All of these and many more were in the Quentin library, or available to us through the state library in Sacramento.

George, too, had encountered Penny Peterson, though Penny hadn't worked George over quite as he had me — George had small bright eyes and a cold, knowing smile — but Penny had tried, and in a small way we both had our revenge on him. We had signed up to sell blood to make a few dollars, and we were waiting in the rotunda of the hospital, when Penny came by. His brows rose, his mouth opened. "How did *you* two get together?" he asked.

"We met in the canteen line," George said.

"Well . . ." Penny studied us. "You look well," he said of me, "but you look a little pale, George."

George indicated the room beyond where the earlier donors were lying around like war wounded. "It's the needles," George said. "They make me apprehensive. Perhaps it's fear of penetration."

Penny took the point, and gave us a composed and disappointed look and walked away. I could almost hear him saying: I was only trying to help them.

George worked in the print shop with me and so did Rollie, who looked like a highly intelligent rat, and had been caught at fourteen in the chemistry lab at Berkeley trying to produce alkaloids similar to those derived from opium. He was using gum he had gathered from the seed-stalks of common lettuce. Rollie had been at Preston when I was there, in the Ding Company, and, like me, he escaped and unlike me, he got away, stayed away, and spent the war in the Merchant Marine. Now he was serving for a burglary. So was George. We ganged around together, and our style of horseplay wasn't much different than it would have been if we had all been attending some upper-class boarding school.

We were all interested in painting. Rollie had come to it on his own, and George was drawn in because we were obsessed and it was something to do. A lot of prisoners become Sunday painters, and hundreds more produce superior handicraft of every kind. The parallel between the criminal and the artist has been labored in other places and the Wit suggested the greatest similarity is that neither wants to work, but given the essential emptiness of prison life, and plenty of spare time, it's hardly surprising so many cons try some creative adventure. Others try to become boxers. Others hit the iron to develop beautiful bodies. The difference between these activities, it occurs to me now, is hardly significant. You have to do something with the time to prevent it from being entirely wasted.

Yet each time there's a prison art show, the media reports it with fresh surprise as if they had discovered the monkeys in the zoo producing works of abstract expressionism. I expect this reflects the exaggerated regard we pay artists and the low opinion we hold of convicts.

After I had served a year and some months, the Inmate Council, who served as pipeline between the administration and the inmate body, organized an art show — the first of what is now an annual event — and we were presented with a rare chance to capture the passing notice of that other, and by now remote, planet we called the free world. Not to be confused with John Foster Dulles's Free World, though it occupied roughly the same geography. It didn't matter that the chance was slender. All our chances were slender. I planned to enter from the moment I heard it was in the wind, but George had some hesitation. "I don't know," he said. "Isn't it a little like a flea circus?" But the Wit, one of several archetypes who were always pounding the yard, said, "You better enter. You might get a chance to eyeball some prime snatch."

The painters — there were probably fifty of us — stirred with excitement. We were like painters anywhere. We worked, studied, quarreled, traded paint and canvas back and forth, and competed fiercely. Most of us had an enormous appetite for recognition.

Paint was impossible to get if you were broke. If you had money you could buy a great many supplies on the handicraft program, but if you were empty you had to find a way around the rules. I had my blood money, four dollars every two months, but this wasn't enough to keep in paint, and I ended conniving them through my cell partner. He wanted a portrait of his mother and I agreed to paint one if he would supply the paints and I would keep them as my fee. I worked from a photograph. That I had never developed the knack of catching likenesses was a condition I managed to ignore until the paints arrived and I found myself turning a rather benign old lady into a sand crab and I heard Mr. Grant, at the orphan ranch, once again say: There's something not quite right about the eyes. Fortunately, my cell partner was good-natured and decided the thought might count.

I produced canvas by cutting up my sheets and taking them to the print shop where Rollie mounted them on heavy-weight bookboard and sized them. Every step of this was against the rules, but this kind of rule breaking goes on at every level of the prison and the Man doesn't care about it if you don't wave it in his face.

I was an energetic painter, with some skill, but little imagination. I tended to produce pictures that looked like other paintings. I also liked heavy, portentous subjects, drenched in romantic atmosphere. I painted Hamlet against Elsinore. Faust against Mephistopheles. I painted myself against a stand of Monterey pines, those same pines that every amateur artist in the Carmel Valley had turned into a cliché. George was amused by this painting, and the Wit called it Shelley by the Seashore, but I couldn't give it up (we painted over our failures) because it appeared almost professional.

When the show was announced I had a number of potential entries, but we were limited to five each. I decided to enter my self-portrait. My intuition whispered that others, those others out there, might not dismiss it so lightly.

This first show hung for only two days in an ed building classroom. Saturday it was open to the inmate body, who managed to control their excitement, and on Sunday it was limited to staff, participating artists, various official visitors, and the judges. The judges were leading Bay Area artists, Yanko Varda and Benny Buffano to name the two I remember, who probably accepted out of curiosity.

Sunday morning, as we waited on the yard to be passed to the ed building, the rumor circulated that the show was going to be covered by *Life* magazine. The painters were electrified. The rumor we were all to be freed this afternoon wouldn't have excited us much more. This possibility of notice by the free world was dear, and *Life* had already run a large spread on Quentin a few years before.

The rumor flourished. Soon we believed they planned a cover story. I imagine each of us saw our faces on the cover of *Life*. I did. What a marvelous thing! Afterward I would always be defined by this affirmation and I would never again feel useless and stunted and soiled.

After lunch we were released to the ed building, and there in a double classroom, where the Inmate Council met, we found a group of civilians. Contrary to the Wit's suggestion, there were no women. At this time Custody was convinced mere proximity to a female of any age or condition would goad us to such frenzy we would attack and ravish her, en masse, even while the guards were beating us to death with clubs.

Some of these were clearly artists. Yanko Varda in particular. I had not seen his kind of theater before. He was then a man in his middle years, who wore his abundant and almost blue-white hair combed down over his brow, like the forelock of a Palomino horse, and this in the time of the great brushcut. He wore a beret, the only possible hat and one I would never have the guts to wear, and a wine velveteen jacket and a fierce yellow ascot. He moved along the paintings, staring at them with meditative attention. We tried to draw conclusions from the length of his trance.

Buffano was tiny, dressed in a plain suit, too large for him as most any suit would have been. He was a sculptor and we knew he had fashioned the bison on the buffalo nickel.

His eyes were bright and he moved quickly. He seemed to look at all the paintings at once, and then, moments later, look at them again.

We sat in orderly rows on wooden folding chairs, which had the effect of segregating us from those free to move around. There was no clear sign of *Life*, but one man wandered around with a speed graphic, taking flash shots. Just these sporadic blooms of light were exciting. At one point he asked Rollie to pose beside his own paintings.

"That's it," Dallas said.

I felt dismal. Rollie had weak, red-rimmed eyes which he sheltered behind green-tinted teentimers, and a chronic and eroding case of acne. How could they want him on the cover? I had assumed they would want me because I had been told often enough I was nice looking. The whole structure of love, merit and attention was founded on this single value, and I had depended on it unquestioningly, simply because I hoped to profit from it.

Those potent bright lights were flashing in Rollie's face, and I turned to George. He was studying me. He had the knack of raising one eyebrow higher than the other, which turned his usual expression of alert intelligence into one of amused and knowing disdain. No amount of practice with my small metal cell mirror helped me reproduce this valuable social weapon.

"How did we get the idea it would be *you* on the cover?" George said.

George always made me feel like a grasping and self-centered shit, which it could be said I was, and I smiled weakly and made some flip response.

I was dealing with a new and harder thought. The judges

were huddled now, talking softly, occasionally breaking to point at one painting or another. I was intensely alert to the potential of this, and it had suddenly occurred to me that not only was Rollie going to be on the cover of *Life*, he was also going to win.

If there was anyone to whom I was certain I was superior it was Rollie, and it was generally conceded, even by him, I was the better painter. But once he showed me something he was working on which was terrific, and I recognized its value and quality and was immediately fearful for my position over him. Later, I asked him what had happened to this painting and he told me he had spoiled it. I was glad.

Rollie came back to his seat beside me, radiant with excitement, as if the flash were still reflecting from his face, and suddenly he was almost handsome. He sat down and whispered, "What do you think that was for?"

I took this to mean he wanted me to say it, but I wouldn't.

There were to be some speakers. There were always speakers. The chairman of the Inmate Council, a clean-cut, crew-cut collegiate type who was a tireless politician, hoped this show would be the first of many. The deputy warden (the warden had ducked) also hoped this show would be the first of many, though his hope lacked the conviction of the chairman's, and he thanked the distinguished judges and he praised the visitors for their interest. He was an old hack, up from the guardline, and this art show, along with masquerades and overnight hikes, was right up there on his list of things he thought he would never see. He seemed to be congratulating the civilians for having risked their lives by coming among us.

A Guidance Center counselor, Mr. Rhodes, was asked

to say a few words. He said he didn't know much about art but he knew what he liked, and if the inmate responsible for these paintings here would contact him after the judging he would like to arrange to buy them. The paintings were mine.

Yanko Varda announced the awards. He started at the bottom, citing several special mentions, and then climbed slowly, with brief bursts of applause, through fifth place to fourth place. The council had voted a number of prizes to spread the money authorized among as many inmates as possible.

When he had awarded second, every painter of any talent at all had been accounted for but Rollie and myself. Dallas turned around to whisper, "That leaves you." But it wasn't clear which of us he meant. Rollie was breathless, seated far forward, hands tense on the back of the chair in front of him.

No one dressed like Varda was without some sense of drama, and he milked the final moments before he turned and pointed at my self-portrait.

"This is the winner."

I flashed joy, a warm confusion, clapped my hands like a child and said, "I won!"

I found myself at the podium thanking the judges, thanking admin, thanking everyone on this beautiful day. It was an odd feeling. Like someone kept in perpetual darkness who is brought for a moment into the warmth of bright sunshine. It is overwhelming.

When, a little later, I talked to Rhodes, he told me, smoking his pipe enthusiastically, how it had pleased him to have cited my work, then, moments later, hear it named Best of

Show, and I realized he was taking a smaller version of the same ride I was taking, and this made me uneasy. Further, it bothered me that Shelley by the Seashore had won. We were very pure and to have honored this painting made the judges look like assholes. In fact, Rollie stood to ask why this particular canvas had been singled out, and Varda replied it was necessary to settle on one painting, but the prize was intended to award the overall quality of my five entries, which he described as "rough, but powerful." Still the ribbon hung on the self-portrait, and the self-portrait, we had all agreed, was suitable only for reproduction on a candy box.

The light faded swiftly as soon as we were back on the yard. No matter where I had traveled this afternoon, I had nowhere to go now but my cell. George looked down at me and said, "I still think it was a flea circus."

And I was the flea who had somehow learned to pull the little cart.

Later George said, "It's Talking Dog. It's not that the dog says anything important, it's that he talks at all."

The next day my triumph was further diminished when I took my paintings to the hobby shop. I explained to the sergeant in charge that Mr. Rhodes wanted to buy these particular paintings. The sergeant glanced at them and shrugged, "What do you want for them?"

"Twenty-five dollars apiece."

The sergeant laughed. "Try again."

This particular sergeant was young, ambitious and smart. He later rose rapidly through the ranks to become a program administrator. There was a certain quality these bright young bureaucrats, those drawn to institutions, seemed to have in common, an alert, authoritarian and homosexual sadism. They looked at you and appeared to make shameful assumptions. They had made themselves strong, or, at least, cleverly associated themselves with a strong position, and you had allowed yourself to become weak. You were the daily proof of their strength.

I looked into his ironic brown eyes and knew my case to be tenuous. If he checked his files he would know I hadn't bought any paint and this meant my paintings were contraband and didn't legally exist. He could have them destroyed.

I made another attempt. "Twenty-five dollars isn't much for a painting."

"Some paintings."

"These just won the art show."

He smiled. "What's that got to do with the handicraft program?"

What did it have to do with the handicraft program? "All right," I said. "What will you allow me?"

He glanced at the work again. "Five dollars."

"Oh, come on!"

He stared at me, showing me a hint of his steel. "Do you want to sell these?"

"All right," I said weakly. "I'll take five."

"No," he corrected me. "You can ask five for the big ones, but only two-fifty for the little ones."

And I accepted this shameful bullying. Later it occurred to me Mr. Rhodes might have had a word with the sarge and asked him to hold the price down. We knew the Care-and-Treatment types and Custody were all buddies together out there at the officers' snack bar. Or maybe the sarge was simply taking a private whack at the world of culture, which has an unpleasant way of making ordinary, intelligent, but not particularly aesthetic people feel like clods.

If this were fiction I'd say here the subject inmate avoided all future art shows. But, of course, I didn't. I entered every one and won several more. And maybe it was better to have won. To have had the chance to pass through such an experience. The Wit told me, "Listen, kid, money talks and bullshit walks." Or maybe he told me, "Keep your eye on the donut and not on the hole."

I forgot to mention the first prize was five dollars, and the photographer present had been free-lancing for the San Rafael *Independent*, the local small-town newspaper.

George gave me trouble. I was the village smart boy in the big city now, meeting someone who could think effortless circles around me. There he was permanently cast in the role I had always seen as my own, and I was back to playing Brassett. He was handsome, popular, brilliant and brave, and again, as I had failed to do with the old thieves, I neglected to ask myself what this marvelous fellow was doing in San Quentin?

Our principal recreation was talk. We talked for years, and like Mick and me in the hole, we told each other everything we had ever done. We cut up every book we read, every movie we saw, and every record we heard on the radio. George was a jazz fan and soon I knew all about Stan Kenton and Boyd Raeburn, even though I seldom heard their orchestras, and I, too, began to pose as a jazz fan, even though a few months before my favorite singer had been Jo Stafford and she had started her career as a Western star. I came under George's influence in many ways. I envied him, I wanted to be like him, and he was hard on me. He suspected my need for approval. Again I can remember him looking down at me with a small wintery smile — his lips always seemed to be unraveling — as he said, "Most people care nothing for what they are, but only for what others think them to be."

And another time when I had been putting on some show, telling jokes and acting out, he had scored me, and I had replied, "I only want to be loved."

And he said, "Yes, and you don't care who does it."

This gives the flavor. I was hungry and I didn't mind elbowing my way to the trough and I didn't mind getting greasy if I could eat, but George made me ashamed of my unbridled appetite. The trough, he seemed to say, was full of slops, and if one could not eat with grace and discrimination it was better to go hungry. I had no ready answer for this then. I have none now.

George also led me into the arid desert, beyond all faith, where Nietzsche was staked in his madness, and we held there what we took to be some rare vantages. The world was full of fools, who were distinguished only by the degree of their blindness. The half-blind manipulated the sightless and were manipulated themselves by their refusal to see. The first function of law was to guarantee privilege and the Church had become an instrument of the status quo. Religious awe had deteriorated to the pursuit of mere goodness. And more of the same.

This line is not unfamiliar, but it was new to me. The heart of it all was that it transmuted selfishness from a gross offense to a virtue, and since I had often been told I was selfish, this was, to the extent I could accept it, very good news. It will surprise no one familiar with that work to discover our favorite book, our Bible, was Ayn Rand's *The Fountainhead*.

So already I was not the boy who had written poems to celebrate the condition that all men were brothers, nor was I the boy who escaped from Nevada vowing to himself he would never steal again. In the world of nonsense the sensible man creates his own reality. George and I were going to steal a pile of money — the details of this would come to us — buy a yacht, and spend our lives drifting in semitropical waters with all the friends of our choice. Dallas would be on the yacht. But Rollie wouldn't. Rollie didn't care. His intelligence was practical and he knew from the beginning there wasn't going to be any yacht.

Incidentally, George dismissed my poetry, which I was still carrying around, in one word. He said it was "weasely."

I want to convey more of what it was like to be in San Quentin, not what I studied, or how I moved from the south block to the east block, and I'm tempted to generalize, to catch the sweep, and to present the prison as a metaphor of our larger society, but this is tantamount to presenting life as a metaphor for life. At some level all metaphors fail and experience is always personal and unique.

The hardest part of serving time is the predictability. Each day moves like every other. You *know* nothing different can happen. You focus on tiny events, a movie scheduled weeks ahead, your reclass., your parole hearing, things far in the future, and slowly, smooth day by day, draw them to you. There will be no glad surprise, no spontaneous holiday, and a month from now, six months, a year, you will be just where you are, doing just what you're doing, except you'll be older.

This airless calm is produced by rigid routine. Custody doesn't encourage spontaneity. Walk slow, the Cynic says, and don't make any fast moves. Each morning you know where evening will find you. There is no way to avoid your cell. When everyone marched into the block you would be left alone in the empty yard. Each Monday describes every Friday. Holidays in prison are only another mark of passing time and for many they are the most difficult days. Most of the outrages that provide such lurid passages in the folklore of our prisons are inspired by boredom. Some grow so weary of this grinding sameness they will drink wood alcohol even though they are aware this potent toxin may blind or kill them. Others fight with knives to the death and the survivor will remark, "It was just something to do."

Well, as the Wit said, Quentin's nothing but California's trash pile. And the priority on recycled garbage wasn't high at the time. This first jolt, though the department was already trumpeting rehabilitation and treatment, I received no attempt at guidance. Other than an honorable attempt to teach me the printing trade, which I have never worked at, they left me alone to do my time. The psych department, those remote wizards, tampered with the heads of only murderers and the grossest of sex offenders. We heard that a Viennese doktor, a pupil of a pupil of Freud's, was conducting psychodrama on one of the wards. We all wanted into it. What a lark to be actors in our own story. But your case had to be high power or you couldn't be considered. The Cynic said, If you want special treatment, next time you're out, rape a policewoman.

For myself, the head of the Psychiatric Department tried to see most prisoners annually, and I recall being interviewed by him once. We called him Crazy David, which didn't have to mean that much, since most psychs acquire pejorative nicknames, but Crazy David often seemed genuinely peculiar. I recall him wandering across the yard with a bundle of folders under his arm, his pipe fragrant, obviously bemused, rolling along like some woolly ruminant who a moment ago started toward that greener grass, but has now forgotten the impulse that first set it in motion. For these and other reasons — he wasn't modern — the prospect of an interview with him caused me no particular excitement. Nothing, for example, like the possibility of an interview with the pupil of the pupil of Freud.

He talked to me in a treatment room off the main clinic. He sat behind a small desk, a sloping pile of folders at one hand, and I sat on a straight chair at the side.

"How are you feeling?" he began. Behind his glasses, his eyes were mild, but I looked into them without any strong feeling of contact.

"Fine."

"Good, good. Do you like your job?"

I didn't particularly, not anymore, but I said, "Yes, sir."

"That's good."

He turned a few pages in my file, and then looked up to catch my eye. His gaze was slightly more pointed. "You should try to do several things each day you find difficult."

Holmes's remark jumped to mind. All his life, he said, he had done two things each day he hated — he had got up and gone to bed. But I didn't quote the Chief Justice. I said, "Yes, sir."

Later, when I retailed this to George and Dallas and Rollie, I lied and said I did quote Holmes.

Crazy David was back in the file. This file, my personal Rosetta stone, was of enormous interest to me, and as David turned the pages I tried to read them upside down. David pulled out a picture I had drawn. It was part of the Draw-a-Man test. First you drew a man, then you drew a woman, then you were free to draw what you like. I had drawn an owl. I thought Crazy David was about to congratulate me, instead he asked me if I had heard the verse about the owl?

"No, sir."

He quoted some lines like these:

> *The wise old owl*
> *Is a clever bird,*
> *He never repeats*
> *What he's heard.*

He ended peering at me with the same mild, remote gaze, until I said, "That's nice."

Then he smiled faintly, nodding at me, "That's all for now. Keep up the good work."

I sense how this appears a writer's scene, worked up with calculated exaggeration to take a shot at the sort of authority figure it is always safe to ridicule, but it is the plain truth. And looking back now, from this other world I live in today, it doesn't seem his advice to me was all that bad, or all that foolish.

If this was the extent of my "treatment," my brushes with custody were equally slight. My one beef was comic. I decided I was going bald. One myth we all seemed to share was the stubborn conviction that while we were locked away nothing would change. Not the world, not us, we would all sleep like Beauty in this malignant enchantment, and return as we had left. It is difficult enough to live in this barren routine without hope of love or comfort; it is awful to think it is wearing away your youth.

The balding panic, like my hypochondria, began innocently. I saw a humorous short before the weekend movie, where a comedian mocked the plight of the balding, and every time he passed his hand near his head, he removed it covered with falling hair. That night in my cell I brushed my hair vigorously, a certain act of hubris, and found the brush full of hair. I was off again.

I was hardly alone. Half the yard seemed to be fighting baldness. One of my cell partners, the most single-minded and determined man I have ever encountered, spent an hour each evening tugging vigorously at his hair. He worked on the not illogical assumption that this stressing would cause each hair to cling so fiercely to his scalp it would never fall out. I met him years later in Folsom. Yes, he was bald.

Another man, in the Nevada prison, shaved his head smooth, greased his scalp with petroleum jelly, and sat in the sun. He was severely sunburned. Either the massive dose of ultraviolet or the burn itself shocked a few follicles, and some hair began to grow in areas which had been barren for years. It was sparse, kinky as pubic hair, but he was delighted. He typed up a report which he attempted to file with the Bureau of Patents, and soon other men with shaved and greased heads were sitting in the sun. Little came of it.

For a different reason I shaved my own head. My logic was scrupulous — why did beards never fall out? Because they were shaved, which at that time they all were, and if I kept my head shaved for the rest of my time I would at least keep what hair I had. You see, I yearned for romance, and I wanted my chance with all my original equipment.

But the day after I shaved my head, I was beefed on the yard by a Lieutenant Roberts. Ordinarily a loot wouldn't bother with anything so trivial, but Roberts was bucking for captain and didn't quite know how to make the jump. He understood, as they all did, that the road to advancement had to be paved with educational credit, and he had allowed his inmate clerk to write his master's thesis, but he'd picked the wrong clerk and was refused the degree.

I was beefed under the section of the rules and regs that ordered each inmate to wear a regulation haircut. This haircut wasn't the mutilation we were required to wear in Preston, but it still wasn't very sharp, and few prisoners wore it with much enthusiasm. There were photos of this ideal haircut posted in the prison barber shop for the guidance of the inmate barbers. They worked in the light of this example like art students dutifully copying the *Mona Lisa*, but, if you slipped them a couple of packs of smokes, they'd copy something else.

I lost my privilege card for thirty days. I couldn't use the library, go to the weekend movie, buy canteen or handicraft, or go to the gym. On weekends I couldn't pass from the upper to the lower yard to use the recreational facilities.

It was a meatball beef, but a sketch of the circuitous reasoning behind it will illustrate one aspect of official thinking. In the old hardrock days, when Law was the issue, no one tried to deny our prisons were harsh and restrictive. This reputation was thought valuable. Those on the prod, about to jump the fence, might think twice, and those who had conquered this temptation and accepted their modest fortune had the satisfaction of knowing that those who had jumped and been caught were getting the shit stomped out of them. It was fundamental.

A shaved head, like the traditional stripes, was an immediate identification of an escaped prisoner, and as a symbolic mutilation it was probably also part of the punishment. However, as prisons gradually evolved into rehabilitation factories, with dozens of innovative and expensive programs to sell to a public ever suspicious and resentful of each new tax drain, the penal bureaucracy intuitively sensed they must now put aside anything suggestive of the bad old days. They became as image conscious as insurance companies and the manufacturers of baby food, and there are few things more visible than a shaved head.

Here is the scenario that agitated the official mind. A mother comes to visit her son and finds his head has been shaved. Does this inmate admit to his mother he shaved his own head because someone told him it would stop his hair from falling out? Many would. But there's always one (and there always is!) who will say it was the work of ten huge guards. Eight to hold him down, the ninth to shave his head, while the tenth and largest kicked him repeatedly in the nuts.

Mother, as some do, transforms her own guilt into rage at these brutes and begins to fire off letters to the governor, to the papers, to her congressman, and a small shitstorm rises in the smooth bureaucratic lake. So what was originally a punishment is now punished.

The Wit told me, What goes around, comes around. And it did with Roberts, who was a prick who had nailed a lot of cons on nitpicking beefs, which stuck only because he was a loot. He was a heavy florid man with a balloon chest who walked around the yard with the self-conscious dignity of a Nazi commander in a B picture. One day a con who had just been released from the nut ward approached him at Four Gate.

"I have something here for you, Loot."

"Yes, what is it?" Roberts asked, probably expecting a snitch letter. What he got was a fresh turd. A real fresh turd, right in his hand.

This story has a further twist. This shit lover was snatched back on the nut ward, and the psych committee met to try to fix responsibility for his premature release. This committee was usually chaired by Crazy David, but when he learned what the subject inmate had done, he turned pale and excused himself. They waited twenty minutes and when it became apparent Crazy David wasn't coming back, the next senior doctor assumed the chair and the committee determined on still another course of shock treatment. A decision Crazy David scratched the next day when he ordered, entirely on his own authority, the subject inmate boxed up and shipped to a real nuthouse. The junior psychs were delighted and the story spread through the joint that Crazy David, the head psych, who was supposed to cure us all, hadn't been able to risk an encounter with a patient who played with his own shit.

>=>=<=<

I didn't live under a constant sense of danger. There were places and situations it was wise to avoid, just as anywhere, and occasionally someone was beaten or knifed, but rarely. I wondered if the death toll at Quentin was as high as that of an average town the same size and decided it wasn't, if for no other reason than because we weren't killing each other with automobiles. As for sex, no one really hit hard, except someone who wanted to go down, and I tried this a few times. It's next to impossible to find a place to be alone, and once I remember standing in a broom closet, with my pants around my ankles, smelling floor polish, while a queen named Betty Boop knelt in front of me. Afterwards he asked, "Did you like that?"

And I said, "Yes," but I hadn't exactly. I liked the stroke of heat lightning, but that was a single moment freed from this desperate shabbiness. Boop was a short, squarely built queen with a ruddy man's face and I wanted him mostly to prove to myself I could have him, but how could I kiss and romance him? All the pretty queens, with whom it might have been different, were locked up on the row with Bob.

The sexual problems which pained me most were more subtle. I usually got along with my cell partners; it's a very close situation and you share a great deal, and I often felt we were friends. Not yard buddies, not even eating buddies, but still friends. And none of these cell partners, with one exception, ever hit on me. The subject was never raised. But then I would hear on the yard that one partner or another was going around telling people he was fucking me. I could see how it happened.

"What about that kid you cell with?"

"What about him?"

"He's pretty sweet looking."

"I didn't say he wasn't."

"You getting any of that?"

"Now what do you think?"

And they would both laugh.

I hated this. There was no defense against it. Several women have told me they put up with the same thing in high school, and in Quentin no one was really immune. We talked constantly of sex and who was stuff and who wasn't and few escaped some speculation, not even the boxers and weight lifters, but you did tend to be a little careful what you said around them. The Cynic said: If you don't want the name, don't play the game, and I would have been satisfied to have had this choice. Neither did I sense the constant threat of riot, though this possibility did seem to grow greater when a different kind of racial unrest entered the prisons. But at this time, in the late forties and early fifties, we were all strung out on the indeterminate sentence, where if you played the model prisoner and designed an artful shuck you might get out in a year or two, but if you flipped and started throwing shit with both hands they might keep you ten years. It happened both ways, and almost all of us were walking this tightrope, and no one was desperate enough to either lead or follow along the path that led to riot.

Still we had one of sorts. It was eerily inconsequential and less a riot than a political happening. It erupted in the mess hall, where riots always seem to begin. For one thing, we're all there, and for another, the one complaint we held in common was our distaste for the food. The food, as I said earlier, wasn't that bad, but this was beside the point. The shaft was this — we had no choice, but always had to eat what we were given, or do without. Something we might have liked on Tuesday, we couldn't hack on Thursday. We had fewer than ten meals, which were rotated in an odd cycle I never understood well enough to predict. These meals were planned by a woman we called the Great Mother, a state dietician in Sacramento, and when she decreed we would have health salad for lunch Wednesday (and every Wednesday forever) she could hardly imagine the sodden mass of carrot pulp, flecked with an occasional forlorn raisin, we were served. All her dishes suffered a similar sea change. Convicts trying to cook from state-approved recipes were like Australian aboes trying to manufacture electronics gear from Japanese blueprints. Further, the cooks always robbed us; from the free man steward to the lowest dishwasher, they cut up the groceries and we ate whatever was left.

The food is always a focus for general resentment, and we bitched about it endlessly, but it wasn't so awful I ever heard talk of riot, and I doubt if we would have come to it if it hadn't been for Captain Dad.

Captain Dad was a tall, heavy man, gone to fat in his middle years, who illustrates the unwritten end of most fairy tales (the Prince grows fat and Cinderella turns snobbish) because he had once in his life stood in that spot where the heroes of our adventures always stand, and he had handled himself well. As a young guard, alone and single-handed, he foiled a bold and determined escape attempt and saved the lives of several important hostages, the warden and several members of the parole board. He rescued the king, saved the kingdom, and they made him a prince. In time, they discovered he wasn't quite bright enough to handle a captain's work and the qualities which had served him so well in the single moment of crisis, served him poorly in a life of day-to-day pedestrian responsibility.

This happened twenty years before the riot we're bearing on, and during this time admin had sometimes been hard pressed to find something Captain Dad could handle which wasn't inconsistent with his dignity as a captain. Usually the mess hall was supervised by a lowly sarge, and even at stress times, big holidays, or the rare rumors of major trouble, the job was only given to a loot. So it was at least a novelty to most of us to find a full captain wandering around the mess hall, watching to make sure we didn't get into line twice, smuggle out bread to make peanut butter sandwiches, or sneak a smoke. Captain Dad was competent to prevent the smoking — it was more trouble than it was worth and few tried it — but he wasn't smart enough not to smoke himself. He sailed the mess hall, hands clasped behind his back, smoking a large cigar.

At first we enjoyed the joke. We enjoyed seeing any rule successfully flouted, but the duck the captain was shooting wasn't just sitting, it was nailed down, and, finally, the joke was on us. We sometimes sat in the mess hall for forty-five minutes after we had finished eating. The benches were hard and there were too many of us breathing the same air, waiting for our own after-dinner smoke. And here comes Captain Dad, blowing his cigar. And that wasn't enough, he started playing the dozens with some of the cons, trading mammies, in that rude joking that treads the very edge of mortal insult. There were still a lot of men around who would fight you on the spot if you called them a mother fucker.

Most of us took the dozens as a joke —

> *I don't play the dozens*
> *Cause I don't know the score*
> *But your face tells me*
> *Your mammy was a whore*

— and we left the deeper implications to the psych dept., but some of us didn't like Captain Dad laying his cigar-stained and custodial tongue on our mammies. Our humor was made from our suffering and he wanted to share the joke without sharing the pain.

I was there the evening someone challenged him. I was sitting left of center in the mess hall and to the front. George was sitting beside me. George had decided that those who wouldn't obey the rules on the yacht (we're cruising off Barbados) would have to be confined to a raft he planned to tow behind, and we were deciding how minimal accommodations on the raft would be. We no longer heard the bedlam; we had heard it every night for two years; nor are we particularly aware of the thousands of men around us — they are always there. We do notice when Captain Dad steams by.

"That asshole," George said. "He's got that thing in the wrong end of his digestive tract."

Someone else, close around us, challenged the captain out loud. "Hey, Fuck Face, put out your cigar."

Captain Dad spun around to give us all the finger. Immediately someone else shouted. "You wanta suck, I got somethin you can suck on."

Again Captain Dad spun and anyone who missed the first finger, got the second. Now two or three cons shouted together, and Captain Dad held his arms wide, rolled his pelvis like a belly dancer and shot his hips forward. *Fuck all of you*, he was saying.

The mess hall exploded. On an instant. The roar was like that of a raging fire and we began to throw our metal trays and cups. The cups had the density of a good rock and the trays were lethal. They were twice the size of a TV dinner tray, fashioned from heavy-gauge stainless steel, and we were skimming them like Frisbees. They could take off your head. At first, Captain Dad was the target, but he ran clumsily, shrilling his whistle, into the kitchen to safety. Then the trays were thrown into the center section where the blacks were segregated, and they panicked and stampeded toward the door, running across the tables. Like terrified patrons in a burning theater they jammed the door and began to climb each other's backs. To add to the panic, the gun bull on the rail high above us, emptied his rifle into the opposite wall. As soon as I saw what was beginning I ducked under the table, and when I looked up a moment later it seemed every con in the mess hall was on the floor, except George. He was sitting up looking around.

When I asked him why he hadn't taken cover, he said, "I wanted to see it. How many chances am I going to get to watch something like that?"

The storm blew out as quickly as it had flared, and by the time the goon squad arrived with their submachine guns we were filing peacefully into the cell blocks. Since we were all guilty there was no effective punishment except to throw the whole prison on lockup and the incident was allowed to pass. Still, two nights later, it blew up again.

We were given a commercial ice cream for dinner, a rare treat, which we understood to mean somewhere a shipment had been condemned, and this dessert was packaged in small Dixie cups. After dinner, as we once again sat waiting to be released, someone picked up his neighbor's empty cup, stuck it in his own, and passed it on. Soon wavering stacks of sundae cups were moving along the tables, while, as if this were some impromptu party game, each man tried to add his own cup and pass the stack without dumping the lot. Harmless enough.

But Captain Dad felt under some pressure. Probably he'd had his ass discreetly chewed — we'd seen no more of the cigar — and was now anxious to reassert his authority. He decided to stop the game. Again he misjudged us.

The only quality we admired in any bull was consistency. So he was a total prick, who would beef you for an overdue library book, that was fair enough, we knew him by his rattles and behaved accordingly. But if one day he let us slide on a major beef and the next day wrote us up for jerking off, we knew we were dealing with a dangerous man, who was, in addition, no more principled than ourselves.

Again, in an instant, our mood turned ugly and we showered Captain Dad with cups and trays, and again he beat his humiliating retreat into the kitchen. This time they were primed for us, and the goon squad ran out on the gun-rail to fire their machine guns into the wall. That wall took a lot of abuse. We quieted immediately. We wanted to play with the Dixie cups, but we weren't willing to die for the pleasure, and this time they did find a way to punish us. They turned off the radios and I missed a pivotal segment of *I Love a Mystery*.

After this Captain Dad was never seen in the mess hall, and soon the grapevine whispered he had been forced into an early retirement, where, doubtless, he used his impressive credentials, to become someone's head of security.

A few weeks after the last incident, inmate masons began to divide this huge mess hall into three separate sections with walls of cement blocks. Still later, an inmate artist was assigned to cover these walls with a mural depicting the history of the State of California.

I appeared in front of the Adult Authority after I had pulled a year. It was the only time I came before these men with anything like an advantage. I had already served a lot of time, longer, it could be argued, than I should have, considering my intent, which, of course, is impossible to verify, but I was young, and very blue-eyed and White American, and, in appearance, at least, I might have been a wayward son from one of their own homes. The members regarded me with some sympathy.

"We understand this is hard for you. You've been locked up a long time."

Doubtless I said, "Yessir." At this time I was saying yessir to the chairs.

They asked, "How do you plan to support yourself?"

"I hope to work as a printer."

"Yes, your marks there seem all right."

I was earning 3s in the print shop, where I worked just hard enough and often enough to keep from being fired and assigned to the jute mill.

"Have you ever heard anything from your family?"

"Nosir."

"Do you feel you're beginning to mature and gain some understanding of your problems?"

"I hope so, sir."

"What do you think your problems were?"

We all knew to be ready for this question. "Impatience, sir, I wasn't willing to wait for anything. Everything always had to be now." It was true enough, as I saw myself.

"And do you think you've learned to wait?"

I tried a small joke. "I've been waiting for some time."

They smiled. There were only three members at this time. An ex-police chief, a former district attorney, and a black councilman from Oakland. The black, as he would have had to have been then, was the smartest, as well as the most liberal, but he also was infamous for chewing out his own.

We heard he called them niggers and raged at them for disgracing their race. The ex-police chief moved me around a little, but never really pushed me. After waiting a year I talked to these men for somewhere between three and five minutes and then the chairman repeated their usual formula, "You go back now and we'll let you know what we decide."

That night I received this:

> INMATE: Braly, M., A-8814
> The Adult Authority has set
> your time at 5 years,
> the last 2½ to be served
> on parole.

Five split, and Big John's prophesy was fulfilled to the letter. I had hoped for a three-split, eighteen months in and eighteen months out. We always found ways to imagine we would be the ones to get those stunning breaks that happened just often enough for us to continue to believe in them. Like holders of a ticket on the Irish Sweepstakes, we fastened our hopeful eyes on the smallest window by which we might imagine fortune would enter. Five-split was an average sentence for the time, and maybe it did represent a break because I was carrying a robbery, and there had been that gun battle on the desert. And even though I told this story to someone every month or so, I sometimes forgot it was also written out, if not quite the same version, in my file. So, all in all, as the Cynic suggested: Five-split's better'n a poke in the eyes with a sharp stick. But I was still left with 18 months, 78 weeks, 548 days to walk away, and by the time I had finished this I didn't always feel as well as I once did. My stomach was often upset, and sometimes

I felt weary. My dream girl was no longer wearing tulle and posing in the moonlight, she had been powerfully modified by George's wife (I saw photos) and now she waited for me in a San Francisco apartment through whose wall-sized windows the Golden Gate Bridge sparkled, or I met her in a jazz club where she was digging, but *never* dancing to, the music of Shearing or Kenton. She looked like Audrey Hepburn in *Roman Holiday*. Many nights I created scenes with her as I lay waiting for sleep. I looked into her eyes, I felt her lips soften under mine, my hands brushed her magical tits and perhaps I had myself say, May I? And she answered: Please do.

Interlude

==

I CAN'T REMEMBER whether I was paroled this first time in the spring or the fall, it was one or the other, and probably I could work it out, trace back to it, but I have anesthetized my memory of these exact dates — the days I entered and left, only to re-enter and leave again to re-enter still once more to leave again, and still return this last time. I have blocked the total of the years. But before I finish here we will have an exact accounting, and for the moment it doesn't matter whether it was the spring or the fall.

When we were getting short and someone asked how long we had left, we said, "Six days and a butt." "Four days and a butt." The butt is your last morning. The time comes when you can say, Next week I'll be out. And then, Tomorrow at this time I'll be out. Your last night, if you're going out on your precious date and aren't going to be overdue, you get a check-out slip. Your last morning you carry this slip from department to department and if you haven't failed to check in all your library books and you've returned the musical instruments you borrowed from the Ed. Dept., and you're clear with Household and Distribution, and you have in your possession all the property registered to you, then each superintendent, in turn, initials your slip, and when this is finished, it's close to noon and you're ready to dress out.

I carried two cardboard boxes full of my paintings — I hadn't done that much writing — and I was halfway across the yard with these, when George came running up. He still had six months left to do.

"Where are they sending you?"

"San Francisco."

"Great. You'll have a good time there."

We shook hands, and I said, "Well, maybe I'll see you."

He didn't respond. Most jail buddies at least talk about meeting outside, but George, despite the yacht fantasy, was never willing to be pinned down to this. The Wit was there to see me off. He told me walk slow and drink lots of water, and if I had to sleep out try to find a place under the bridge. And the Cynic was there too. Take it easy, kid, it ain't hard to make it out there if you're not afraid of a little work, and you don't try to play catch up.

I walked through the first of the between-gates and entered Receiving and Release. This was the room where I had heard Gerry say it would be awful to die here. He had known something about himself, but had still lived long enough to get out in eighteen months, but then a few months later I heard he was dead. Louis was still here, predicting flood. The property envelope, sealed two-and-a-half years before, was opened and my comb, with broken teeth, a ring I had stolen somewhere, and several mechanical pencils were handed back to me. I was dressed out in a cheap woolen suit (maybe it was fall) and given a Social Security card and forty dollars. Another forty was waiting for me at the parole office where I was expected to report before the day was out. The forty held there was to guarantee I would report at least once.

I had been locked up a few months over six years. I had been eighteen that morning I walked in from the Nevada desert and I was now twenty-five. My head was full of ideas I had picked up from George and the many books I had read, but my emotions had been largely sealed away where no change was possible. I did not feel any large excitement. My mood was one of quiet anticipation. I was still far away from the apartment overlooking the Golden Gate and the girl who looked like Audrey Hepburn. One thing, however, I wasn't bald.

I took the bus to San Francisco, checked my boxes in a locker at the depot, and, on impulse and because I could, I decided to walk down the length of Market Street to the parole office which was housed in the Ferry Building at the edge of the bay. It was a strange walk. I was shocked at how dirty the streets were and the people seemed nondescript. For years my impressions of this world had been formed by magazine ads and the weekend movies. As their illusion gained substance, if only through repetition, my memories of this ordinary world had faded away. Now I suffered the shock of instant disillusion, and this, too, was the real end of a fairy tale.

My parole officer, a former cop, had no interest in me. I signed papers, received the balance of my release money, and was told, "Good luck."

"Where should I live?" I asked.

"Get yourself a room in a cheap hotel. You've got a job waiting. When you get paid you can look for something permanent. Look, you and I aren't going to be any trouble to each other if you remember just one thing, get your report in every month by the fifth."

For years I had been told exactly what to do. I had walked from the most rigid of routines into this strangely empty freedom. I rented a cheap room, recovered my boxes, and went out to walk the streets. I found myself near the top of Nob Hill, where the pavement sparkles outside the Fairmont Hotel. Here was life as I felt I could live it. I repeated my litany: I was young. I was good-looking. I was smart. I could make something happen for me.

I walked back down town and ate dinner at a cafeteria and went to a movie. The picture was *My Six Convicts*, filmed in Quentin, and I watched an actor named Harry Morgan trying to escape from the upper yard to the lower yard, and when I saw this I laughed out loud, and someone behind me leaned forward to ask, "When'd you get out?"

That first morning and every morning for several weeks I woke exactly at six-thirty when the big bell had begun to pound in the blocks. Rise and shine. It's daylight in the swamps. I took the Mission bus out to Daly City where I had a job handing up lumber to carpenters who were putting together a housing development. I wasn't used to the pace of this work. In Quentin we had two speeds: slow and very slow. Anyone too eager was invited to slow down. Here the foreman expected me to put out. Twice he found me sitting down and the second time he told me, "Get to work or pull your time." I pulled my time.

I found another job the next day, painting showcards for

a dime store in the Mission District. I wasn't much of a card man, but the dime store wasn't offering scale, they weren't offering a third of scale, and I managed to hold this job for a year. I sat down in the basement on a teetering stool that was once part of the soda fountain and turned out such gems as:

— and here in the warm closeness of the stockroom, smelling of Three Flowers brilliantine and Christmas candy, I met the girl I would marry. She did look a little like Audrey Hepburn; tiny, very young, pretty. I don't think we loved each other.

Before this I had something going with a girl I met in the adult education classes I immediately went back to. She was a twenty-seven-year-old virgin and the first time I got her up to my room with a promise of steak, which I burned, we started to make love on the floor, kissing and grabbing, but when she began to respond so I knew it could really happen here, I went soft. She didn't push because she was afraid herself, though she found an oblique way to tell me her fear was more acceptable than mine, and I put her on the bus and went for a long walk. I had tears in my eyes. I had been lying routinely. To cover my funny woolen suit I said I had bought it in South Africa, the most distant place I could imagine, and to cover my near total ignorance of women I said I had been married, but my wife had died, and for this I borrowed the death of Wren's wife in *Finley Wren*. Now I was exposed.

Too often I had heard Alice telling me how I was hurting her. How could I climb on this shy and inexperienced girl? Yet I so believed the myth of total maleness as men like Hemingway had sung of it I thought I should have been able to fuck a bear trap if someone glued a little hair on it. Now I imagined I couldn't fuck, would never fuck, and would be forced by this inexplicable and shameful treachery to live alone, a poor freak, without the company of the girl I had always counted on to make my life worthwhile.

As it happened I did fuck this same girl a few nights later, on a pile of tires behind a restaurant where we had just had dinner, and if I hurt her I saw no sign of it. She called me the next day to tell me she had a discharge, and to ask me what I thought she should do. I told her I knew nothing. I had never been married, but had spent the last six years in prison and was as innocent as she. She was silent a moment, then said, "I didn't quite believe you."

I thought I was a good liar. "Why not?"

"I've read *Finley Wren*."

"Oh."

"It's all right. I liked it. I like to feel life inside me."

><><><

San Francisco was a lovely city in those years. On Sundays I bought an all-day ticket on the Muni buses, and rode out to Playland and the zoo. I walked up to the Cliff House to watch the seals and walked through Golden Gate Park where there were free band concerts in the afternoons. Then rode down to Fisherman's Wharf, where you could buy freshly cracked crab in the street and eat it looking up at Telegraph Hill and Lucy Coit's monument to her dead husband. Sometimes, but rarely, I went into North Beach and sat in bars where it was said Steinbeck sat when he was young. I might have made friends here, but I had no ease of manner. I sat frozen in my self-consciousness. I did make a single bid for fortune. I entered several of my paintings in a juried show at the San Francisco Art Museum, but they were not accepted. I didn't bother to pick them up.

The first thing that attracted me to the girl I married was her name. Her father had called her Vitoria, but her younger sisters, unable to pronounce this, had hung her with Veto and it had stuck. Her name then was Veto Russo, and my favorite saxophonist, recording with Stan Kenton, was Vito Musso. She was the oldest of three sisters, and the second sister had already escaped into marriage. It wasn't wonderful in the Russo home. The father, an immigrant from Genoa, was a tyrant, who liked nothing about America except the wages, and to see his daughters turning into jitterbugs was driving him wild. Veto had some balls and she defied him— she had her hair cut very short and wore the New Look, skirts almost to her ankles, and when she met me, there in the stockroom, she decided I was her ticket into the real world where she would be a married adult, and not a kid in her father's house. I don't think we'd have done it, except her mother became excited and immediately sent out several hundred wedding invitations, and this became the reason we had to get married.

Veto was bright and awesomely reckless and if she was

now free of her father, she wasn't free of me, and we fought a great deal. I think Veto understood she was never going to be able to break loose — we never lived more than four blocks from her parents' house — and it was making her crazy. It was a sad mismatch for both of us, but, despite this, we had some fun together, and both of us were finally free to have all the sex we wanted. This was another reason I marched like a zombie into this marriage — because there would be a small, soft girl in my bed every night. We hardly devoured each other. After reading of those magnificent couplings in historical novels, the swollen lips and diamond-hard nipples, our lovemaking seemed pale, and I think we were both disappointed. But we made a baby, a little boy, who was born after we had been married a year. Veto called him Steven after Sister Steven, a nun at the Catholic school she had attended.

I hadn't lost my obsession with clothing. The highest style of the day was a gray flannel suit, a pink shirt and a black knit tie, but I told myself I had learned to live without this exquisite uniform. Far across the Pacific, the Marines were landing at Inchon, and all this meant to me was there was plenty of work. I paid no attention. Sometimes a *Newsweek* or *Time* would fall into my hands, and I never glanced at the national or international news. I read of music, books and movies. I was interested in the matings of movie stars and whether Doris Duke would finally find happiness with her fourth husband. I couldn't drive, but I loved cars. I hoped for distinction.

When the Cynic warned me not to try to play catch up, he was aware I would find myself far behind my contemporaries, my doubles, who had spent the last six years learning and earning. There was no easy way back, and it could be said I had never been there. The life I saw reflected from the advertising everywhere around me was a life I could see no way to obtain. I wanted things. I wanted clothes, a car, a hi fi, I wanted my share of that river of products Americans had begun to produce. We judged each other by these things. At one point the proudest thing I owned was a Ronson lighter, the model they called The Adonis, and I smoked more often simply to display it. It broke almost immediately. Later, when I was back in jail, the Cynic told me they were made to break.

Another thing bothered me, I had almost stopped painting. My rejection by the museum disturbed me, and, a little later, something even more significant happened. I designed a menu for the Hungry I when Enrico Banducci was first converting it from a private club to the successful restaurant it later became. In payment I was allowed to hang my paintings for the opening. I was very excited. This could lead to the break I dreamed about. This was North Beach, one of the great capitals of the art world, and I sat there that first night with Veto and a few friends convinced I was entering a new life. As the club gradually filled an amazing thing happened. No one paid the slightest attention to my paintings. They could have been wallpaper. They didn't look them over and dismiss them. They didn't look at all. One older man made a brief casual circle, standing a moment in front of each canvas, before he went to the bar and ordered a drink.

One day when I was in the basement of the dime store, sitting on the fountain stool, writing out twenty 5x7s, each with a large red 5¢, George walked in the door. He was wearing gray flannels, a pink shirt, a black knit tie and suede shoes. In the pocket of his gray flannel coat with the padded shoulders and the wide lapels he had a Drine Alpha inhaler. The manufacturers of the Benzedrine inhaler had altered their formula to weaken it, but Drine Alpha was still charged with the raw drug. I hadn't taken this stuff since Nevada, but I was no longer worried about my heart.

George had found me by an incredible strategy — he had looked me up in the phone book, called Veto, and she had sent him to the store. I invited him home for dinner and we walked up Mission Street as I told him about the Veto Russo/Vito Musso joke, and how Veto had great legs like inverted Coke bottles, but couldn't cook anything except meat loaf. We didn't eat anyway, only the cotton out of the inhaler, and sat all night and talked. Just before dawn we went out to ride the Oakland ferry, and, after that, Veto and I went home and fucked for the first time as if we really meant it. She cried out as if surprised at what was happening to her and I drove, wild with joy, right to her center. After, I asked her what she thought of George.

"Well, he's very good-looking, but I don't like him."

"Why not?"

"He doesn't like me. Why should I like him?"

"Of course he likes you. Why wouldn't he?"

Drine Alpha was on sale in any drugstore and Veto and I began to use it regularly. We hardly ever drank because we couldn't afford to, but an inhaler cost sixty-five cents and would keep us both high for days. At first, we tried to take it only on weekends, but Monday morning was hard to face and a little more turned torment into a treat. I breezed into the store and spent the day ecstatically lettering. I enjoyed it. Each card, no matter how trivial, challenged me and I set myself to letter it perfectly. But you can't use strong drugs and maintain an ordinary routine. Your rhythms become those of intoxication and recovery.

I sometimes didn't sleep for days, then collapsed for forty-eight hours. Whenever I dropped the cotton I rose on a burst of warm confidence. I was no longer shy. No longer lazy. I spent whole nights painting. I began to write again and my focus seemed precise and I was sure the things I made were valuable. But when the crash came it was dreadful. My mouth filled with canker sores like stigmata and I knew I was worthless. I had deliberately destroyed my mind, fused my nerves, and turned myself into a sodden vegetable.

You can't swing on this pendulum and work in the ordinary world. Soon I was missing a day, then two days. I was habitually late. I learned to sleep sitting on the fountain stool. Gradually my guilt over all this pushed me out of my job. It was not sane. I was a bargain to them and I knew it. Still one day I didn't go back.

I got another job, and again I started well and then gradually lost momentum. If anyone had asked me why I couldn't hold a job, I would have answered seriously: Because I can't get up in the morning. But, also, there was this difference between the life I had always promised myself and the one I was living. What could happen to change anything?

When I lost the second job, I left Veto and ended living for some weeks in an empty house up on Russian Hill. The house was tied up in probate and I used the basement as a place to sleep, and washed up in a service station a few blocks away. It was here I started again as a burglar. I found my first job across the street. Russian Hill is an expensive neighborhood and this large home seemed temporarily empty as if the people were gone on vacation. It was hardly a real burglary, but I found food and liquor and a zircon ring which I thought was a diamond.

I can't remember how I really felt. I know what I told myself. I was a hunter and this was the elemental, the only real life. Here I was "a pair of ragged claws." And yet I hurt no one. I didn't steal from real people, but only from places of business which I knew to be insured. My only victims were the insurance companies themselves, and it amused me to think I was valuable to them as a negative advertisement. How could they sell insurance against burlgary if there were no burglars?

But something happened at this time that impressed me quite differently. After Steven was born I went back to Veto and we tried to resolve our differences for his sake. Our apartment opened on a small rear court we shared with a grocery store, and I managed to loosen some boards on the side of the grocery so I could enter anytime I liked. I began to "weed" this store. I took meat and eggs and whiskey, but nothing else. Then one night, looking around, I found the canvas cash bag, and the temptation was too strong. There was six hundred dollars in it.

The next day I was in the store and the owner was behind the counter. He looked like hell and was telling another customer how the money he had been saving for his wife's operation had been stolen, and he didn't know what to do.

I've noticed a tendency in these pages to give myself a little the best of it — some bullets are harder to bite than others — so when I say this made me feel awful, you will be able to judge how awful, when I go on to tell you I didn't return the money. Still, I remembered.

Something else happened. I have already described the time in Sacramento when, in the midst of a burglary, I suddenly understood I was going to San Quentin. The voice that spoke to me then, that hidden part of myself, had not had much to say lately. When I was still in San Quentin I used to go through an exercise I called Truth Court, when, periodically, lying on the edge of sleep, I would become plaintiff, prosecutor and judge in a trial to determine the precise difference between what I said I was doing and what I was really doing. These Truth Courts provided me with valuable compass readings in the voyage I felt I was taking, but here, in the free world, this courtroom had remained dark. Then one night as I was walking along the Embarcadero looking for a place to burglarize, my voice spoke again. It said: *When you're back in Quentin, you'll have time to paint.*

The night I was caught my intuition warned me again. I was out with George. When he had first appeared I thought we were going to finally become friends, but George had remained remote. I saw him from time to time, but we never had much fun together. I sensed him judging me as I had judged myself in the Truth Courts—I was all mouth and no ass. I stayed with Veto because I was afraid to be alone. I left her only to go back because I was afraid no one else would ever have me. I refused to try to exploit my talent because I was paralyzed by fear of rejection and failure. I sensed all this in his mind.

Then one morning he called me. "I know you're capering," he said.

"Congratulations."

"Do you want a partner?"

"Sure."

We met downtown and since it was early afternoon, decided to go to a movie. We found a rerun of *Red River*, one of our favorite pictures, and watched John Ireland and Montgomery Clift, firing alternately, keep a tin can in the air for thirty seconds.

Afterward George said, "That picture is a con job. It's only *Mutiny on the Bounty* towed out into the desert."

We decided not to steal in San Francisco. I explained to George, "It's too built up. You bust into a place around here and you've got your ass stuck in someone else's bedroom window." So we took a bus to Palo Alto. We spent the night ransacking a suite of medical and dental offices and started home just before dawn carrying a stolen briefcase which we had stuffed with money, various drugs and almost a pound of dental gold, which George planned to use to cast some miniature sculptures.

The moment we were outside on the quiet residential streets, I began to grow anxious. This was not a smart place to be. Palo Alto was a college town, and a high-class residential community.

"We'd better hide somewhere," I told George, "and wait until morning."

"No, I want to get home."

We were both worn, unshaven and our hands were dirty. "We can't just sit in the bus depot," I said. "The fuzz'll be in there every half an hour."

"We'll walk to the edge of town and hitchhike."

"Okay," I agreed reluctantly.

We walked on and soon saw the lights of a small all-night

coffee shop. George said, "Let's get some coffee. It'll pick us up."

"It's not a good idea."

"I don't care if I have to do ten years in San Quentin, I want a cup of coffee."

That should have told me what forces were at work here, but I didn't hear precisely. I said, "Okay, but maybe we should leave the briefcase outside."

George looked at me sharply. "What's the matter with you?"

My intuition was screaming, but I was so easily led I simply followed him into the shop and we ordered coffee and bearclaws. The counterman looked us over before he moved to serve us. George had brought the briefcase in and as we left he said, "It's your turn to carry this thing." I picked it up.

As we learned later, moments after we left, the officers on prowl stopped for their own coffee break, and the counterman told them two strangers had just been there with an expensive briefcase, and neither of them had looked much like a lawyer.

We spotted the prowl car a moment before they spotted us, and I tossed the briefcase into some bushes. But they knew it existed and they looked until they found it. When we were searched at the station it turned out George had been sticking things into his pockets. He had one of the screwdrivers we had used to jimmy file cabinets, and several credit cards he had picked up while we were ransacking the desks. So they could put us inside and they had us nailed. As the Cynic told me later, The police can afford dozens of mistakes; you get only one.

Once again I was fingerprinted and mugged. The cop

who took the mugs also took the trouble to buffer the harsh floodlights with some scrims he had fashioned. "I hate those stark mugs," he told me. "You could photograph President Truman like that and even he'd look like a criminal."

I called Veto and she began to cry and then I was crying and I didn't care that George was in his cell listening. Later on, I accused him of having led us directly into jail. He made no answer.

Second Jolt
==

I WAS FREE a few days over eighteen months. Beyond marrying and fathering a child I had done little I had dreamed of doing. Now I was abandoning my son, just as my father had abandoned me, and I faced even more empty years before I could hope to start again. How did I absorb this crushing blow? I didn't. Once again I dreamed of escape.

Looking back I can see how it was necessary. Villon wrote: We live in hope, we die in despair. The living can nourish the wildest fantasies, and often go mad to avoid denying them. Our madness was to imagine we could break this jail and find our way to those warm waters where the yacht was sailing. We made a few half-hearted efforts. I tried to dig through the brick walls with a small drill I fashioned out of a coat hanger. This was discovered and we were thrown into a max. tank. George accused me of leading him into even deeper trouble.

Still we might have made it if we had been willing to hit a jailer, and we went so far as to make a sap by stuffing soap into a sock. But we were haunted by two alternating scenarios. In the first, we wound up and hit the guard as hard as we could, and he turned around, his mild eyes blinking, to ask: "Now why did you do that?" In the second his head split and he fell dead.

We never tried it. Failure had already worn the edge from our spirits. One day I told George, "You know something? We're both thirty."

"You think we'll get out that soon?"

Veto came to visit. She had her black hair tinted with a silver preparation and her fine eyes were weary. "Are you sleeping at all?" I asked.

"Only when I fall out," she said.

She smuggled us some Drine Alpha, and we took it and stayed up all night writing limericks on scraps of paper. Later I covered myself with a blanket and began to jerk off. Almost it seemed I was home with Veto, and I began to cry again.

We spent six months fooling around in Santa Clara County Jail postponing our trial, trying to find some way to escape, and, finally, we copped out, and our court-appointed attorney, a nice one this time who liked us, tried to tell the judge we were intelligent, and the judge snapped, "Ants are intelligent, too," and sent us back to Quentin.

Back in Quentin, once again in the Guidance Center, we continued to dream of escape. Again and again I went over the routine, looking for the hole I knew must be there. But every guard on the Quentin wall is armed with a high-powered rifle, and I was not ready for a risk as great as it would surely take. Maybe in a year we would find ourselves in a position of trust. I continued to dream of escape until I knew I had surely served over half of the time they would take from me, and then, slowly, I freed myself of these fantasies. My other fantasies persisted — they were also necessary — and many a night I made myself very small and walked through or under the bars. I wondered how many weeks it would take this tiny man to reach the front gate and freedom.

Penny Peterson was still working in the Guidance Center and he looked at George and me in a sadly knowing way. When he asked me what I had done out there, I said immediately, "I got married."

And he said, "Why'd you do that?"

In some ways it wasn't awful to be back. My friends were there, and I had some new stories to tell. Here was a life of which I was certain, and its harsh limits were also a form of security. This was not our real life, our real lives were once again projected into the future, and limited only by our fancy. We were now secured against failure in the present. We could neither succeed nor fail here, we were in stasis, and preserved against failure and loss until, once again, we were set free.

Any advantage I had had my first time in Quentin was now sharply reversed. Every detail served only to draw the net tighter. For one thing, the briefcase we had carried contained a small bottle of morphine sulphate. We had taken it because it was a glamour drug. Neither of us had ever taken morphine, or any opium derivative, nor did we know anyone who did. It was with a number of other drugs, and we took it because it was there.

The morphine became critical. It was then what heroin is now, and the prison Establishment was alert to the implication that morphine could be both a symptom and a cause of criminal behavior and it was, in significant addition, a politically loaded issue. Several state senators were basing their political lives on the fight to make sales of these opiates punishable by death.

This is typical of the deadend dialogue I was led through again and again.

I see here you were in possession of dangerous drugs at the time of your arrest?

Yessir.

Are you an addict?

Nosir.

Then you intended to sell them?

Nosir.

If you aren't an addict and you didn't intend to sell it, what were you doing with the morphine?

There was no answer to this. My denials were dismissed. I was expected to lie and in every contradiction between my version of events and that recorded in the file, the file was taken to be primary.

That's what it says right here. Why would the investigating officers, and the probationary report lie?

Not lie. Misinterpret.

These men are experienced professionals.

Who wouldn't accept my version of these events because it wasn't typical of their experience.

If you don't admit you're an addict, we can't be expected to help you.

Dangerous drugs! I was beginning to wonder if any of those responsible for this drug hysteria had ever taken them. How did they know so much? About this time I read a report in a medical journal, stolen from the C.M.O.'s library, where two doctors speculated that systematic addiction and withdrawal might, since every organ was stressed during withdrawal, add to one's lifespan. No one picked up this to blast on the six o'clock news. The Cynic told me, First they frighten people, then they make careers protecting them. The Cynic tended to overstate things, but I was suspicious. I remain suspicious.

My file, which now paralleled my life like some shambling, distorted and malicious doppelgänger, caused me further trouble. During my last sentence I had been classified as a First Termer, an innocent. The Nevada conviction had been subsumed because it was clear then the events which led to convictions in both states had been part of the same relatively brief chain of events and I had not been free between the two sentences. Now that consideration was dismissed and I found myself classified as a Third Termer, one of the almost lost. This was arbitrary, the result of a casual reading by some classification clerk in Sacramento, but once entered it was impossible to have altered. No one I complained to cared enough to try to find a way it might be changed, and I didn't yet sense how I might make them care. Three-time losers were considered poor prospects for rehab and we were seldom selected for any of the pioneer programs California was then trying one after the other. We were shuffled aside, dismissed, warehoused, and allowed to walk away the years until we had served enough time to assure the Adult Authority they couldn't be criticized for once again giving us a chance on parole.

I was classified Third Termer at twenty-six, which must be close to the record. My number was now written: A-8814-A, the terminal A to indicate the second conviction carried on the original number, and I was transferred to Folsom Prison.

The night before the gray goose rolled, George sent me a can of Prince Albert pipe tobacco. Inside was a St. Christopher medal and a limerick designed around the nickname he had hung me with. Sam.

> *There was a young convict named Sam,*
> *Thrice caught by Deputy Dan,*
> *Who was so unwholesome*
> *They sent him to Folsom*
> *And no one ever saw him again.*

Just entering Folsom is desolating. You roll through two sets of double gates set in massive stone walls, and it seems you are leaving the world behind, saying farewell to everything soft and sweet, leaving forever the natural land of oceans and mountains, of women and children, to enter some underworld. The bus paused in the second set of gates and some trusties loitering there jumped up to look through the windows at the fresh meat. They seemed grotesque.

Suddenly the apparent ruin of my life overwhelmed me and I held my tears with difficulty. How could I deserve this. What had I really done? But also how could I deny what I had brought down on myself? The first time I had wandered into jail I had been a boy, seized by an adventure, who had no idea what he was getting into. This time I had known, known well, and still it didn't stop me.

Was I lost? A psychological reject, a programming error, marked as surely as any congenital cripple, who burned away his vital energy in some senseless conflict buried below my ordinary awareness, so I could not even grasp its design, let alone relieve the devouring pressure? Would I never learn to fear the real consequences of my symbolic acts? Was I afraid of my life? If I could remain free to become myself, would I attract some powerful and murderous antagonist, who was hidden in my own heart?

I could make myself no answer. The only hope I could offer was essentially negative. I could endure. And some quality in my makeup caused me at regular intervals to face my true situation. I had an instinct for the truth, no matter how harsh its implications, and this was an instinct I couldn't turn away. When I was in despair, I called before myself all those who had lived and died in circumstances even more wretched than my own.

It took six weeks for my troubles in Folsom to climax. At first I liked it there. Folson is to the north and inland of Quentin and the weather is better. I played a lot of chess and worked in the library lettering titles on the spines of rebound books. The bookbinders worked across from me, and argued endlessly as to who was a convict and who was an inmate. An inmate had surrendered, but a convict hadn't.

Taking that rule, Folsom was full of convicts, but a great many had abandoned hope, which made them quiet. If Folsom had a motto it was: Do your own time. But the surface quiet in Folsom was deceptive and there were some very strange men in this cage with me.

My trouble came because I refused to observe color lines. I fear I prided myself on my willingness to have black friends, hardly the rarest of conceits but still relatively unusual in the early fifties. Jazz was one of the mediums through which difference was being broken down and I had spent some time hanging around a Filmore district after-hours jazz club called Jimbo's Bop City, and I had learned to talk the language. Blacks were special avatars of the life force, they knew things we'd forgotten, and I was pleased and flattered to be associated with this talismanic people, who were clearly the wave of the future. Such was the line and, aside from it, I liked some of them.

I liked some I met in Folsom and walked the yard with them, talking about Coleman Hawkins and Lester Young, and how to defend against the fianchettoed bishops of the Queen's Indian opening. But Folsom was a hundred years away from San Francisco and in parts of its dark heart the Klan was still riding. My open association with blacks was interpreted in the light of sexual obsession, and I was looked upon as a white woman who was openly screwing spades. One night there was an unsigned note tossed in my cell.

> Listen, punk, you keep hauling
> coal and one day you'll
> wake up dead.

Custody apparently heard the rumor I was going to be knifed and snatched me off the yard into the Adjustment Center. This was a euphemism for a new kind of solitary unit, and not a very reassuring one; however, we weren't adjusted, but simply confined away from the main population until boredom alone drove us into some form of compromise. But here, for me, the screw was given a particularly savage turn. The duty officer who took me off the yard was a grossly fat and florid loot called The Peg. Prejudice is too mild a word to describe his elemental hatred. He glared at me, eyes boiling.

"You know how close you came to getting your pansy ass slashed? Fucking niggers! It would have served you right."

I had sense enough to keep my mouth shut. I was dismayed by the force of his emotion, and, in an odd way, I envied it. I felt he could have blown me away like a leaf in a blast of hot wind. Yet the trick he now played on me was essentially petty. He locked me up with the most dangerous men.

The AC unit was laid out to contain a number of tanks, like a large county jail. Each tank was self-contained with its row of cells, its narrow day area, and, when the weather was good, we were allowed an hour in a small recreation yard. Each tank had a different category. Instead of holding me by myself in protective custody, The Peg locked me up in high-power with the psychos, the killers and the double-Y chromosome monsters. Since I had not been warned, I had no idea of the danger.

I walked in and was immediately taken up by a large black who told me he was an American Indian whose friends called him Cherokee. "You want to be my friend?"

I wanted to be left alone, but I didn't dare say as much.

"I take care of my friends. I am a powerful man here. These others will tell you."

I looked at the others. A dozen men were walking back and forth in front of the cells like soldiers on watch. They avoided each other automatically. One was a boy I had known slightly in Preston, now a man, and he glanced at me and nodded slightly as if begrudging me this much recognition. A short heavyset Chicano approached with some slips of paper.

"Hey, man, you wanta get down on this football ticket. You pick the weekend games, the man who picks the most, he win all the smokes."

"I don't have anything to smoke."

"You can play on the cuff."

I didn't want to say I neither knew nor cared much about football.

"I've got nothing on the books."

The Chicano smiled, "We can work something out."

Cherokee seemed to swell and grow darker. "Split the scene, Chili Bean." There was nothing frivolous in his manner, but the Chicano seemed neither frightened nor offended.

"Tough enough, Cherokee, you tighten your action."

Cherokee invited me to walk and we spent the rest of the afternoon pacing while he told me how it felt to be an Indian and watch them kill all the buffalo. He watched me closely and I held my expression carefully neutral. He seemed to understand no one really thought he was an Indian, but he knew he could force at least the appearance.

We went out to dinner in a small mess hall, and Cherokee was right beside me. We were given pork steak and Cherokee asked me, "You want this?"

"Don't you eat meat?"

"I don't eat swine," he said precisely.

"I have all I want."

"You might as well take it."

"No, thank you."

He stared at me for a moment, then picked up the pork and dropped it on the floor.

After dinner we were locked into single cells and I was grateful for the chance to relax. I had picked up a worn copy of *Time*, and I lay in my bunk reading it. This world seemed so distant, so wonderful and so dear. I didn't worry about my situation. I had been walking around these places for a while.

The next morning Cherokee was called out on the sick line and I fell into conversation with another, smaller black, who soon found a way to tell me he had killed three men. One in Quentin and two in Folsom. He spoke with pride and told me how and why he had killed them. They had insulted him and his pride had demanded their deaths. He was twenty-seven and they called him Snuffy Smith. He touched his smooth cheek, and said, "I'm just death with a little skin stretched around it."

He didn't seem deadly. He was pleasant, intelligent and good-looking. He owned a chess set so we settled down on his bunk to pass the time over a few games. I had studied this game off and on and I had little trouble winning. This seemed to surprise Snuffy and he began to look at me with some respect and talk about bearing down on my ass. I looked up at one point to see Cherokee standing in the doorway of the cell. I smiled and nodded. Cherokee simply stared at me.

In the middle of the third game Snuffy was called out of the tank. I sat there, studying the board. Cherokee filled the door again and I knew immediately I was in trouble. He'd tied a red bandanna around his hand. I began to slide toward the rear of the cell, and Cherokee launched himself like a panther and smashed me in the mouth. The bandanna was so he wouldn't cut the back of his hand on my teeth. After this first blow, the fight became every fight I've ever been in. A blurred, confused grabbling and twisting where neither of us was able to swing freely and most of the blows were to the body.

A curious thing happened. At one point I had a perfect shot at his nuts. I could have crushed them with my knee. But I somehow knew this wasn't serious yet, and if I hurt him in that way and angered him he could kill me, a murder for which he might not even be tried. The bandanna was the clue. There was something too deliberate about this preparation. He was only administering punishment to regain any face he felt he had lost in the tank. As soon as I understood this, I began to ask him to stop, and he did.

He stood up, breathing heavily. "You can't fuck with me."

"I don't even know you."

"You *know* me."

He scooped a handful of the scattered chess pieces and threw them at me. "Snuffy ain't shit," he said. "You tell him I said so."

When Snuffy came back he seemed to understand immediately what had happened. He touched my crushed mouth with one finger and said, "Poor baby."

Then he began to tell me his shank was being held for him by the A.C. trusty, and it usually took a day to arrange to have it passed. "Cherokee know that. Otherwise he wouldn't have jumped so salty." It seemed to anger him most that Cherokee had beaten me in his cell. "Black motherfucker, fucking over my house like that. If he's Indian, I'm Irish."

After a few days, Snuffy stopped talking about taking any revenge against Cherokee, and Cherokee never spoke to me again. He spoke to no one, he was a total loner, and Snuffy told me I was almost his only attempt at contact in months. Later, when I was back in Quentin, I heard Cherokee was up on the psych ward for treatment. Then I heard he had been killed during an electroshock treatment.

Snuffy convinced me I needed his protection. "Can't no one like you just come walking in here and not get down with someone. That Peg's an evil motherfucker, he knew what he was doing. But you'll be all right as long as my hand's on you. I'll look after you, and maybe sometime you can look after me." He winked slowly. "You know what I mean? I ain't in no particular hurry."

I agreed. I was so scared I didn't care any longer, and what difference did it make? This was my life, why not accept it all? One afternoon Snuffy hung a blanket in front of the bars, kissed me, which surprisingly I didn't mind, and then looked at me with a shy, sheepish, somehow heartbroken expression, and bent down to blow me.

My case was heard by the disciplinary committee. The captain in charge asked me why I was wearing a wedding ring. I told him I was married.

"It says here you're single."

The file again. "I got married when I was on parole."

"There's no record here."

"I didn't have permission."

"It would still be noted."

"If you look on my mailing and visiting list you'll see I have received permission to correspond with my wife."

The captain was clearly unsatisfied. He wanted me to be responsible for what had happened. He wanted me to be that person such things should happen to. If it was my fault, it wasn't theirs. However, the committee recommended my return to San Quentin.

> CHRONO — 103-B   5/3/52
> Subject Inmate, Braly, A-8814-A, clearly
> meets all criteria for placement at Folsom,
> however his youthful appearance may make it too
> difficult for him to adjust in this setting.
> Subject appears to be a pseudo-
> intellectual who may have
> homosexual tendencies.
> REC. Trans. to S.Q.

It seemed as if the first time I was in Q everyone was trying to become a boxer. This time everyone wanted to be a musician. I was no exception. I wanted to be hep until the Wit told me it was no longer hip to say hep. I checked out a flute and began to learn. Soon I ran into another archetype, the Hipster, a musician who didn't happen to play. The Hipster told me to never snap my fingers on one and three.

Veto wrote regularly and visited often. Because I was locked up she was eligible for state aid and she had enough to get along on. She was still hitting the Drine Alpha, and nights she sat up sleepless she sometimes wrote long, rambling letters, describing, if she could think of nothing else, the books she was reading.

George went to work in the hospital as a psychometrician, and didn't often come on the yard. Sometimes he would cause a ducat to be sent me and I would pass through to the hospital to visit him in his office, where we fried steaks on a tiny hotplate, and drank ephedrine, the nearest we could get to amphetamine. It brought a hot flush and a brief, uneasy sense of excitement. We stopped talking of the yacht. We talked of the novels we hoped to write, the movies we hoped to film.

I landed a good job myself as one of two institutional sign painters, and we had a small shop to ourselves above the handicraft department. Here I had the room, the materials, the time to paint, but I never settled to it. Over the four years I worked here I did produce a number of paintings, but paintings designed to sell on the hobby shop. I made clowns (I must have painted Emmett Kelly twenty times) and postcard landscapes.

Whatever was in me yearning for special expression I blew into my flute, which I never learned to play with any easy skill, though the Hipster told me for a meter beater with a tin ear I didn't play too badly. I became one of the crowd who hung around the band room and were always forming and reforming small jazz combos. Flute was a rising horn and I got a few chances to play.

Quentin was still a quiet prison despite the chronic overcrowding. Once in a great while someone would try to escape, or a fight would break out on the big yard. I can't recall a single killing. Once some nut tried to rob the inmate canteen at knifepoint, and then escaped into the East Block, where they found him hiding in the shower. Some other con, in this same block, mugged a guard and took his money and his identification. Custody thought this the prelude to an escape attempt and for days the goon squad was everywhere. They finally recovered the ID, but the con was never caught.

Most of us were trying to figure out some way to keep smoking. Tobacco was not only our exchange, it was also our principal pleasure. To be able to stroll from the mess hall onto the yard, pull out a tailor-made and light up was to say you were doing all right, and, most likely, before you'd taken that first drag someone had asked you for the butt so you smoked, savoring it, while others waited on your pleasure. It was common for five men to stand on the yard in the early morning, stomping their feet against the cold, sharing a single cigarette.

This time, I had told myself, I wasn't going for the okie-doke, I wasn't going to stand around the yard talking Cadillacs and rolling Bull Durham. I wasn't going to accept the standards of the joint. I wasn't going to compete for some tiny advantage. But it is very hard to be empty. To just wait. Any life requires some expression of itself and I needed to have something I could think of as pleasure. So I spent a lot of my time painting clowns and New England snow scenes, painting more portraits from photographs, and air brushing the leather work produced by the hobby workers just to keep in smokes.

And, meanwhile, those months in San Francisco began to blur and fade, and often it was better not to think of them. I didn't pull particularly hard time, and, after the first year, my misery was seldom acute, but I seldom felt really well either, and I didn't have to look in the mirror to know I had begun to age. By the end of this jolt, the boy laminated under the plastic of my ID card looked so little like me one guard accused me of carrying another's card. Shortly after this incident I was ducated to Identification to have a new mug taken.

I continued to read. I loved fine adventure stories, but they were rare. Diligent hacks turned out competent books every year, but Raymond Chandler wrote no more than six or seven novels in his working life and I read them all again and again. I had no taste for writers like Louis Bromfield and J. P. Marquand, and I wasn't wise enough to try to penetrate such classics as *Madame Bovary* or *Remembrance of Things Past*. Even when I began to find it difficult to discover new authors I could enjoy, I still avoided these monoliths. I hoped for diversion, a ride on the magic of others, and, meanwhile, my own fantasy machine continued to grind out my old favorites. I walked through walls. I teleported myself. I became small, invisible, or enormously strong. I had begun to polish these daydreams and some of them became whimsical. I would, for instance, imagine every piece of paper with my name on it destroyed. I would be a non-person, and how would the prison handle me? It amused me to imagine how they would prove I existed.

Nothing large happened this jolt. I didn't fight. I was never beefed. I had a good job and no trouble with it. I sat in the concert band and tried to hold up my part of *The Destruction of Atlantis*. I walked back and forth across the yard. Once a week I changed my sheets. Those ten meals passed through me again and again. Once in a while my cell partners would change.

I find it agreeable to speak of these other men. There can't be many who've never seen a photo of the standard cell in one of the old-fashioned cold-water prisons like San Quentin. These cells were originally designed for only one man, but in the modern prison business there has seldom been any shortage of the basic product, and we were always doubled up, two to a cell.

Few married couples live as closely as cell partners, and they, at least, chose each other, but cell partners always came by chance. The only criterion was that we must be no more than seven years apart in age, and Chicanos were celled with Chicanos, blacks with blacks, and the rest of us were lumped together in a rotating lottery which might find us thrown in with a good dude, who washed his feet and read quietly or napped a lot, or we might find ourselves boxed up with some raving dingaling a half step away from the nut wards.

It made a big difference whether you moved into their cell or they moved into your cell. If you lost your partner to transfer or parole and your cell was empty, you hoped for a few days of privacy. You could shit in peace and slobber and groan when you took your hank. But you knew you couldn't be left alone for long. The joint was too full. Each day narrowed the odds. Then one night at lockup you discovered someone's bedroll tossed on the empty bunk. Immediately you look around the tier for a strange face. If he is standing there already, he's looking for you, as anxious probably as you are. You nod at each other, exchange names, and try to form some impression of this instant buddy the Housing Loot has tossed you. We all wear the same clothes, but there are many variations within the uniform. Pressed clothes and shined shoes carry one message. Worn blues and scuffed shoes quite another.

When the bell rings, the bar is pulled and a thousand iron doors slam. You stand count. You grip the bars with both hands. This is to prevent the guard from counting a dummy as a live body. If you're dying and can't crawl from your bed for count, the guard will tell you, "Show some skin." They want to see you move.

You indicate whether you want to stand count squeezed between the bars and the end of the bunk, or in the aisle where you might be able to slip back for a quick piss. It's a small courtesy, but it's your right because this is your cell. You have two more rights. Your choice of the upper or lower bunk — the lower was favored, you weren't always climbing up or jumping down, but I found the light better in the upper — and it's also your choice whether you want to divide the two shelves in the rear one each or half and half. Since your gear is already in place, the new partner takes what's left.

You help him make up his bunk. It's simply too awkward in this small space to handle it alone, and throughout the time you cell together you will perform this ritual once a week on sheet-change day. Everything else is done by turns. While one washes, the other waits. For a while a new partner will hang back and let you wash first. Gradually, if you're getting along, you'll establish mutual habits. After while, it no longer matters who was there first. If your shit stinks, he'll tell you, "Mix a little water with it."

If you're the one with the cell change, all this is reversed. The cell-change ducat is often a surprise. They're passed out in the morning, just after wake-up. A large electric bell sounds with the insistent and strident hammering of a fire alarm, and wrenches you, like a snared rabbit, out of sleep into the reality of still another prison day. It is seldom a day you have any reason to look forward to, and, like hundreds of others around you, you roll over to sink back into sleep. You're playing roulette with your instincts. If you miss unlock it's a beef. The tiers are released one at a time into the breakfast line, and at each unlock there is the shattering perididdle of the slamming doors, coming always closer. When you can sleep through this, you've done some Sundays, and often you wake the second time with only moments to grab your clothes. It's a rare morning you don't pass someone sitting on the tier lacing his shoes.

But if you're hit with a cell change, it comes moments after wake-up, and you have no time to adjust to this reality before you must be up. You roll your blankets and collect your cell property in your pillowcase. Few have much. I moved with a slender packet of letters, Veto's mostly, a few books, a comb, a razor, my metal cell mirror, my radio headset, my copy of the Rules and Regulations of the California Department of Corrections and whatever canteen I had at the moment. Cans of Nestlé's Instant Cocoa, small jars of Kraft cheese, peanut butter, jam, a few packs of Pall Malls, hair oil, toothpaste and brush.

You say goodbye to your cell partner.

"See you around the yard."

"Yeah. Take it easy."

"You, too, man."

You are used to these changes. Your friends always come to you within the reality of the prison and you are used to making do. You cast the important roles in your life, your eating buddies, your walking buddies, those you like to sit with at the flick, from whatever raw material is available. What you cannot bear, unless you are the rarest of men, is to be alone. Your cell partner has heard your stories, you have heard his. Now you will both find new ears.

When you find your new cell you are anxious to read your

new partner's character in the evidence there. He is at work, but his presence remains. Is the cell neat? Is he a hobby worker who will spend the nights pounding leather? Is he a gunsel with boneroos and a reputation to protect? You hope you won't find pictures of Jesus, or pictures of Elvis, or pictures of hotrods. You hope he's a quiet, ordinary convict, who bathes at least as often as you do, has his own smokes, and doesn't talk too much.

After years of this enforced intimacy with dozens of different men I gradually concluded that beneath all the special pleading and cultural difference, beneath the bullshit and the often rough charm, despite their different rebellions and easy moralities they were all much the same, all much like me. And like you. We were all on this planet together and the ways in which we were similar were far greater than any way in which we were different.

One told me about the jobs he had worked. I learned to appear to listen while detaching most of my consciousness. I left a private on duty to follow whatever heroic narrative I would be expected to punctuate with my response, and while most of me was off seducing Ingrid Bergman or accepting an Academy Award the private stayed behind to listen and when it was time, he signaled and I said, "No kidding?"

These job stories weren't designed to show him in any particular light and the detail was ordinary, unheroic. He claimed to have driven trucks, worked the harvests. He had pumped gas, fry-cooked, and worked car washes. All the faceless, interchangeable jobs you can drift in and out of. After a while, I began to wonder and I kept a loose record of the time involved. When I abandoned this record he was already three hundred and fifty years old. I never understood why he was telling me these gray lies. Perhaps he simply needed to talk to me and these were the only things he could think of to tell me and as long as I pretended to listen some connection, vital to him, was intact.

I had another partner who never took showers or changed his socks. He never removed the socks and he slept a lot with his feet hanging over the edge of the bed, inches from where I had to stand to wash or shave or make coffee. I learned to breath through my mouth. If this weren't enough, he had a small windup phonograph on which he played Western music.

Yet this same man painted miniatures of fairy-tale cities, gardens and fountains, slender towers topped with heraldic pennants, linked by delicate bridges and flying arches.

Another was called Daniel Boone Pine, and he was far from his home in the mountains of West Virginia. His stock showed in his thick black hair, his fine pale skin and very blue eyes, but he held himself indifferently and the vigor of his hair wasn't echoed in his face. His expression drifted between resentment, querulousness and bewilderment.

Daniel was a multiple rapist, and, though he was in his early thirties, his victims were all over fifty. We had all heard of granny dodgers, they were large in our folklore, but they were seldom really encountered, a shy type, rare as a genuine shit fondler, and here was one in my cell. He was a soft, slow-spoken man and I never saw the passion that must have once animated him.

He was trying to writ-out, and was acting as his own lawyer. His writs were an odd jumble of borrowed phrases, the sonority of legal cliché, and his own rough style. The thrust of his argument was not innocence (though he never, not to me, admitted his guilt) but based on the slender contention that his court-ordered commitment to the Patton State Hospital for examination, a period of two years, constituted imprisonment. Under California law such time is dead time. If a serving prisoner flips so seriously he is transferred to one of the institutions for the criminally insane his sentence automatically stops and only resumes when he is returned to the prison. This could be years, and some, of course, never come back.

Daniel argued that this practice was unconstitutional on the grounds that it constituted both double jeopardy and cruel and unusual punishment. To me this argument seemed responsible, but his writs were routinely denied by the state courts. He pinned his hopes on federal judges.

Among his papers was the transcript of his original trial. This vital document can be obtained from the courts for a twenty-five dollar copying fee, an obstacle that prevents more than a few from writing writs. One day when I was locked up in our cell, and Daniel was off somewhere, I read this transcript and made a note of the following passage.

The complaining witness is sworn and gives her name as Betty Miles and her age at fifty-six. Betty's not bright and the D.A. leads her patiently through the details necessary to establish her testimony. It's a warm afternoon, and, Betty, dressed only in shorts and halter, is taking the sun on her porch. The defendant comes up the walk and begins to try to sell her a vacuum cleaner. When it becomes apparent she is alone, he attacks her.

D.A.:	Did you say anything to him?
BETTY:	Yes, I did. I asked him what he wanted with an old woman like me?
D.A.:	And did he answer?
BETTY:	No, he didn't say nothing.
D.A.:	And did he then perform the act of coitus upon you?
BETTY:	What?
D.A.:	Did he then insert his phallus into your vagina?
BETTY:	What?
D.A.:	Did he then put his male thing into your female thing?
BETTY:	Of course he did. What do you think I come up here to tell you?

The writ writer expects to leave at any time, any moment his conviction will be overturned, and he will be dressing out for home. And, sometimes, this unlikely lightning strikes. Writ-writer Sullivan, held in solitary, wrote a writ of habeas corpus on shit paper, served it, and won his release. If Daniel had not had his writs to fool with and pin his hopes to he would have had nothing to do and many years to do it in. A bizarre sex offender finds it almost impossible to win parole. Another acquaintance had raped a nun. Over the years, while he served twice the usual sentence for forced rape, he continued to protest it had been mere circumstance which had caused him to jump the nun. He had been horny, out looking and fate had dealt him this Bride of Christ. When he was finally paroled, he was back in months for child molesting.

I saw Daniel again, five years later. I was now a camp clerk, in Q to appear before the Adult Authority, and I caught Daniel in the lunch line. He seemed unchanged and he told me his case was going well. He had a writ before the federal district court and expected to hear any day.

Another man saved Pall Mall wrappers. He smoked them and he picked them up wherever he found them on the tier or the yard and he had others saving them. He carefully unfolded the wrappers, pressed them, and when he had hundreds, he made them into picture frames. There is a way to fold each pack so it can be braided with the others, and the frames were large and elaborately layered.

The pictures he finally framed were the kind of photos you take by machine, three for twenty-five cents, in penny arcades and bus depots. He had three different poses of his girl friend who hadn't written in a year, and these tiny, yellowing shots were almost dwarfed in the large rococo frames. He spent months on this. Then a former buddy came in from his old neighborhood and told him his girl had been married for six months and was expecting a kid. That night he methodically destroyed the frames and the photos.

One of my rational fantasies — there was some slight hope of it — was they would somehow slip up and put an attractive queen in my cell, and this, like so many of my projections, came true, but in its own way. The queen was grossly fat, farted like a mule, and lay around at night in an outsized pair of women's panties, embroidered with the signs of the zodiac.

I watched one cell buddy learn to paint. I usually had a few supplies, though I did most of my hack work in the shop, and he began to fool with them just to have something to do. He had worked as a mechanic and he approached painting as deliberately. He checked out some standard how-to books, and following directions carefully, he was soon turning out respectable renderings of red barns and my own canned snowscapes. He did neat, clean work.

He told me he was going to set up a stand on the highway, paint all day and sell his work to the tourists. He felt he might make a decent living. "Beats fucking with cars," he said.

He was paroled several years before me, and the second Christmas after he left I got a card from him. The art was one of his own paintings, a nice covered bridge, and in a brief note he told me his plan was working and if I was ever up around Sacramento to stop by his store.

I admired the way he did this entirely outside the structural affectations of the artist and I laid this against some other news I heard from a journeyman sign painter passing through our shop on his way to Folsom. He watched me work. I was never content to just letter, I used outlines and inlines, and various kinds of circus trim. Finally he said dryly it was almost always a mistake to hire apprentices who drifted into sign painting because of an interest in art. "Give me any kid who likes to work with his hands and I can turn him into a crackerjack sign painter, but the artists" — he made it sound like a disease — "they're always fucking around trying to invent some new alphabet."

I was stung and said that the artists were troubled by too much imagination. He shrugged and moved his hands to suggest I had only confirmed the truth of his observation. When

I thought these things over I realized imagination wasn't the problem, it was the desire to be thought imaginative.

I celled with the Hipster for a while. He told me you're either on the bus or you're off the bus, and that while I was usually on it, he was usually off. "It doesn't make any difference, man, if you're not on some trip. Now I don't dig religion and I'm not crazy about sex and I don't get off getting drunk and whipping on people. So dope's all that's left. Do a little geeze and lay back to dig the sounds. Watch the scene. It's always the same show and it always ends the same, but each time it comes down it comes down a little differently. Does that make you wonder?"

One night he brought two small tabs of morphine, one for him, one for me, and fixed us with a ragged hypo taped to an eyedropper, and by the time he got this thing into my rolling and elusive vein I was so frantic I don't know whether I felt anything or not.

One of these cell buddies I'd be glad to have for a friend today. He was also a rapist. Rape's a tough charge, and the rapist often feels, with some justice, he shouldn't be locked up with thieves. The thieves feel they shouldn't be locked up with rapists, but they would miss them when they needed someone, anyone, to look down on. And all rapes are not the same.

Jim's was a near-comic blunder. He jumped his neighbor, a woman in her thirties who spent the days drowsing in front of the television in her nightgown. Jim had often visited her and they had sat together, drinking beer and watching Queen for a Day.

Jim was married, but sex with his wife was spasmodic and

imperfect. He was a fat, awkward and shy man, who, during the dry periods in his marriage, fantasized over the lady in the next apartment. He was painfully fair in his retelling, and it was never clear whether the neighbor had contributed anything to these fantasies. At the time, I assumed she had. This was the vicious cliché that controlled our attitude toward this kind of clearly unplanned rape — sure, she waved it in his face — and for Jim's sake, though he didn't insist, I was willing to accept it automatically.

However it was, one day he fell on her and his life went off on an angle he could have never imagined. He plunged through the floor into the pit. He was hustled, paralyzed by shame, through the legal process, and, because money for his defense would have beggared his wife, he copped out. Then his wife sued for divorce. His career as a computer tech was ruined, and his mother wrote to tell him how it shamed her to have the postman delivering letters with the San Quentin return address.

His situation wasn't any more desperate than most, but we, at least, had had some days, weeks or months, even years, to consider what we might be risking. Jim had blown his life on the impulse of a moment, and he was punished, corrected, if you will, just as if he had acted entirely and deliberately on his own, out of the context of his culture and our history on this planet.

These considerations, incomplete as they are, are not difficult to view as abstractions. Happy citizens are daily mutilated, and our sanity requires we view these occurrences with a certain detachment. But when you know someone as intimately as I came to know Jim, detachment becomes impossible, and it was difficult to see how imprisonment could help him.

It was hurting him. He was sent to Quentin because the method for sending him existed; the social construction, secured in law against any easy re-examination, allowed only this solution. This human buck was passed from one group of experts who didn't know what they were doing, to another group of experts who also didn't know. And where this process became evil — and I suggest evil to be a chronic insensitivity to the real feelings of others — is when all these officials were compelled to pretend they did know what they were doing.

Yes, we were in the hands of faith healers, and when we broke and stumbled down the aisle, eyes streaming, crying, "Heal me!" then we found they couldn't.

When I entered the California prison system there were just three prisons. When I was finally discharged, almost twenty years later, there were thirteen prisons and more were planned. It's expensive to build and operate prisons and each new unit added to the correctional bureaucracy. More guards — more sergeants, more lieutenants, more captains, more program administrators, wardens, associate wardens and superintendents. More correctional counselors, clerks and storeroom keepers. More vocational instructors, teachers, doctors, dentists and medical techs. More psychologists, psychiatrists, sociologists and psychometricians. More chaplains, librarians, stewards, cooks, and recreational supervisors. And, always more and more prisoners. The jails of every county were packed with the convicted waiting to begin their sentences in one of the state facilities. Sometimes they waited months. And as each new prison opened the relief was only temporary. Soon the jails were crowded again. The Cynic had an idea about this. You ever notice how when they want to build a new prison all of sudden paroles are hard to get and they're busting dudes back on violations for spitting on the sidewalk, and, pretty soon, they've got us warehoused ten deep, then they go to the legislature and cry about the over-crowded conditions which only a new prison will relieve.

During this second jolt it seemed the world was about to go mad and blow itself up. It was the era of the bomb and the bomb shelter, and we didn't always feel too badly about this because we thought Quentin offered fair shelter. When San Francisco was destroyed, and the guards panicked, we would be safe behind these massive walls and free to start a new society.

Meanwhile, in the event they didn't drop the bomb, I thought I better try to get some help. By now every psych in the joint had group therapy sessions, and while these were largely limited to the same special interest cases who had formerly enjoyed the psychodrama, George had the connections to get me in. He arranged an interview with an agreeable psych who collected unusual prisoners, and I was pleased with his interest in me and he was pleased with my interest in his program.

It's grossly unfair but an inmate with some charm and intelligence can usually gain advantages hopelessly beyond the reach of the average con. An abuse hardly peculiar to prisons. The doctor doesn't think: Here's a man who isn't boring. He thinks: Here's a man who's really open to treatment and maybe he's someone I can help.

Group therapy was held for an hour each week, and the group I joined numbered ten. One had killed his wife.

Another had killed his wife and their three children. Another had revenged himself by burning down his neighbor's house. Another had killed a cop in the course of a robbery. Another had raped twenty-three young girls. Still another was a statutory rapist, who was himself not much older than the age of consent. Another had killed a friend in a knife fight over a broken bottle of wine. Another, after the death of his wife, began to sleep with his three daughters. The daughters were apparently content with the arrangement, but a neighbor overheard them arguing as to whose turn it was.

By the time we were all gathered, sitting in a circle on wooden folding chairs, usually ten minutes of the therapeutic hour had already gone by. Our circle here, like Arthur's table, was supposed to have no head, for the remaining fifty minutes we were all equally free to say anything we liked, but naturally we polarized toward the therapist. His equal voice might be heard by the Adult Authority. We all knew the Adult Authority took special interest in these programs.

A word about the therapist. He was a psychologist and I expect he had his master's. He was young, working his first job out of school. Once, in a moment of confidence, he told me his main interest had been football, and that was very much the type he seemed — large, blond, handsome and athletically graceful. He dressed beautifully and was almost always pleasant. Occasionally, but rarely, he could be witty. The position he had given himself was difficult. His therapeutic stance was passive.

Every session began the same. We sat silently. We smoked and stared at the bland cream walls. Sometimes the therapist would attempt to melt the impasse by asking briskly, "What were we talking about last week?"

The Wit would say, "Our chances for immediate parole."

And the therapist would smile dutifully, and ask again. Often no one remembered. Or we all pretended we didn't remember. But if someone volunteered: "Wilson was talking about his wife . . ." A girl now seven years in her grave. The therapist would settle around and try to lay the weight on Wilson, and maybe Wilson would continue his painful recapitulation of the events leading to his wife's death at his own hands, and maybe he wouldn't. Maybe he'd just continue to sit. We weren't, as we said, warmed up.

Often half the hour would pass in this willful silence. We had been told that even as we sat silent the therapy was working. If we each accepted responsibility for the waste, dealing with this responsibility would help us grow. But time was the one thing we had to waste. And the one thing we were truly seeking here was not an understanding of our problem, but the appearance of the search. This was obvious from the question we asked again and again of the therapist.

"Does this therapy help us with the Adult Authority?"

The therapist has an answer to this. "Do you think it should?"

"I don't know about 'should' — does it?"

"I don't really know."

"What do you think?"

"What do *you* think?"

"Well, let me put it to you like this, do you make a report to the Adult Authority?"

"Not directly."

"Who do you report to?"

"The head of the Psychiatric Department."

"And does he make a report to the Adult Authority?"

"That's my understanding."

"Well, when you make this report to Crazy David for him to tell the Adult Authority, what're you going to say about me?"

"What do you think I should say?"

"You wouldn't say what I think you should say?"

"How do you know?"

These same questions and counterquestions came up again and again and the therapist sat there, Socrates in the agora, and calmly batted them back. I can't judge the effectiveness of this method. Certainly there isn't one of us who isn't marked by the use Socrates made of it. But it became my ambition to force the therapist to ask me a direct question.

When we finally did warm up and begin to talk, our direction was often idle. Someone might wander into a discussion of the way the Texas prisons compared to these in California, or how someone long ago had failed to give them a break, or why the Giants were certain to win the National League pennant. Sometimes, but rarely, someone would begin to talk openly. I think more than one of us wanted to. Once Wilson, who had killed his young wife, broke down and cried. I worked near him and as we left therapy that day he asked me not to mention the incident.

We didn't trust each other and that was one reason these sessions remained so tight. We knew anything we said was noted and would be retailed as gossip. We gossiped constantly, rumor moved through the joint like fog, and almost no one was entirely untouched by it. The emotions of grief and uncertainty were no part of the pose we struggled to maintain with each other. Our ideal convict, like the Hipster, was a zombie of coolness. Hard, smart, utterly certain. This attitude was designed to say: You can herd us like animals and feed us on slops, but you can't break our spirits. We could hardly leave this attitude behind for an hour of therapy a week. Particularly when the therapy itself seemed so elusive. How did it help to talk about these things?

Still, some of us did talk, usually softly, staring at the floor. These men, now so extraordinary, who had started out to be regular guys, told how the transformation had been worked on them. The most tragic and infuriating of these stories came from the young statutory rapist. In California any act of intercourse with a girl under eighteen is rape.

This boy, call him Willard, grew up in a small central California town, an agricultural community. While still in high school he fell in love with one of his classmates. They were both sixteen. Her father was implacably opposed to Willard and when he surprised them one night making love in the back yard, he blew the whistle. The girl tried to testify to her willingness, but she was brushed aside, and Willard was sent to Preston. He managed to stay in touch with the girl and when he was due out on parole she ran away to meet him. They checked into a motel. It was here the father found them. Again Willard was charged, again the girl's protests were brushed aside, and this time Willard was sent to San Quentin. Now he was assigned to group therapy to discover the nature of his problem and how he might deal with it in the future.

I can sense myself sitting there every Tuesday for three years. We met early in the morning and I can still hear the sound of the buffer wandering back and forth across the brown linoleum out in the hospital corridor. Beyond the frosted and barred windows that led to the hospital yard I sometimes heard the hospital clerks and orderlies playing tennis. George was often on this court. After several years the therapist no longer seemed so fresh, and I think his enthusiasm for his job here was slowly draining. However, his socks still matched his ties. There were days when I came here for no better reason that the glimpse I could catch of Jake La Motta, as we called Crazy David's confidential secretary. She was the only real woman I ever saw, except the main floor nurse, a very tall girl with no tits, whom George said he had had once on the table in O.R., and she had whispered obscenities in his ear. And, sometimes, since I was in the hospital, I dropped by to talk to another psych who had befriended me. He was much smarter than my therapist, and while he never came right out and said my therapy wasn't very useful because my therapist was dumb, he allowed me to form this impression.

We played a funny little game with each other. He had two ashtrays. A little plastic job, a copy of an Edith Heath original, and a metal soup bowl. The soup bowl was for the inmates. This bothered me as much as my unequal chair in the board room, and when he wasn't looking I would switch the two ashtrays. When I wasn't looking, he'd switch them back.

Almost everyone in the joint was taking the line that they had come to this because of their neuroses. I watched my former crime partner Mick, who was back, turn from a fierce young hardass into a quivering jelly of complaints and uncertainties. This was better for those he might have mugged in another future, but how was it better for him?

I lettered a sign for George to post in his office. NEUROSIS FOR RENT. And the text went, in part, "Do you feel dull and ordinary and responsible for what you have done? Do you need something, or someone to blame . . . ?"

Finally the therapist broke down. I had outwaited him. One day he asked, "Why do you think you steal?"

And I answered, "Because I wanted the money?"

And he laughed and said, "Sure you did."

It's possible that the twenty thousand men said to be confined within the California Department of Corrections were there for twenty thousand different reasons. This would be a manifestation no more extraordinary than the number of stars which appear to be in our universe. What I finally learned in therapy was that the reasons, whatever they might be, I was in prison, were irrelevant beside the condition that I was there. What difference could it make? I was here. The way to stay out was hardly elusive or subtle. I had to go to work and stop stealing.

Things gradually got better in Quentin. They began to change our socks every night. Before you went to sleep you hung the pair you had worn on the bars. In the morning a fresh pair had been tossed in your cell. Whoever did this performed like the shoemaking elves in total anonymity. Then Christmas eve of 1957 when I came into the block for evening lockup, scrawled on the blackboard which usually held notices like NO WATER!, was the following greeting.

MERRY XMAS
FROM THE
SOCK MAN

I can't remember writing anything this time except a number of melodies, and sometimes I thought I might write words to turn them into songs, but I never did. The Hipster told me the only trouble with singers was that sometimes you found yourself listening to what they were saying. My hair continued to fall and I took this to be the visible record of my spiritual shrinkage. Monks paced the same quiet rounds I walked and their spirits were not diminished. Thomas Merton had committed himself to a life of discipline harsher than mine, but he had chosen.

That single thing that grinds you down and finally begins to erode your confidence, your vitality, your most basic sense of yourself is the moment-to-moment condemnation implicit in this situation. Even when the prison begins to seem like the only world, you know it isn't, you know there is always a larger world, full of nice people, who would not understand how you had become a part of this small, disgraced minority.

I defended against this, like most of my brothers, by becoming a cynic. We knew the world was corrupt and the square john was a fool who carried the capitalist, the bureaucrat, the welfare claimant and the politician on his patient back. Our nation, in the larger sense, was a do-gooding bully, who said one thing and did quite another, and, in the smaller sense, was made up of income-tax frauds and office workers who stole postage stamps and paper clips. We were alert to the whole spectrum of hypocrisy and it provided a significant crack in which we could make our lonely defense. We were upfront, natural men, who lived out the truth of our human condition.

But when we went in front of the Adult Authority we were eager to join this chorus of hypocrites, and, in many ways, this was the worst time of all.

From the moment you enter, and during all the time you serve, until your sentence is finally fixed, you are always waiting to appear before the Adult Authority. The average inmate appears once a year and you are no sooner denied, flopped over, knocked down with your rent paid for another year, than you begin to wait for your next appearance. It's out there, beyond Pluto like some great comet, moving toward you, bringing the precious date on which your life, your real life, will start again.

We never knew just how long we would have to serve — my own basic sentence was one year to life, which left the A.A. a lot of time to play with — but most of us knew in a general way about how much time we would do. There was nothing that interested us more and we logged years trying to thrash out a basis on which to predict the Adult Authority. This was our great debate. We knew which programs to try to associate ourselves with and we knew which ploys were now exhausted. We could gauge public pressure and the changing winds of penal philosophy, and we knew which individual members were apt to be liberal and which were conservative. We charted their idiosyncrasies. We hoped they were feeling well.

In short, we usually knew within a few months how long we would do. Despite this, every time I appeared in front of the Adult Authority I found some reason, however wild, to imagine they would free me. These were not dreams of invisibility, this was real hope. No matter how I counseled myself against this irrational optimism it always came to me. It made me crazy to know that these other humans, these walking, talking, shitting and ulcerating humans, could, if the whim took them, order me set free, and no one, not the entire guardline, could change their order. Again and again, as I lay on the edge of sleep, I walked into the boardroom and took them by storm. I was Demosthenes whipping up the Athenian spirit. How could they deny me? I was Voltaire showing them the painted scenery, spinning the bull roarer, working the machine that lowered the god, exposing every trick played in the whole sorry show, until they came to realize history could not condemn me. Or I was Joan before her English judges, my unequal chair was her stool, and this time their hands were stayed by mercy.

I wasn't even able to make a favorable impression. My supposed potential now worked against me. Others had succeeded with less. They saw hundreds of men every month who had had the shit kicked out of them every day of their lives, with no break in sight, and here I came, who could work, but wouldn't. An evasive smart-ass who couldn't meet their eyes. It was a rotten experience. They sat there and knew you had to lie to them.

We had our body of wisdom and our intuitions as to how they must function, but they also had learned something about us. They had been subjected to the most artful and elaborate cons until now they took nothing on faith. They knew we would say anything to get out. Every man who came before them sat there with a single purpose — to somehow leave that room with his freedom restored. Few cared how.

When I appeared with three years served, I was certain I was going to get my time. I had worked one job, my grades were decent, I had had no beefs. I walked in confidently, and came out ten minutes later feeling as I did after I had sold a pint of blood — weak, clearheaded and empty. That night the slip came in the evening mail. They are folded and stapled. If you're flopped over, they simply write *Denied* on an angle in red pencil. You don't have to open the slip to see this. I tossed mine in the toilet. Another year — at least another year — of morning bells and paintings of Emmett Kelly, a year in which I would pass that mysterious border between twenty-nine and thirty. A year in which Veto would finally stop writing. I would see fifty-two movies, of which twenty would be B Westerns, and eat meatloaf thirty-seven times. I would jack off approximately two hundred times, examine my hairline at least once a week, and my stomach would continue to bother me, and my crotch would begin to rot.

When I saw the Cynic on the yard the next morning I told him I'd been flopped over and I thought this the grossest injustice since they nailed up Jerusalem Slim, and he made a tiny circular motion with his thumb and forefinger. "What do you think this is?"

"What?"

"The world's smallest phonograph playing 'My Heart Cries For You.'"

But you're never shot down for long. In a few months you begin to think of your next appearance, when you will have strengthened your primary requirement — you'll have served one more year. There's only one thing to bring before the Adult Authority, the Wit said, and that's enough time. It takes many months for the official process to catch up with your apprehensions of it, but, finally, three months before your next scheduled appearance, the orchestration begins.

One morning you have a ducat to a pre-parole interview, and at the appointed time you wander over to the counseling office and begin to wait. Anyone who has dealt as a supplicant with any government agency has endured this waiting.

It becomes easy to imagine that behind each office door is Dostoevski's embittered clerk, sucking on his rotten teeth, brooding over his liver, punishing the world for his own misery, and there are always a few of these, but most are in no hurry and they assume you're not in a hurry either. You have lots of time.

At first I approached these interviews with excitement and optimism. Finally, I hoped they wouldn't go badly. At first I was anxious for the counselor to see I was different than the others. Finally, I hoped he would imagine I was simply one more inmate, for I had learned it was particularly dangerous to be considered any kind of special case. We all knew the story of the con, a simple thief, who inherited a million. Rather than release him early to enjoy his fortune, the A.A. kept him several years longer than he would have ordinarily served to secure themselves against the suggestion they had been influenced.

I always drew the same counselor — caseloads were determined alphabetically — and he was a kindly and dull man. I watched him grow older, always trapped in a river of routine paperwork, not smart enough to master the competitive exams which would have entitled him to promotion, and still too young to retire. He could not help me. He knew it and I knew it. He was broken, far more than I, to the realities of this prison machine.

I sit beside his desk and try to read snatches of my case summary. He offers me a smoke, takes one himself and lights us both. "Where do you think you'd like to go if they grant you a parole?"

"San Francisco."

"Ah, yes, you were there before."

"Does that matter?"

"I don't know. I don't suppose so. Do you have a job offer?"

We all thought a job offer valuable in winning parole, but it's very difficult to get a potential employer to promise to hire an inmate who may not appear to actually work for two to three years. Such offers were usually put together by the family, calling on old friends, and often they were dummy jobs, simply gestures. The Adult Authority knew this, and the Cynic, for one, thought the job offer could be a tactical error since it carried the suggestion one might be manipulative. Very few cons had the connections to carry a valid job offer to the board. I certainly didn't.

The counselor goes on, "Do you think you'll be able to find a job if your parole is granted?"

Who's going to say No? I always said, "Yes."

"Is your marriage intact?"

"More or less."

"Does she write to you?"

"Not often anymore."

"Do you think she expects you back?"

"I don't know. I'm not sure I want to go back. We weren't that happy."

"It's a place to stay. Does she — ah — live alone?"

"I think so."

"The Adult Authority may ask you these questions."

He was telling me as directly as he thought prudent to answer the Board more positively. He rocks back and looks at me. He's seen me before, and, probably, he expects to see me again.

"They may let you go this time. You've got some time in. Your record's clean. I'm going to recommend parole, but I don't know if it will do any good."

"I know."

"Good luck, then."

Later this same month your work supervisor makes out a special report. Very like a report card. He grades you in several categories — quality, quantity, attitude — from one to five, and there are four lines for his comments, which are necessarily telegraphic: *Good worker. Much improved. Seems to have settled down. Going along all right.* Or. *Negative attitude. Only works when supervised. Steals. Talks back.*

If you're close to your super, one of his willing horses, he might explain to you how you deserve ones, but he is going to give you twos and keep his evaluation moderate so the Adult Authority won't imagine you have been able to con him. One of my supers explained how it angered him to be unable to write a direct and honest report, but the Adult Authority routinely accepted the negative and suspected the positive reports. "They're so jealous of their authority they resent any implication that the institutional staff, who see the men every day, might have a legitimate hand in the decisions they make. They think we're such fools any scam artist can con us."

It was amazing to learn that the staff saw the Adult Authority to be just as remote and arbitrary as we did, and they had their own version of our debate — how best to help those inmates they thought worthy?

In the psych department another report is prepared, one you will never see — the file clerk there is an incorruptible free man — and one certain to sound negative, whether it was intended to be or not. There is little you can say in the language of their discipline which doesn't sound ominous.

FALSE STARTS

Subject inmate is a sociopath with a highly organized system of repressed hostilities. His successful adjustment to the rigidities of the institutional setting must be viewed negatively. Uses his verbal skills to disarm any attempt at analysis. Prognosis must still be described as negative.

In the library an inmate clerk checks your card to tell the Adult Authority what you've been reading, and in the chapel of your choice (I had naturally set myself down as atheist, but here, as in Ireland, you must be either a Protestant or Catholic atheist) someone writes a brief report on your religious participation. The board is not enthusiastic about Pauline conversions. Still, every once in a while someone will try to run this number, but it's not regarded as a classy route to go. The Block Loot writes a few lines. *Clean cell. Cooperative.* Your disciplinary record is condensed. *Last infraction 4/7/48, violation of CDC-140, Failure to wear reg. haircut.* Your family writes in, as all do, to say you are needed out there. All this is gathered and condensed six weeks before your hearing.

Now you wait. You have been waiting since the moment you entered, but now the momentum gathers and with it comes the crazy conviction you have a chance — a good chance! — to be freed. There is a formula which cannot fail, if only you can discover how it must be said. You are Aladdin before the sealed cave. "Open barley!" "Open bulghur!" There is some magical combination which will cause this great rock to roll clear.

The Adult Authority, like visiting heads of important states whose inconvenience in the smallest matter might be reflected in negotiations of the gravest importance, is treated with great deference. Hearings never start before 10:00 A.M., but the inmates scheduled to appear first are routed out at 5:00, fed, and held in readiness against the remote chance the Adult Authority might start early. They never do, but whenever they enter the hearing room and press the buzzer, an inmate is immediately provided.

It takes most of the day to go to the board. You begin waiting at the first staging area, the captain's office, hours before your appearance. In time, you move between gates. Here you sit on two long benches like paratroopers waiting to jump. And the debate goes on. Maybe you sit next to someone who wants to run over his story, and you ask the hardest questions you can imagine the A.A. might ask. Some think the prepared story is dangerous. It might sound canned, insincere, and one can trip on the rigidity. The Cynic warned me to go loose, and, like a great shortstop, be ready to field anything hit to me. But it's impossible not to speculate and run trial hearings. Your nerves are tightening. This is enormous.

Men returning from the board come back through the outer gate a few at a time, and someone will always ask: "How do they seem?"

And the Wit will answer, They don't seem like adults.

"How are they, really?"

"Tearing ass, baby."

"Do you think you got your time?"

"Who knows. I can't read those suckers."

The Cynic believes everything depends on how they feel. If they slept well, enjoyed the hookers in San Francisco, and were pleased with their breakfast eggs, if their lunar and emotional cycles were high and their ruling planets in harmonious concord, then, and only then, you had a slight chance.

Next you move out from between gates over to the ad building where the hearing rooms are located. Here you are beyond the last wall, held only by the armory tower, and, over the green lawns, the neat beds of flowers, and the roofs of the officers' homes, you see the San Francisco Bay. Once a year, twice at most, you see this, Angel Island and the Richmond shore, and the sweet freshness of this other world washes over you like love. It would be enough to sit there and skim flat rocks across the water.

In the ad building you are seated in the corridors in the order of your appearance. As each man goes, all the rest move up one place. Everyone is quiet, drawn in, staring at the floor, and even the Wit has stopped making jokes. A secretary may sway past and her smell comes to you like something remembered from a dream. You watch the others come out of the hearing room. Many are white-faced, a few visibly angry. Others shake their heads.

The last chair is the hot seat and here, finally, it is you who are waiting. Your hearing may last ten minutes, but it may be as brief as five minutes, and it is hard to see how they are able to turn the crank so swiftly, to digest your file and decide your fate in these few minutes you have waited a year to earn. The Cynic says this proves it's all dumb show and empty form, your time is set in Sacramento by anonymous clerks and all you can do in the hearing room is fuck up. If you keep your head low and your responses simple, you'll get whatever sentence was recommended by the Sacramento bureaucrats.

The buzzer sounds, the guard nods and you're on your feet. I can never remember entering the board room. Suddenly I'm there, and they are looking up at me, and the member I've drawn says, "Please have a seat, Mr. Braly," and there is my chair, just as I left it last time.

At first there were three members, then six, and, finally, nine. You see only two, and often everything depends on which two. I am clean and neat, but not slick, and my haircut is responsible. One member is in my file and the other member is in the file of the man who will come behind me.

My member looks up to say, "You've done very well this last year."

"Thank you."

In my case doing well doesn't mean much. I'm thought to be adjusted to the institution, if not quite yet institutionalized, and my good behavior is taken as no guarantee I'll continue to live quietly once I am free. A precise intuition.

"We see you're participating in one of the therapy programs."

"Yessir."

"What do you feel you're gaining?"

I want the courage to say *Nothing at all*, but instead I begin to chant Insight, Maturity, Coping with Anxiety, Coping with Anger, Rejecting False Passivity.

"Do you feel you've reached some understanding of your problem?"

And there it is again.

My problem is I can't get up in the morning. I want, but can't believe I deserve. My problem is I'm a rational and good-hearted man who does irrational and harmful things. My problem is there is no one out there in the wilderness who can tell me what my problem is. My problem is my life is already half over and I haven't allowed myself to begin living it. My problem is I'm terribly afraid I can't solve my problem. I feel I can, though I tremble for myself, and I live in this hope, but I have felt so, hoped so before and I have been wrong. My problem is that I don't know what to say to you to explain myself. I meant no harm. I mean no harm. Please let me go now before it is too late for me.

But I didn't say this either.

"If we should decide to release you now, do you feel you can cope with your problem?"

"I hope so."

"We do too. How will you support yourself?"

"I have a trade."

"Yes, we understand you do well at it. Do you plan to reunite with your wife?"

"If she wants it."

"All right, we'll let you know what we decide. Keep up the good work."

I don't need to tell you what the Cynic concluded when you were told "keep up the good work." Shot down again. Another year to walk away. Maybe you should try to get out to camp, or transfer to Chino where the weather and the food are both better. Maybe you should start going out to the gym to try to get some exercise. Maybe you'll try to write a science fiction novel about a man who can teleport himself out of his jail cell into the Cirque Room of the Fairmont Hotel, but who arrives there in his prison blues with A-8814 stamped above the shirt pocket.

But one of those years, as almost everyone does, I made it, and again I left San Quentin in either the spring or the fall.

Second Interlude

THEY FIXED MY TIME at seven years — four and a half in and two and a half out. I believed I was very different when I left this time. I was thirty-one and I thought I knew how to knot a tie. You realize the extent to which you have melded with the blue uniform you have worn so long the day you drop it and kick it aside to be tossed into a large hamper, to be washed and issued again to the next one who comes to play the part. Your new clothes are seldom in style, and I dressed out in a loosely cut suit which had been beached somewhere by the flood of the Ivy League look, and sold at discount to the state. I didn't mind.

I left, coincidentally, with Colby Burtis, a black musician I sometimes jammed with in the band room, and we rode the bus together to San Francisco. As we were pulling over the bridge, Colby nudged me and pointed to the man sitting just in front of us. He had a small button sewed to the back of his collar. Colby started to laugh. "What's it for?" he whispered.

"To hold your collar down."

"Oh, man, you think our collars are going to pop up because we ain't got no button?"

I started laughing, too. The more we looked at that button the funnier it seemed.

Colby and I thought it wise to separate before we hit the parole office. One of the conditions of our paroles was that we would avoid associations with other ex-convicts. We shook hands.

"Hey, man," Colby said, "maybe I'll dig you around the scene."

"What do you plan to do?"

"Work a bit, buy an axe and see if I can get with some group."

"Maybe I'll catch you blowing somewhere."

"Yeah."

This time I drew a younger and more aggressive parole officer. He looked at me with a flat, untrusting gaze and made it clear my leash would be short. I was damaged and suspect goods, a third-termer with one busted parole behind me.

I hadn't heard from Veto for months and I didn't feel drawn to her. If we had lived together these years we might have hammered out the basis for some peace between us, but the chance had been lost and I didn't care enough to want to revive it. Again I took a cheap room and spent my first night wandering the city.

One of the great games we played in the joint was to imagine what we would do our first night out. I'm going to get a good room, take a big healthy shit and a long hot shower, catch a shave and go out to the best restaurant I can find and order the biggest steak on the menu. This is possible if you want to spend all your gate money the first night, but soon fantasy slips in, and the waitress is a fine chick, and you come on to her and discover she's really a jazz singer, weathering a dry spell between gigs, and you arrange to pick her up when she gets off, and the two of you hit the after-hours spots, dig the sounds until dawn, when you walk arm-in-arm up Telegraph Hill to the very top where her pad overlooks both bridges and most of the bay, and there on the coffee table are *The Prophet* by Kahlil Gibran and Walter Benton's *This Is My Beloved*. She pours wine, rolls a joint and puts Bird on the record player. You kiss and she sighs and says, You must of really been lonely, baby. And when you make it, you don't come immediately as you will for weeks, but ride on and on, Oh, Lord, as her apartment windows slowly turn bright with the sun.

Nothing like this happens. I was too shy to speak to anyone. I wandered down into North Beach and went to a jazz club where I sat at the bar and stared at myself in the mirror. A male Cinderella, already a little too old for the part.

The next day I found a job in a small one-man sign shop. When I told the owner I'd just got out of San Quentin, he smiled, spread his hands, "There's nothing here to steal, but a few cans of paint." However, in his mind, I'm sure he took ten dollars a week from the figure he had planned to offer me.

I've never found it hard to get a job. A certain kind of marginal employer knows you're desperate and will work for less than you may be worth. Maybe you'll pan out, maybe not, but he's sure to get a few months' work while you're still fresh out and really trying to make it. If he's a real asshole he may keep you in line by threatening you with your parole officer. But these are the dues you expect to pay. You can't jump out to start even. I went to work for sixty dollars a week. Scale at that time was a hundred. But I wasn't that much of a bargain.

After two nights in my hotel room I began to think of Veto differently. How could it hurt to see her if I could also see Steven? We weren't enemies, Veto and I, we didn't know each other well enough. It wasn't even that I didn't like her, I simply didn't want to live with her. So I reasoned. But my real motive was uglier, ugly because it was so craven — I thought she might let me fuck her. I didn't really want her, but I thought I might use her to regain my confidence. Her warmth might thaw me. I was naive. She was in no position to volunteer these missionary services.

She had moved during the years I had been gone, but her mother hadn't moved and I knew her new address would not be far from her mother's house. I took the bus out through the Mission District and soon found the address. A small brown bungalow, almost as tiny as a child's playhouse. No one was home. I left a note saying I was free along with the number at the hotel. When she had stopped writing I had assumed it was because she had moved someone in. I sensed another strong presence around this house, and I rode the bus downtown thinking it just as well. I went to bed to read myself to sleep.

Fifteen minutes later the phone rang. It was Veto. She had been out at her mother's and had come home to put Steven to bed. Why didn't I come back out? I dressed, with some uneasiness, and rode the bus back to the Mission. Some messages were beginning to pass between those barricaded parts of me, and I knew I was blundering, taking the easiest way, but nothing I tried to say to myself could halt my confused retreat. And it's not just to see it so negatively. I had had nothing. This was something. But even as I moved toward it I knew it would not be enough.

Veto didn't look well. She was bone-thin, her eyes feverish, and she had been speeding all the years I had been gone. She lived on pills. Whites to wake up, yellow jackets to sleep, and a special present she called a Christmas Tree, a cap filled with red and green spansules, when she wanted to leave it all behind to float in the warm water.

We kissed hello, a dry tentative kiss, and she took me into the bedroom so I could see Steven sleeping. He was a beautiful little boy. I stood and watched him. "Could we wake him up?"

"We shouldn't."

We went into the living room, where a television played without sound. She had given away all my paintings because someone had told her they were ugly and cynical. She had replaced them with Keene's big-eyed kids. Ceramic clowns and French poodles stood on the end tables. I could sneer privately at her taste without considering the hundreds of paintings I had personally added to this great river of junk.

I had thought she didn't know I was getting out. She did. She had called the parole office twice in the last few days and they had refused to tell her where I was staying. She knew I was being freed because they had cut off the state aid. The wife of a prisoner is not entitled to anything, but his children are, and all the time I had been locked away she had collected a small monthly check, just enough to live on with some help from her mother, for Steven's welfare. Now that I was free the state expected me to assume the burden of his support. So, I discovered, did Veto.

She responded to my clumsy advances by telling me flatly, "You can have me if you promise to stay."

"Don't you want it?"

"Not particularly. The nature's gone out of me."

"You're exhausted."

"Sometimes. Will you stay and help take care of Steven?"

"Yes."

She stood up and began to unbutton her blouse. "I'm going to ask you to wear a rubber."

"Okay."

"Don't take this wrong, but I have some here."

"Your life's been your own."

"Has it?"

"You've made your own choices."

I always had an answer, but what had happened to Veto was another one of those grim ironies. During my first years back in Quentin I had been too desperate to let her go, and, thinking of the older woman in Wilder's *The Bridge of San Luis Rey*, who had tried to hold the attention of her shallow daughter by writing her marvelous letters, I had showered Veto with mail. Three, four letters a week. She became acquainted with the mailman and began a long affair. I'm sure she would have married him, but he was already married, with kids of his own, and she was his side dish.

We made love on the rug and it wasn't much fun. She had nothing for it and made no pretense. But I lay there beside her, stroking her shrunken breasts, telling myself a story about how I'd move in here, get her off the pills, be a father to my son, and find some success in this, but, instead, I went on the pills myself.

Steven was the only bright thing in the months that followed, and we had fine times. For the rest I worked in the little sign shop, and since I was now rushing and crashing again my work was uneven, and at times I felt I was close to losing even this job. I set up a studio in the garage and began to paint, but my confidence was tentative. When I was speeding I felt a sense of sureness I took for power, but I was no longer quite so naive and I knew some of the ways careers in painting were made, and aside from the question of talent, which was always moot, I didn't have the temperament. I observed that most people tended to like the work of artists they could recognize, the style must be familiar, but not too familiar. I watched van Gogh shoot up in the wake of the Irving Stone biography, *Lust for Life*, overexpose (those sunflowers were everywhere) and begin to fade while Utrillo began to swell into the vacuum. There were a few star parts, niches to be filled with the current icon, in every field and no shortage of applicants. For myself, I could never stick with a single style. Each day was different, and no vision compelled me.

I learned more about style in another way. Ivy League came in while I was locked up, and George and I scorned these styles as narrow, repressive and lacking in gallantry. We would always wear the bold collar, and the generous tie in the Windsor knot. Once home, I found Veto had managed to save one of my old ties. It was broad and bright red and I began to wear it again by way of saying nothing has changed, and this is my own, my natural style, this and not your mean narrow ties with the pinched little knots.

Then one day, when I had been free about six weeks I glanced down at my shirtfront and there was a vast unseemly river of red tie. Ivy League had begun to look natural to me and I suddenly realized I didn't dare be even that different. Not in any way so obvious.

I was different, though, and I couldn't deny what had happened to me. One morning going to work when I was waiting on the corner for the Muni bus, I was joined by a group of high school girls on their way to class. They were friends, all pretty, and they stood there talking with such enthusiasm and animation they made me feel finished, passed over, settled for the rest of it. I wanted them all, their bloom was so bright, but already I felt I had no right to such feelings. I could not join them on the journey they were each ready to take. I had missed that journey and now it was too late. And, then, the voice whispered again: *If you don't get out, you'll be here just like this ten years from now.*

I lost my job and found another, working for a small manufacturing display firm. The pay was better, and the work interesting. The useful men in this shop were competent at a dozen different trades and I could have learned a lot if I had had any common sense, but I was on the speed cycle of arrogant highs and worthless shallows, and soon I was on sufferance here. I began to oversleep and miss a day here, a day there, and, soon, before the axe could fall, I drifted out into my other life.

I ran into Colby. He'd teamed up with another musician, an alto player, but so far the only gig they'd found was a job tarring and graveling a roof. The three of us worked it together, split fifty dollars, and went over to North Beach to find a jam session. I had been to the Beach now and again, but always as an isolated observer. Now, suddenly, I was thrown into its real life and a new world opened for me.

The beatnik with his sandals, his beard and his "Like, wow!" had just stepped into the pages of pop history, and here I was in the hairy heart of it. For a year or so we were a large social club holding a street carnival, all poets, the freest of lovers, singers of the only song, who were about to recreate an entire society. We were the ridgepole of the world, the essential happening, and we supported each other's pretenses and sheltered each other's defects, and most of these soi-disant rebels were being supported with monthly checks from home. I wasn't and that soon made its own problem. But how small this consideration (it's just bread, man) seemed besides this discovery of another land where I was automatically a prince.

From the first night when I wandered in carrying my rented flute with Colby and the Alto and we jammed in Miss Smith's Tea Room, sawdust on the floor, with a tenor player named Kovin, who was really down with it, and his old lady on piano, oh, wow! jamming with her old man just like Judy Tristano, and, afterwhile, someone showed up with a bass, and we played most of the night for drinks. Afterwards Kovin told me, "You played some nice stuff on 'Stella,' but your trouble is you don't practice."

I walked to the bus with Colby and he said, "That was okay, but we can't live on beer. Tell you the truth, I don't even like it."

For a few weeks I stretched myself between Veto and North Beach. I would pretend I was going to look for work and head instead to the window seat in the Coexistent Bagel Shop to share a bottle of root beer with Sandoz, who was always sitting there, and dig the action on Green Street. When you sat down next to Sandoz he began to talk and he talked constantly until you left. I never decided whether he was so brilliant I couldn't follow him or he was just wandering absently, in a verbal fever, from one subject to another. He touched the magic names: Hume, Berkeley, Kierkegaard, Sartre, and I kept thinking here I am sitting in this wonderful place listening to a man who smokes Delicados and says Wittgenstein as casually as most people say Whitey Ford. I remember two things he told me, a teacup dipped from a Mississippi. Once he said, "The thing that killed jazz was jam sessions." And another time, "One day we'll all play King of the Mountain on the level."

One night on the way home, without forethought, without consideration, I broke into a large printing plant and took the petty cash. The next day I met Judy.

At her boldest and most self-assertive Judy could seriously call herself The Love Goddess of North Beach, and in her low moods she told me how ashamed she had once been of her hairy legs and her big tits and how she had been raped at eleven by someone who had explained to her how it was her own fault because she had shaken her ass at him.

She was sixteen when I met her and it would be hard to say which of us was most full of themselves. I remember standing with her one evening in the underbrush at the foot of Coit Tower. We had just finished fucking leaning against a tree. In the middle of it I realized the revolving light out there in the black waters of the bay was a guard light on top of Alcatraz, the federal prison.

We stood there afterwards hand in hand and she said, "Do you know how I first knew I was going to be a bombshell?"

"How?"

"Because I was born in nineteen-forty-one, and do you know what that is backwards?"

"Fourteen-ninety-one?"

"No, nineteen-fourteen, the year the First World War started."

"How about this one. You're sixteen, I'm thirty-two. Sixteen and sixteen is thirty-two."

"Oh, wow!"

One day I told Veto I was going to take a room in North Beach. It was a fluke of her temperament to never value me until I was about to leave, and then, too late, she tried to find ways to keep me. She followed me down to North Beach, saw Judy and knew what she was up against. We were both, finally, sad about parting, but didn't know anything else to do. She told me Steven was going ape, but even that couldn't draw me back.

I took a room in the Columbo Hotel and began to cook on a hotplate. Judy, who was still in high school, came and stayed with me on weekends. The first time she brought steak and salad stuff and began to fix food. She was cutting up a bell pepper to put in the salad, and I told her, "I hate bell pepper."

"You can pick it out."

"I hate it so much I don't even like things that have been near it."

She still put the pepper in the salad and I didn't eat it. We sat and glared at each other. She had luminous brown eyes, but when she was uneasy or willful her mouth became pinched.

Judy had been fucking for several years but she hadn't yet come, so when she did begin coming with me, we decided we were in love. We were that year's magical couple and we gave off a nice light. People liked to have us around. Judy wanted to be an actress and belonged to a little theater group called The Interplayers. One night when we were the last to leave I left the door open. After I put Judy on the bus, I went back to the theater and climbed the backstage ladder to the roof, where I walked across the rooftops to the other side of the block. I broke open a skylight, lowered myself into a clothing store, where, against all the odds, I found someone's nest egg — thirty-two hundred dollars. It was the most I ever scored.

We threw this money away. Judy spent over five hundred dollars in a single afternoon at I. Magnin's, buying clothes. The more she bought, the more she wanted. "I can't stop," she told me. "I just want to consume gifts." This was the moment of living fantasy. The saleswomen fluttered around us, looking at me from under lowered lashes, as I paid with hundred dollar bills. We wandered in a warm daze. In I. Magnin's we played up the difference in our ages. I was the sugar daddy, and she the almost dangerously young candyass, but when we went over to Hastings to buy a suit for me, I gave her the money and she acted the very rich young girl who has found a stud she wants to dress decently enough to be seen with in the evening. She made remarks such as, "Don't you think you should have both the cashmere and the vicuña?"

I talked her into leaving home, leaving school, leaving her cherished first real part in Miller's *A Memory of Two Mondays*, and running off with me to Mexico where we could live in a mansion and hire hungry Mexicans for a few bucks a week to haul our shit away. We bought an old Chevy for two hundred dollars and, learning to drive on the way, we started south. Finally, I felt I was free, living my own life with my true life companion. We would sleep together now every night forever.

Judy said, "I just can't spend the rest of my life with you."

"Why not?"

"I may need to renew myself."

"How long do you plan to give me?"

She studied the question. "I think ten years. Yes, ten years. I'll be twenty-six, that's not very old. Then I can have other experiences and come back to you later."

"I'll be bald by then."

"You'll never be bald."

It was true. After I had been out a while, my hair had started to grow back, and I had thrown off the chronic complaints that had dogged me around San Quentin. I felt good. I was hunting again. I had a lovely girl with skin as fine as satin, who could make me feel like every hero I had ever read about. I remember one day I was sitting playing the flute — "The Waltz of the Flowers" from *The Nutcracker* — and I looked up to find Judy studying me with soft eyes. She said, "How will I ever replace you?"

We never got to Mexico. I chickened at the border when I suddenly realized Mexico was full of Mexicans, it was their home, and, also, we had spent most of the stolen money. We drove into Arizona where I tried, without much success, to steal some more money. At first, Judy had been unhappy when she discovered I was a thief, but she adjusted to the idea and, finally, she told me, "I don't care how you get money as long as you get some."

I did break into a large drugstore in Tucson, and spent most of the night sorting through the pharmaceuticals. I took every drug whose name ended in -ine. Amphetamine, Dexadrine, Benzedrine, Methadrine and a few other variants. I had a monstrous stack of ups. In one of Dragnet's great moments of unconscious self-satire, Friday and his partner enter a user's apartment to discover his stash. "Look at this Frank," Friday says, caught between awe and disgust. "There's enough here to keep him high for years." That's how much I had.

At first Judy tried speeding with me, but then she said, "I don't think I like what those things do to me." A few weeks later, she continued, "And I'm not so sure I like what they do to you."

"I'm not addicted, you know. That's bullshit."

"What's the difference, if you take them all the time?"

"I don't take them all the time."

"I keep finding them in your shirt pockets."

"I take them for a few days, then I clean up for a few days."

"Then start again."

"Yes."

She frowned, and her mouth looked pinched. "It's all funny rhythm to me, baby. When you're on those things you know everything, and that isn't enough, I have to know how you know it."

The truth was I was afraid to steal without them, and I didn't know how to stop and look for work. I didn't want to work. I wanted this to go on, just as it was, but I was strangely edgy trying to steal in Arizona (who knew what their jail was like?) and I insisted we return to California. We picked Santa Barbara, a lovely white-and-green town on the Pacific, and I paid a month's rent with our last hundred dollars.

The ways in which I have been mad, or, more concisely, those times when I have supported systematic delusions, have always seemed subtle. Not so surprisingly I have always considered myself sane, and never so sane as when I was acting most irrationally. Always the walled man (assuming he was sane!) cowering behind my blind spots was able to send out some messages, but when I was speeding these reports from the interior fell off to an occasional frantic word or two.

I was intolerant of intolerance. I wasn't a fool (the degree to which I wasn't a fool amounted to greater foolishness, for I sneered at common apprehension and hard-won sense) and I saw how the entire subject of drugs had been co-opted, mythologized and structured into a cottage industry by a small group of enforcers and self-styled experts, who had developed finger-touch control over the largest lever by which we could be manipulated — fear of our own destructive impulses, and the recent suggestion that dope hysteria has often served as a mask for xenophobia only strengthens the point.

I know what goes on in my mind, but I'm strong, and

civilized, and I can control myself, but what about you, Old Buddy? You coke up on those devil drugs, and you're liable to come crashing through the wall to burn up my living room, smash my balls, rape my wife and eat my kids.

Well, I knew better than this and I wanted to live in the white focus of energy the speed released, and when I needed to generate the courage necessary to go out to break into stores, I always started in the morning so I would be free to enjoy the first rush. Usually when it came (your skin grows taut and the hair rises on the back of your neck) I would start to paint and quickly become obsessed. I would work all that day, all that night, transfixed in the grip of this chemical inspiration, trying to finally realize some monstrous truth. By the second night I would be grinding my teeth, chewing the sides of my mouth, gripping the brush like a handaxe, while the paint literally dripped from the canvas to the kitchen linoleum. Always it needed just one more touch to catch fire, become realized, and Judy, who had been sleeping uneasily, waking again to see the light still on in the kitchen and perhaps frightened and a little envious of the force of my obsession, would come out into the kitchen, take me by the hand, lead me to our bed and pull me down into her strong, sweet body and I would start to drift out there into that vast shining whiteness, until the walled man turned in terror from this great strange singing nowhere and I would simply come, come quickly, and out in the kitchen my ruined canvas remained as the record of still another failed journey.

After this I would find myself out trying to steal, often on the third night without sleep. We were always broke, my options were burned, and I searched for a target, any target, in a wavering haze where I saw lights flash where no lights were, heard voices calling me from the shadows, and large parts of my consciousness separated and drifted away from the focus of my determination. I seemed too hot, my hands and feet tingled, and I was morbidly conscious of odors. An incoherent whisper (the walled man was raving) played eerie counterpoint to my practical thoughts. I wandered the streets, trying to appear at ease, and I blundered repeatedly and took awesome chances.

One night I broke a safe in a drugstore, using the small pry bar they kept in the storeroom to open crates, and, once I had a peel started, I continued the opening by driving in a number of softball bats I found on display. Here was the expert safecracker at work, spilling fire clay all over the tiled floor, tracking it with his heels, pounding in ballbat after ballbat like an insane beaver, until, finally, I broke the lockbox and opened the safe. I took three hundred dollars in bills and change. We could live for a few weeks.

When I found my way home, usually just at dawn, Judy was never too happy with the amounts I had. I had expert safecracked her, of course, and she couldn't understand why, if I was going to take the risk, I didn't try for something larger. The something larger was still standing ruined in the kitchen.

Now I began to try to sleep, but speed grinds on long after the fun is over, and I sometimes had awful periods. I lay exhausted, but some feral center was artificially lit and couldn't yet relax. I drifted there on the very edge of sleep, hearing the black waters roaring to take me to hell, and I would dream I was suffocating, and use all my strength to hurl myself out of sleep, sitting up, often crying out, heart wildly pounding, and, sometimes, this happened again and again until I was trembling with terror. Judy would be awake and I tried to apologize to her.

"It doesn't bother me," she said. "I just hope you'll learn to leave that stuff alone."

She was strong, and if she had been even stronger we might have had some chance, but now she went into a decline of her own. She had drifted into the local little theater group, a vigorous and creative company, and they had cast her as Stella in their production of *A Streetcar Named Desire*. It was her first adult role. The Interplayers had used her as one of the little girls, with breasts bound, in Lillian Hellman's *The Children's Hour*, and as a nymph she had decorated paradise in Shaw's *Back to Methuselah*, but she had never carried any of the critical weight of a production, and she wanted to be taken seriously. She wanted to star. Now some part of her wish was on her, and, in the middle of rehearsal one night, she suddenly took sick. We rushed her to a hospital, and they, baffled by her symptoms, gave her a bed.

As soon as my immediate panic eased, I began to doubt her illness. I was, however, much too self-centered to consider the critical part of Stella, the whole syndrome of success and failure, and the equal fear of both, which I knew so well — I thought only she meant to desert me, and I behaved like an asshole: wounded and accusatory if I were straight and breezily cavalier if I were speeding. I told her doctor I doubted she was really ill, and he, after several days of negative tests, shrugged, "It's odd you'd come to that, but you should remember whether her condition's pathological or psychological, she's still in some distress and needs support."

This I couldn't give. How could she leave me to lie there getting fat in the hospital at fifty dollars a day? I was in distress, I needed support. How was I going to pay the bill?

I speeded up and went lurching out to steal the money. I broke into a medical-dental building. Five years before, when I had last been free, these buildings had been easy marks, with several hundred somewhere in every office, but now they had been burned up by people like myself looking for dope and an easy score. I went through the entire building and came up with eleven dollars.

I tore the offices apart. I *knew* there had to be money here. I had the fancy I could sense it and, as the night wore away, I became crazed with this obsession. I went through the filing cabinets, folder by folder, emptying them on the floor. I ransacked the desks, dumping the drawers. I stripped photos, diplomas and credentials from the wall and pulled up the rugs. I found nothing more.

Several times I realized I was taking things from my own pockets, fingering them and putting them back in a different pocket. Like Beckett's crazed old man shifting his rocks, I was moving some paper matches, a handkerchief, the few bills I'd found and anything else I had from one pocket to another, around and around my body. There was no sense to this, but whenever I stopped paying attention I would go back to it.

I finally gave up and forced myself to realize there was no hidden money. When I left those offices the floors were white with scattered papers. On the way home, I stopped for a milk shake, and the counterman stared at me with some alarm, and I realized I was still shifting the contents of my pockets. I continued home, trying to remember to control my hands, and behind me something whispered: *Mal, you better aboomaroom aboom. You better humarum aboomaroom.* And below this, very distant, a mad little waltz played and played like the music of the bus wheels when I was small and we were moving once again.

When I was home I discovered I had thrown away the eleven dollars. I sat on the living room couch feeling empty. The waltz had turned into a distant humming. I couldn't imagine going out to look for the money. I had to twitch my way into sleep. There were still a few things left to eat, some canned soup and a sack of red beans. I would rest just two days, then speed up again and go hunting. This time I'd dare something large.

I slept the balance of that night, most of the following day, and woke ravenous. I heated a can of tomato soup and put the beans on. I was still tired, but I felt calm now. Tomorrow or the next day I would be strong again. I lay down on the rug and began to study my paintings on the walls around me. Someone knocked on the door. Detectives. Among the things I had tossed out of my pockets, along with the eleven dollars, was a slip of paper with my address on it.

The Third Jolt

SANTA BARBARA was a pleasant town with pleasant detectives, who looked the house over, found the shoes I had tracked in the fire clay, and placed me under arrest. As we were getting ready to leave, I said, "I have some beans cooking."

And one of the detectives said, "I took care of them."

We drove through the green streets, and I sat in shock, staring at the handcuffs I had thought I would never wear again. I closed my eyes. You fool! You poor fool! Whatever was wrong with me it was far more serious than I had imagined.

I could face the possibility this disaster was random. All random, all Monte Carlo. A man has a last drink before walking home and is killed by the falling cornice of a decaying building. Did that last drink kill him? And if he had been killed by a meteorite which had traveled light years to keep his appointment in Samara, was this process essentially different from the movement of a detective stooping to pick up one scrap in that sea of paper I had left on the floor of the doctor's office? I could have believed it was random if I hadn't also thrown away the eleven dollars.

I had been exhausted. With the willful mode of my personality stunned and nodding at the controls, did some other construct within my identity seize this opportunity to make its wishes manifest? I didn't know, I still don't, but I found the coincidence suspiciously smooth, and I remembered walking into that all-night spot behind George when I knew exactly what was going to happen.

This whole line of thought was strongly reinforced by my emotions in those days just after my arrest. Beyond the anguish of loss and the certain knowledge of still another failure, the emotion that commanded me was simple shame. My glib and essentially gutless impersonation of Nietzsche's Superman collapsed with a whine and I was left with the bedrock realization it had been many years since I had even earned my own food. I had felt free to reason from a position beyond the social contract while everything I desired for my life was a product of that contract. The things I wanted could never have been created in a society where everyone felt himself free to behave as I had. And, most damning, I could never survive as the lone hunter I had idealized. My first day in the jungle would also be my last.

Even if my heel print had not put me standing next to that busted safe, I was a parole violator again, and now also a statutory rapist. They were calm about the latter, and when I offered to cop out, make it easy for everyone, they told me they didn't plan to press the charge. "We've talked to her," the detective told me. "She's as grown-up as you are." I smiled weakly.

As a reward for copping out they let me call her at the hospital. Her voice was small, quiet, faintly hard-edged.

"How are you?"

"Better . . . physically."

"I'm not getting out, you know."

"I know."

"I'm sorry I fucked up."

She sobbed, then cleared her throat. "I've been waiting for you to come to get me. Instead the police have been here."

"How did they treat you?"

"Okay."

I paused, then asked the question I had told myself I must not ask. "Will you wait for me?"

She didn't answer immediately. "How long will you be gone?"

I thought I might do between six and eight years. I said, "Eighteen months."

"I know that's not long, in a lifetime, but it seems a long time."

"It'll pass. I don't expect you to stay home with your legs crossed, just don't make commitments."

"I'll try."

"Will you come to see me?"

"Yes, of course." She began to cry. "This is awful."

She hated to cry and I listened to her trying to control herself. Finally, she asked, "What cleaners did you put my good coat in?"

I told her. The detectives were waiting, pretending they weren't interested, and I felt I had to end the call.

"I have to go," I said. "I love you."

"And I love you."

"Goodbye. Please come and see me."

"Yes, I will."

I knew from the beginning this was destructive. I knew she wouldn't wait. I knew she couldn't wait. And why should she? To reclaim this damaged man? I knew I was deliberately structuring a situation where her only reward for the constancy she did manage to show me would be her guilt when she finally had to drop me. There was no way she could free herself and not feel like a shit. Only I could do that for her.

And for myself, I was only postponing what I knew to be inevitable. Sweating out letters, knowing they would come further and further apart. Pleading for visits which would only heighten my anguish because I would read the changes in her, changes I had not shared, changes which were swiftly moving her away from our brief life together. More than all of this, I had nothing to offer her. I had to cut her loose, return her to her own life, spare her guilt, give her this brief cauterizing pain, and remove this shadow over her future happiness. But I could not. I couldn't do this any more than I could have killed myself. I hung on desperately, falsely, without hope or pride, finally without love, and everything I had foreseen happened, just as I had known it would, and I lost her. And I might not have.

I was crushed, dismembered, mutilated, smashed up so badly I ached for months. Night after night when the lights went out in the tank, I curled in my bunk and turned to the steel bulkhead, to cry. In the daytimes when I felt I was about to break down, I would rush to take a shower so I could cry openly there in the cover of its waters. I was desolated by the loss of all that was real between Judy and me, and sickened by the silly preening bullshit falseness.

One moment sums both these things. We had dipped briefly below the Mexican border to spend a night in the little town of San Luis. We had fucked sweetly, listening to people laugh and sing in a nearby cantina. "It's blue down here," Judy said. "Deep blue."

"What color was it in California?"

"I didn't always get colors." She was silent a moment. "Do you think afterwhile I'll see many different colors?"

"Sure."

She laughed. "Do you know what they called me in boarding school?"

"No."

"Moonbeam McSwine."

In the morning we had breakfast in a small café, where the counter stools weren't bolted down and the pie and sandwiches were wrapped to go in newspaper. Two Mexican men stared openly at Judy, and an American in a leather jacket, who wore a holstered .38, studied her covertly. I went to a bodega to buy a pair of sunglasses. I returned wearing them, and was aware Judy was watching me through the window as I walked across the street. When I sat down beside her, she put her hand on my arm and whispered, "You look like the Marlboro man."

That was it, wasn't it? The Marlboro man and the Love Goddess and the rest of the world was there only to serve as the measure of our special qualities. A permanent audience.

It was true enchantment and when the spell shattered, the Marlboro man was gone and in his place stood a gutted and gray-faced prisoner. When Judy came to see me the first time there in Santa Barbara I saw clearly in her dismayed expression how much I had already changed. Now I was finished. How much better if I had never gone out? I had set myself the limits of a brief vacation, a short dance in the sun, and now I had scurried back to my real life. But this was a life I didn't have to bear. I could die. Except I couldn't imagine it. Suicide had always been my ace. The final freedom no jailer could successfully take from you. You could always die. They might take your belt, your sheets, your shoelaces, but how could they stop you from standing on the top bunk to dive headfirst into the shitter?

But I couldn't imagine being dead. I had just folded my hand. With one card to fill a royal flush I had drawn the deuce of clubs, lost my life, and still I could dream of the next hand by which I might rise to glory, even when I knew, with the best luck in the world, it would be five years before that hand could be dealt me.

So, once again, I would escape. I heard there were no bars on the prison ward at the Santa Barbara County Hospital. If I could make it there, I might get away. Out into the warm night. Never to steal again. Live quietly, work hard. It was over, I knew the silly melodrama was over. It was truly over. Something had happened to me.

To get to the hospital I decided to eat soap. I had heard stories of how beans cooked in a poorly rinsed pot had caused regiments of soldiers to become violently ill with the symptoms of food poisoning. We were furnished Fels-Naptha, a strong laundry soap, to wash our socks, and I took a bar of this and soaked it in water to make softsoap. I ended with half a number ten can which I forced myself to drink one afternoon. I sat down to wait, hoping the soap wouldn't kill me or make me so weak I wouldn't have the strength to escape. After half an hour I belched once or twice. That was all. I decided if I was healthy enough to digest a quart of softsoap, I was too healthy not to try to live.

If I couldn't escape, I could still dream of magic, but, even here, at my secret center, something had changed. One night I realized if I could really become invisible, or obtain even the slightest of the powers I could imagine, I would automatically lose this ordinary world because I would have moved on into some other unimaginable continuum where I was now possible, and this fond place, this green and familiar earth, would be lost to be as surely as it was lost to Faust. You may come to know, but everything you learn will change you until it is no longer *you* who knows.

I realized I could have been a competent sign painter with a wife and three nice kids, or a man who moved crates in a warehouse, lives in a furnished room, and spends his days off sitting on a bench in the park feeding the pigeons. I could have driven cab, washed dishes, or cleaned the streets if I hadn't been obsessed with the notion I was an artist. Well, who wouldn't want to be an artist? It was a nice clean job, with some chance of excitement, and you were your own boss. But with all swell jobs there were fewer positions than there were applicants, more dreamers than dreams, and if this were the case for me it was time to find it out. I either had to shit some real art or get off the pot, put my money where my mouth had always been, and, if nothing else, it would give me something to do when I was back in Quentin.

George wrote me. He was luffing along in San Francisco, and he called me an "eight-bladed, gold-plated Boy Scout knife" by way of citing the special quality of my self-destructive urges, and chided me for running back to San Quentin without him.

When I dressed into Quentin I was an old-timer. When I tossed my own clothes into the hamper, the very last of the Marlboro man left with them. I sat there on the same wooden bench where I had sat three times before, and crossed my legs and folded my arms. This was not the man Judy had loved. Already this was someone else.

And the Cynic said, "Oh, shit, man, what are you doing back?"

"I don't know."

"Well . . ." he looked down, then shrugged. "You got any tall tales to tell?"

"Yeah, one or two."

The Wit asked, "Couldn't you stand the heat?"

"I guess not."

"It's the buttoning and the unbuttoning that gets me."

"They have zippers now."

"It's not that different."

My number was written A-8814-B, to include my new conviction. I was classified as a Fourth Termer, one of a tiny hard core of apparently hopeless cases, and shuffled through the various entry processes like a case of condemned canned goods. Deep in the eyes of those friends still here I saw how I had betrayed them by failing, sucked still more from their slender fund of hopefulness, and caused them to wonder if any of us could make it out there. Now instead of the gunfight in the desert, I told about North Beach, where I had been a prince, and how I had scored the Goddess of Love, and deep in my head, instead of imagining I could, like Lamont Cranston, hypnotize anyone with a single compelling glance, I formed and reformed my own version of "Once upon a time and a very good time it was there was a moocow coming down along the road ..."

Until I realized this was the precise masturbation, this unbuckled dream of greatness, which had caused me to fail again and again. Because I didn't understand how you could work at an inspired masterpiece, which *must* simply flow from you, and not turn it into one more trick, an excellent trick, perhaps, but still a shrewdly structured device to trap and manipulate our yearning for excellence, while your cold hands danced together in the empty air. While Oz roared and thundered you were always stuck behind the curtain, working the levers, vulnerable to any innocence, including your own green heart.

Then I asked myself an astonishing question. What do you really like to read?

Well, many different things.

But who's your favorite author? Who gave you the most pleasure? And don't tell me Shakespeare.

All right. Raymond Chandler.

It was true. Marlowe, hunched over a chess problem in his furnished apartment, or sitting in his office watching a bottle fly do wingovers while humming the prologue to *Pagliacci*, was as real to me as Ivan Karamazov. Marlowe's central decision, brought to him again and again, was what must a moral man require of himself in an immoral world, and that seemed to me as profound as any question in literature. So I took Chandler as my master, and decided to write mysteries.

I had another reason for abandoning painting to try writing one last time. I could find some success at writing before I left the institution. I wouldn't have to wait all those years to start over, with no better hope of success than I had been able to give myself on these last two paroles, where, if I was now cold-eyed, I had to admit I hadn't had a chance. If I could write, if I really could, I might leave with a career already fashioned. It was a wild gamble, but it would satisfy my need to try to help myself, and what did I have to lose? I had already lost everything.

Still I didn't immediately start writing. Months drifted by while I wrote Judy to tell her I was writing, and then one night the mail officer dropped a letter on the bars. It was one of mine to her and it was now stamped: NO LONGER AT THIS ADDRESS.

It was finally over. I couldn't cry anymore. I was truly relieved. She was free, and, in my own way, so was I. Later that same evening I tore up the letters she had written me. I didn't do this in anger, but simply so I would not have to be reminded. It was over and now I could swim forward in this empty calm. Goodbye, Dear Heart.

The next evening I started my first novel. A murder mystery set in North Beach.

The largest sacrifice I made to become a writer was going to work as an inmate clerk. I had to have the use of a typewriter and this was the only way open. I signed on at the ed building, in the Voc. Ed. section, and continued to work here, in increasingly more responsible jobs, for several years. All those trivial chores I had sluffed off years before at the Redding *Record* came back to me now and I learned to perform them patiently. I am not a neat man, but I learned to impersonate a neat man for as long as I had to. Each night, and every spare moment during the day, I spent writing. I wrote all weekend. Soon a book was growing under my hands. I was sure it was a bad book. But when some old buddy commented on how I had changed, I drew to myself the same pressure the Babe had put himself under when he had pointed out to left field that long-ago afternoon in Yankee Stadium, and said, "I'm going to write my way out of this fucking joint."

I don't think I could have finished the first book without the help of my cell partner, a really sweet man, and it was his function to read *each* page as I finished it and adore it. If he ventured to offer the slightest criticism I plunged into immediate panic. The book was worthless, it was shit, and how could I ever finish it. I had never once brought anything to a successful conclusion. How could I imagine I was different now?

My doctor friend in the psych dept said, "You're older. This seems to work for some. You see how the Gods churn away your life," and he smiled faintly to mark his use of this figure from the language of other priests. "And the immortal child begins to yield to the mortal adult. You come to a point of awareness where you must either embrace a state of partial disillusionment, or turn deeper into the delusion. You are deciding to become sane."

"If I'm sane why do I dream I'm tied to a tree like Sebastian while people shoot arrows into my balls?"

He rose, glasses flashing, like a great crewcut trout. "What?"

"Do you remember the finish of *Anthony Adverse* where he's chopping down a tree and a rock embedded in the trunk causes his axe to deflect and bury itself in his inner thigh? He bleeds to death there under the tree."

"Yes."

"I've felt that axe a hundred times. Doesn't that seem a little corny?"

"Well, perhaps . . ." he smiled. "You know you have a trick head. You've been told often enough. I wish I had time for you, but I'm going to take an administrative job in Sacramento, and I wouldn't tell you to see anyone here, except, maybe Oddjohn, and he doesn't have the time to take you on."

"I'm all right. Look, I had some nice things happen to me. I want to get back to something else like that. I think I know how I can do it. I think I have a chance."

I didn't tell him the precise vision that held me because I was afraid he would think it simply sentimental. One afternoon in Santa Barbara I was sitting on the couch and Judy was running a vacuum over the rugs. She didn't like doing housework and her mouth was pinched. A wave of love came over me, and something inside spoke wordlessly to tell me this was my own, this love for this companion, and I saw how we might live together for years in homely contentment. My main question to myself these days was how much had this vision frightened me?

When I finished a first draft, my cell partner asked to reread it, and I lay in the top bunk, staring at the bland cream ceiling, listening to the dry *whisk* as he turned the ms. pages. He read all evening, stopping only once to piss, and, finally, a little before lights out he finished and said, "You know, it's okay. It reads like a real book."

All my friends read it, or pretended to, and most liked it. It was written for them. It became what we called a "trip" book, one where you could blunk out and simply drift through the atmosphere of the North Beach nights, the sex, music and drugs, pulled along by some fairly unlikely events. The protagonist was an alto player, who, companioned by a lovely and hip young girl (guess who?), wanders into a murderous maze.

It was a slow night and a bad set. My reed was soft and the drummer was bugging me. He was a meter beater who came on super hep with a beret and a spidery tuft of hair under his lower lip, but he played like he was busting up his set with a ballbat . . .

I still have the ms. and I'm not ashamed of it. My cell partner was right. It is almost like a real book. And, at that time, I couldn't imagine what was the matter with it.

Having started to swallow the reality of these clerical duties, I found my labors, as if they were a continuing test of my new determination, had to increase still further before I could go on. I had been one of several junior clerks and my duties had not overwhelmed me, but this job didn't pay and soon I would need some money to send my ms. to the Magic City. I had nothing and I knew no one who would send me the five dollars I needed for postage. The only way open was to take a more difficult and responsible job, which would pay me six dollars a month. I went to work as printing control clerk, handling printing requests from all over the state. I maintained stock inventories, ordered supplies, authenticated copy and nothing could be printed without a work order from me. One day I nodded and ordered an additional ten million CDC 103-A's for the second time, and, a few days later, the stock clerk asked me to come down to the shop and invited me to tell him where the fuck he was going to put this great mountain of chronological reports? At six dollars I wasn't overpaid.

It would take two months before any of my wages could come into my hands, and I used this time to rewrite. I began to gain some understanding of the problems of this typical genre fiction. The art lies in controlling the pseudo-naturalism. If the characters become too real, their actions, necessarily dictated by an arbitrary plot, begin to seem implausible, and the reader, offended and disappointed, stops lending the energy necessary to support the fantasy. If, however, the characters are sketched too thinly, too falsely, they quickly join the gallery of mechanical types who populate true hack writing. Plot, as I was soon told by those who knew, must rise from character. To reverse this order, as I had, is to rupture your story below the waterline where it can never be successfully patched.

When I finished my first, I immediately started another. I had sworn to write two books before I gave up — a man who worked across from me had already written eleven novels and was hard at work on his twelfth, and still hadn't sold anything except a few radio scripts in the twilight of that market. However, two other friends, who worked on the San Quentin News, had both sold novels in the last year. It did happen. It could happen. Still it was a small, mad hope in my heart, and I had formed a contingency plan where I worked my way out to camp, ran away, bought ID, and shipped to New Zealand, where I still remembered

Van Heflin in *Green Dolphin Street*, standing on those lovely cliffs while rainbows played in the mist thrown by the waves. It was a rapture just to dream of swimming in that surf.

My second book began to grind down and fall apart at around a hundred pages. The characters couldn't eat the plot. I gathered everyone into a Truth Court, where I admitted I was not clever at plotting and that maybe I shouldn't try to follow Chandler after all. There was a secondary problem. I had *sworn* to finish everything I began. Now I argued that all arbitrary formulations, these beds of Procrustes, could be harmfully false if not tempered with intelligent discrimination. I junked the second book and began a third.

Here the plot would wander wherever the people needed to go. I wrote also of something I knew — a drifting kid who winds his way into jail to face a test of his manhood. I made up the state, I made up the town and I made up the jail, but the people were real, and brought me another kind of problem.

All inmate manuscripts shall be censored under the supervision of the Warden of Care and Treatment, and no manuscript shall be approved which is libelous, pornographic or critical of the policies of the California Department of Corrections or of law enforcement in general. No manuscript shall be approved which appears to glorify criminal behavior or places drug use in a favorable light. No manuscript shall be approved which might prove to be offensive to any race, religion or organized group.

This is a paraphrase of the section in the Rules and Regs. of the Calif. Dept. of Corrections governing the censoring of inmate manuscripts and, obviously, it could be used to prevent the submission or force the revision of *Anne of Green Gables*. Despite the formidable density of this regulation, censorship wasn't a major problem for the prison writer, if he remained reasonable and didn't become too successful, until the Chessman scandal.

Our opinion of Chessman wasn't always high; we felt he was a showboat, who might still live if he could find the sense to compromise and provide Pat Brown, who clearly didn't want to kill him, with the political room necessary to commute his sentence, but one buddy, who went to death row every week to project their movies, told me, "That man is all guts."

And now I see how that was so. He acted out the drama of the individual vs. the state, played his role without compromise and died bravely. I saw him his last night on television, which had now replaced the cell radio in our modernizing prison, and he came out and sat on a desk to talk to reporters. He was at ease. I could sense how he liked the attention. He'd only been locked on death row for thirteen years. They asked if he expected to die in the morning, and he smiled and said, "Yes, they have me now. I think it's over." When they broke for a commercial it was to advertise an air freshener. They gassed him the next morning. Someone told me when they locked and dogged the metal door, tears had formed in his eyes, but, when the gas had come billowing from under the chair, he took a long deep breath.

The questions surrounding Chessman's execution have not yet been fairly dealt with. However, it was the censorship imposed on him which made me apprehensive. He taught them the power of the written word when he came to prominence with his first book. He had shouted from his cell and the world was listening. With the money he earned he was able to hire fancy legal help to strengthen his defense, and a movement to protest his execution began among some liberals.

The department moved to counter this by cutting his power at its source. They forbade him to write and they confiscated his second book because he had written about death row. What else was he to write about? When he managed to recreate this book, keeping his copy safe through repeated and frequent cell shakes by the brilliantly simple stratagem of typing on carbon paper, one page to a sheet, and when he had smuggled (the grapevine said one of the doctors had done it) this completely rewritten manuscript to his publishers, the department sued to recover the ms., and, failing this, they brought a second suit to claim the royalties. They argued they had the legal right to employ inmates in situations, such as the clothing and furniture factories, where a profit was turned for the state, and this right could, by logical extension, be stretched to cover any monies an inmate might earn during his period of confinement. In short, they were asking the court to act as if they believed the state had assigned Chessman something to do while waiting to die, to write this book, and turn over to them any money it might earn. A federal judge dismissed this suit contemptuously. And it seems to me this miserable attempt to silence a condemned man and hustle him to his death is the sorriest abuse of free speech since the notorious Sedition Act, and I hope this *memento mori* has the power to bring some reflex of shame to anyone who lent his hand to it.

This large struggle affected us in smaller ways. The super of ed., who wanted to be a warden, decided to clean his house of writers and caused the goon squad to shake down the ed building and take anything that looked like it was becoming a book. They raised a netfull — sonnets, sagas, a clutch of the dirty stories we wrote and rented out for a pack a night, and two novels under contract to be published. It was a twenty-four-hour shitstorm. The publishing writers began to scream as if they were being gored and they reached the assoc. warden of C and T, a pretty good head, who privately told the super of ed. to calm down and give the manuscripts back providing they were typed on paper the inmate could prove he had purchased on the inmate canteen. Here I had been lucky. The only bond sold on the canteen was Plover Bond, and it was not supposed to be stocked anywhere else in the institution, but there was a small stack held by the ed. supply clerk, and I had managed to connive several reams to produce apparently legal ms. My first instance of successful forethought. I had to rewrite my dirty story, but didn't mind because I had thought of a more imaginative use to make of the Great Dane.

I thought I was different, but the joint was still much the same, and again it began to wear me down. I crawled around, listening to the unchanging talk . . .

"Look, why don't you break down and give me some pussy?"

"Stick pussy, that's what I'll give you, some nice stick pussy."

"Come on, that's just a handle to turn you over with."

> "I've got your handle
> Dangling low,
> And when you want it
> Let me know."

Pardon me, gentlemen, and I see you are gentlemen by the knife creases in your starched overalls, and the discreet glimmer of your Timex watches, I thought it might interest you to know how I took the twenty thousand dollars and bought chairs for the standing army, and sausages for the little girls in Corona, and then the season after that I worked a blind wheel in Tucson, and, after that, I had three fine chicks, all tricking sailors in Diego, and I bought myself a stand-up fiddle, mohair, you know, and a big dark-blue Eldo, and a white fuzzy hat, and I wouldn't be here with you today except my hat jumped dead off my head and seized a policeman by the ankle. Save me the short, will you?

I didn't smoke cigarettes now. I wouldn't hustle for them. I couldn't spare the time. I smoked state-issue tobacco in an old pipe, and I was used to it. I did, however, develop other time-wasting vices. I joined the drama workshop and tried to become an actor. I continued to hang around the band room, and, afterwhile, simply because I had been there a long time, they asked me to emcee the warden's shows for various fraternal organizations. I was suddenly interested in political power, and I used my new understanding and determination to push my way into places where I had no business.

I seldom replayed my old fantasies, except those that were sexual, but I developed a new kind of what-if, each based on a single unlikely stroke. What if, for example, they discovered some way to truly rehabilitate us. If all men could be made equal, all competitiveness removed from our natures, and the sorry and troublesome march of our history slowed to a pleasant walk on a nice afternoon, then what would happen to the Dept. of Corrections?

I imagined the rate of recidivism, always somewhere over 50 percent, slowing to finally stop. Coincidentally, since the counties also have the magic mind-cure, the new arrivals dwindle away. Then parole, discharge and death begin to drain the prison populations, until the day comes when there is only a single convict left, like Dreyfus on Devil's Island, and I pictured the might of the department bearing on this single man. A hundred rifles would watch over his sleep, a thousand guards supervise his showers, and supply his needs. Psychs would test and interview him, and sociologists collect his statistics, while the chaplains prayed with him and the doctors maintained his health and the dentists took turns working on his teeth. Every week he appeared before the Adult Authority, and the director, the director himself, received daily bulletins on the state of his welfare. He is preserved like a living fossil, and, twice a week, schoolchildren from all over the nation come to stare at him through plate-glass windows.

When I had the money for postage I sent my ms., now called *The Young Dancer*, to Willis Kingsley Wing, the agent we were all using. A week later he wrote back to say he would be pleased to represent me. I knew this was a break, but I didn't overread it. At that time Wing had a nice lady in his office named Pat Kuhnel, who worked with the Quentin writers, and I had the feeling we were her charity. We later exchanged dozens of letters and my guess was at least partially correct. She was kind enough to go out on her lunch hour to Dunhill's on Fifth Avenue to buy pipe tobacco, when I had stopped smoking state-issue.

I went on working on my other book, and I had my problems with it. Michelangelo is supposed to have lightheartedly explained his genius at sculpture as simply knowing what to remove. I didn't know what to remove. I put

down everything I could remember or imagine and the pace
was glacial and the ms., on twenty-pound mimeo paper,
began to resemble a phone book. None of my captive read-
ers, who had really enjoyed *Dancer*, liked it much.

I walked the yard with my friend Nimar, an Arab with a
big belly, a bigger nose, and savage intellect, and he told me,
"I can't stand that little punk."

I started to qualify, but Nimar waved it away. "I know,
I know, the white-blooded little worm will turn, but I'm not
willing to read four hundred pages to see it. Who gives a
fuck? And, worse, it's a lie. Punks stay punks. People don't
change."

"Some people do change."

"Not very damn many. You tell me someone you know
who's changed."

"Me."

He looked me carefully in the eye. "I didn't know you
before. Ah! Can't you make the little punk more
interesting?"

After a month I had a pleasant letter of rejection from an
editor at Mill-Morrow. He thought I wrote well, but plotted
poorly. He would like to see anything else I wrote. Still
another month later I had another letter, not quite so generous, from someone at Simon & Schuster, who thought I
had, like most amateurs, neglected plot to concentrate on
atmosphere. A note fastened to this from Wing told me he
had decided to try the book as a paperback original. I
decided the *Dancer* and I had struck out. I had nothing
against paperback publication, I had nothing against serial-
ization in the San Quentin *News*, but I thought plot and
violence were the most important elements of the paper-

back original and I expected swift rejection. There was a flaw in my reasoning.

One afternoon as I was walking across the yard the constant music broke for an announcement:

A-EIGHTYEIGHT FOURTEEN, BRALY, REPORT TO RECEPTION. A-EIGHTYEIGHT FOURTEEN, BRALY, REPORT TO RECEPTION.

A visit. It could only be Judy. Veto had divorced me six months earlier. I knew no one else, except George and he wasn't over here walking into the steaming mouth of the dragon. I ran to the ed building for my razor and down into the basement to shave. I looked like shit. Gray-faced, worn, twenty soft pounds heavier, and, further, I thought I saw something beaten in my expression. The empty look of the lifer who is doing it, as the Wit said, on the installment plan.

Parsons came in to take a piss. He was one of the two publishing writers—a smart, tough, competent man. "Got a visit?" he asked.

"Yeah."

"Know who it is?"

"There's only only one person it can be."

He smiled, "Well, whoever you think it is, you're wrong. It's Knox Burger, the editor of Gold Medal Books. I just finished talking to him."

"Jesus Christ."

"Indeed."

I rushed out to the visiting room, and as I stood there waiting on the visiting room bull I smoothed the sides of my hair and straightened the collar on my denim shirt. One section of the visiting table was visible, and as I looked it over, automatically checking the chicks, I suddenly found myself staring into shrewd hazel eyes. I was being studied.

He was only three years older than I, already bald, handsome despite this, and when he rose to shake my hand I noticed he carried a cane. "You know your book is in our shop?"

"Yes, Wing told me."

"I haven't looked at it yet, but it's had several readings and my people like it. They see some difficulties, but maybe we can find a way to work on it with you."

Holy shit!

I launched into a fervent declaration of how much the slightest chance would mean to me and how hard I would work to justify it.

Burger looked down, obviously to protect himself from the intensity of my need, and said, "I can't make you any promises."

He was really here to see Parsons. I was an afterthought. Still we talked companionably for ten minutes.

A few weeks later I received a four-page, single-spaced editorial letter, containing an exhaustive and highly perceptive critique. He praised the energy and charm of my narration, and suggested a number of ways the plot might be shored up. However, he couldn't offer me a contract at this time.

I must step outside the prison for a moment to place Burger in proper perspective. I had made a most valuable friend. A man of rare sympathy, whom I would try sorely. Many of his fellow professionals considered him one of the best editors in the business, with a quick eye for new talent, and he was, just at this time, publishing one of Vonnegut's earliest novels, *Mother Night*, as a Gold Medal original.

I was ready to give up on the *Dancer* because my new book was now finished. Now I had to deceive the censor. The assoc. warden of C and T was the official censor, but the actual work was done by the librarian, a strange obsessive man, who was a filing freak. He had an office staff of three inmates who did little more than maintain his filing system. Everything, every scrap of paper that passed through the library, was copied and filed. When he spoke to you on interview he made notes of the meeting and these notes were filed.

Parsons told me, "Make him an outline for his files. He loves that. You can slant the outline away from the rough stuff, particularly the sex and drugs. Then, if you're lucky, he'll only read the outline. Meanwhile, he's on your side because you've fed his obsession. Do you know he has files on anyone who has ever published anything out of here? They go back years."

There are a lot of books written in Quentin. They marched out all the time, and most came limping back. The staff could hardly take these books seriously, they simply assumed we had ideas above our station, and it was reasonable the librarian would take any opportunity to avoid reading a four hundred-page ms. by an amateur.

Besides this strange man had always liked me from the Sunday afternoon during my first jolt when I had stood up in a Seeker's meeting to read a thousand-line poem on the mystery of evolution. I had made him a copy for his file. He had often helped me order special books from the state library at Sacramento, and was only disappointed I had avoided his Great Books Discussion Group which met monthly to chew over Plato, Augustine, Aquinas and other heavies.

I wrote a careful outline, and consigned my book to its fate.

Nimar said, "You may have fucked up."

"I don't see how."

"Well, he liked that first book. What if he hates this one?"

Once again, I started another book. I scrapped *Dancer* to the foundation. I had wit enough to realize the North Beach atmosphere, still not widely exploited, formed the basis for Burger's interest, and I decided to keep the setting, but to make the characters richer. What plot I did have I stole from Victor Hugo. The man he called Javert, I called, in my re-creation, Lieutenant Carver. An addicted narc.

It was on one of these days I moved to the honor block in the old west wing (the Guidance Center was now in Vacaville) where life was easier. And on one of these nights I wandered down to the band room and they had some new music in. We played Ellington's "Satin Doll," and it reminded me so strongly of Judy I was miserable again for several days.

Then one night at mail call I had another long letter. On the first page before I could even begin reading my eye leaped to the single word "contract" and I immediately began to cry with joy. Some idiot voice in my head said over and over: *You can live. You can live.*

I was celling alone there in the honor block and none of my buddies were close around me, except the inmate band leader, a brilliant jazz trumpet player, but one of the most sour and cynical men in this entire army of sour cynics, and, yet, I *had* to tell someone.

I ran to the bars and called, "Charlie. Hey, Charlie!"

"Yeah," his voice came back.

"Charlie," I shouted it out, "I sold my book!"

"Groovy, man," he said wearily.

My New Life

==

THIS WAS THE START of a new life, my real life, where I would finally win fame, fortune, even my freedom. Now the world might know I was a man of some merit and not a failed thief and a desperate fuckup. Now Judy would know. Not that I would ever tell her, but she would find out. Someone would say: Remember that dude you ran off with a few years ago? I just saw his picture on the cover of *Life* magazine. Yes, he won the Art Fernard literary award for the most modifiers in a single sentence. And she would think: He was my friend and I left him in that awful place.

It's not news that we don't start new lives, or that the longest journey of discovery ends in much that we have always known, but the energy and the optimism that informed me that night has never entirely faded, and one thing was very different — I was about to earn some money.

The next day when I was accepting congratulations in the

ed building, the man who had written eleven novels, and was working on the twelfth, came over to shake my hand. "Jesus, man, that's just wonderful."

His eleven novels were neatly bound and stacked in his locker. He worked constantly, and had studied every form. He typed a hundred wpm and seldom made a typo. Each of his eleven novels had drifted from house to house for years with no takers. He had only one problem — no talent. I recognized how easily I could have been he. I wasn't being rewarded for the quality of my resolve, or for hard work and fatihful application — in all these things he far outstripped me — but because I could somehow do it, and he couldn't.

I wrote George, who was still living in San Francisco, to tell him I had written and sold, however modestly, a novel, and he wrote back to say our friendship, if I still wanted to think of it that way, had never seemed worthwhile to him.

The man who had written eleven novels wasn't the only one from whom I drew instruction. I also learned from Crazy Smith. Crazy Smith was flattening out a one-to-five, doing every day of the five, for counterfeiting the Great Seal of the State of California, which I must suppose is the only time this particular statute has been used to convict a man, but Crazy hadn't duplicated the Great Seal because he admired the art work, he had been attempting to forge state bonds.

He wasn't truly crazy, but no one called him sane either, and he wasn't very smart, but if some drug had been found to add twenty points to his IQ, I believe Smith would now be one of our great literary artists. He loved to write and he wrote with boundless optimism and energy and every tenth page would flare with power, but he was an *idiot savant* who didn't understand how he produced these gems, and the other nine pages, with the spark missing, were simply overwrought.

We were both taking a verse writing course from the Extension Division of the University of California. We shared the same teacher and shared our fantasies of her. We knew her only by her pale-violet marginalia: *Lovely line, nice image,* or *Your ear is beautifully tuned to the magic of vowel music.*

Verse Writing/UofC Ex./Lesson 5/Braly, A-8814

Write a short poem demonstrating the use of the Alexandrine:

PRIMER

Mother said stars were the tears of angels
and she wore her hair in a strangled bun
fixed with a pin like the head of an ant
She said the sun was the glad face of God
She told me Lift my face, See how He cared —
These were the things we shared. These were
    the things we shared!

These poems were manufactured and our teacher, who signed herself to us, in small violet letters, *mpi*, read the inner emptiness, but praised the attempt and Crazy Smith and I collected these comments like flowers, like Our Lady's favors, and proudly displayed them to each other. A modest contest.

Crazy wrote a poem on bedbugs. He described how he had been lying in his bunk one evening when he had caught a bedbug foolish enough to slip out of its fastness while the light was still on. He was about to destroy this pest, when he began to wonder if he had the right to take its life. It was only doing what it was programed to do, occupying its slender station in the Great Design, and if he held its life at no value, how, then, could he assign value to his own? He went on like this, and, as he formed this debate in his head, he held the bedbug loosely in two fingers, and, as he chased Truth through one level of abstraction to the next, the bug split.

The poem was splendid, and *mpi* praised it as absolutely first-rate and gave him an unprecedented A+. Crazy took this to mean *mpi* liked poems about bedbugs, and he raised armies of them. Warrior bedbugs, rich with blood, leading their people out on the great plains of Crazy's chest. He evoked priests who told parables of the Cosmic Bug, and he created philosophers meditating in the pages of great books. Poets and orators, heroes and navigators, all these and many many more poured from Crazy in a series of poems as richly varied as Eliot's similar sermons on cats, but Crazy Smith's elusive genius failed to ignite, and most of these poems were dull and mechanical, and *mpi*'s comments grow more and more confused.

I never finished the course. When I began to get editorial letters from the Magic City, I found I no longer had time to collect these pale-violet flowers and I gradually stopped writing poetry. To my regret. However, it was just. I didn't read it.

Now I was working on a total revision and handicapped because I didn't have my own typewriter. I had to slice time to use the machine at the ed building and I tended to slice too thin. So Nimar bought me a typewriter from another con for three cartons. You can't sell your type-writer. It's issued to you, registered in your name and, when you shape up the day of your release you better have a type-writer, or a bag of typewriter parts, or the charred frame, or a very good story. The man Nimar bought the portable from was a fool, who only sold because he *had* to pay some gambling debts or someone was going to give him a knife to take to the hospital, and he immediately ran up more debts, and asked his mother to send him a new typewriter. He was going to import them for a living. But when the new one arrived, the property officer asked: "Where's the old one?"

And he said, "It was stolen out of my cell."

The first I knew there was all this heat on typewriters. The goon squad was checking permits, and the block officers were shaking down. I ran out on the yard to find Nimar.

"That typewriter's smoking. I don't even want to be near it."

Nimar said, "I'll find out what went wrong."

He went over to the captain's porch and got the story from the head clerk there, who said, "A word of advice, get rid of that machine, even if you have to eat it."

Nimar took it down to the metal shop and stood there to watch while they broke it down and melted it into an anonymous lump of slag.

My contracts came in a few days later. They were han-dled by the same man who always wrote my board reports, and he was pleased to be involved in something this positive, but he warned me, "Don't expect the Adult Authority to share my enthusiasm."

I took copies of any papers I had been allowed to keep to

the librarian as a gesture of diplomacy. He was delighted. "Now I can start an active file on you."

I remembered Parsons mentioning these files, and I asked about them.

"I have files on every man who has published here. Would you like to see them?"

"Yes," I said, uneasily.

He brought a half-dozen folders and I went through them carefully. The stories covered thirty years and were all the same. Inmate writers who had found some success, published a book or two, and several had scored huge windfalls through the sale of film rights, but all of them — every single one! — had gone out, eventually failed and returned to the prison. I remembered Gerry, my walking buddy that first time in the Guidance Center, I remembered him telling the trans. officer, "Yes, I've written twenty books." And there he was on the Quentin chain, busted up and heading back.

As I studied these files, the librarian typed my name on an index label and glued it to a new folder. When my advance check came — five hundred dollars — he asked me for a copy of the check record, which I typed out for him, even copying the bank's identification numbers, and when the money was on my books, I ordered a typewriter, an Olympia portable, through the inmate canteen. I was free.

While all this was going on I made several board appearances. Just walking through. One member acknowledged: "We see you've sold a book."

"Yessir, and I've just sold another."

"That's noted. Congratulations."

I hadn't expected it to make a big difference at this point.

It wouldn't have made a big difference if I had risked my life to save the warden, if I had rushed into a burning building to carry him out in my charred arms, because I simply didn't have enough time in. These years passing now — thirty-three, thirty-four, thirty-five — could not be salvaged, but I still hoped to win back a few years before I turned forty. For a great many reasons, most not hard to imagine, I didn't want to turn forty here in San Quentin.

Meanwhile, I had scored one of the supreme political plums of prison life. I was the emcee on the warden's show. Almost every Friday night through most of the year some fraternal organization, the Moose, the Elks, the Masons, the Kiwanis, the Soroptimists, or service organizations such as the Berkeley cops, or the Fairfax Chamber of Commerce came to tour the institution. It was all department PR, and carefully controlled. They entered after the evening lockup when the dings and nuts, the red shirts and the winos and the dinos were all safely boxed in their cells, and they stood and looked out at the big yard — largest exercise yard in the world — and walked to the North Block where they rode the elevator to death row to take a look at the gas chamber, painted apple green. Then they were fed, sitting at the tables where we sat, and, finally, we put on a variety show.

It was some show. We had a Western group, a Mexican group, a jazz group, a harmonica player who slurred through "Cherry Pink and Apple Blossom White," an operatic tenor who imitated Mario Lanza imitating Caruso and a concert pianist who played part of Tchaikovsky's Concerto No. 1. We had an artist who made chalk drawings to the accompaniment of Thelonious Monk's "Round About Midnight," and a comic who lived in hotel rooms so small the mice were hunchbacked, and a good band, lighted by an occasional big-name soloist serving on a drug bust. There was a tap dancer who time-stepped to "Tea for Two," and a spoon player, and an impersonater who did John Wayne, Walter Brennan, Jimmy Stewart, and a violinist who played "Humoresque."

I emceed this circus. I emceed it, I told myself, because after the free people had split, we ate whatever they had left. Meat, tiny servings of steak, which didn't taste like liver, and potatoes Lyonnaise, gone cold, fruit salad, real coffee. This is why I did it. Sure. This is why I sat through several hours of incredible cacophony in the band room, while each of us practiced something different, four trombones, five saxophones, three trumpets, two drummers, my single flute, all playing triple *f*, and this is why I dressed carefully in a tuxedo, designed to retail at \$22.50, to study my emblematic face above the soiled white tie, and walk stiffly, a broom up my ass, out under the warm lights, awkward, ill at ease, far from home, to try to establish some rapport with this vague sea of free faces. I did it because I was rewarded with the leftover food and because between introductions I could stare at the girls in the audience through tiny holes we had bored in the wings.

Bullshit, the Cynic said. You want to be seen. It makes you feel alive. You want to be up there. You think when you put on that cheap tux a little of yourself is returned to you. Well, I'll tell you something, buddy, it's bullshit and you're so hungry for attention you'd eat shit if anyone would watch you do it. You think you look dap in that tux? You look like a waiter in a failing restaurant. If you had half the class you aspire to you'd moon that audience and laugh all the way to the hole.

For six months I clung to this position tenaciously. I knew I was no good. I didn't have it. When I walked to the mike I could overhear the musicians making fun of me. I told myself they made fun of everyone. It was their job.

When I finally forced myself to quit, half thinking the musical director would ask me to carry on at least until he could train someone to take my place, he accepted so swiftly, with such obvious satisfaction, I realized he had been trying to think of a way to get rid of me without hurting my feelings.

Nimar was delighted at my success. He believed in success. But not everyone was delighted. My desk mate, Howard Cipinsky, managed to control his enthusiasm. Howard had won the Medal of Honor, swimming into the black waters of the Rhine River to rescue two of his buddies, who had been shot there and were about to drown. "How did you ever do that?" I asked.

"I don't know. You can't not do it. It's there and you know someone has to try."

Howard had been a square john, on the civil service ladder himself, until the day he won the daily double at a Jersey track. The double paid six thousand dollars and this sudden warm infusion of unencumbered cash had turned his life upside down. It takes a long time to wear the luster from a Medal of Honor and Howard had tried a number of hustles from bad checks to armed robbery before a judge had finally given up on him and sentenced him to San Quentin.

Howard hated Perry O'Brien, the Olympic shot putter, with whom he had gone to high school. "All he can do, I mean, *all* he can do is throw a little iron ball farther than anyone else in the world. Can you tell me what's the value of this? He throws this ball and people line up to offer him scholarships in the best universities, corporations bid for his services and offer him vice-presidencies, chicks fall over for him. And what is he really? What is he really worth? How does it make sense?"

One afternoon as I was working on my final draft, as I did every afternoon, I looked up to discover Howard staring at me. His expression was somber. "You know something," he said. "I hate that fucking book of yours."

Shortly after I had finished my final draft and sent it off to the magic city to become a Gold Medal paperback original, the Class. Com. reviewed my case. Before, when they'd thought of it, the Class. Com. had dismissed me a pseudo-intellectual, but now that I had written and sold this modest book they dropped the pseudo. They reduced my custody to Minimum and recommended camp placement. If the Rover Boys from the Department's Sacramento Offices, a traveling truth squad, rubber-stamped the action, I would take one more step toward my freedom.

A few weeks later I was transferred to a road camp in Northern California to work as the camp clerk. There was no better job a prisoner could hope for. I said goodbye to Howard and Nimar shook my hand, offered me a cigar, and said, "Keep hacking, and let's keep in touch." The Wit told me, Don't go out there and develop a case of rabbit fever. And the Cynic said, I knew they'd never send you to camp until your reasons to stay were more compelling than your reasons to run. You may have these things, but only after you have learned to live without them.

Camp Clerk

CAMP WAS PARADISE. We were stationed high in a green saddle on the north slope of Lord Ellis mountain, twenty miles
from the Pacific, thirty miles from the Oregon border, and
in the mist, which drifted up each morning from the ocean,
the stands of second growth rimmed the camp like a forest
in a dream, and when I walked these same woods in the
afternoon, my tennis shoes light on the beds of dried pine
needles, while the camp dog ran seven circles around every
radius I hiked, the clearings were like ovens, simmering with
the bakery quality of warm decay. The air was sweet, graced
with salt from the water far below us, and I found myself
living here in a state very like happiness. I remember sitting
on the office steps in the sun, watching Tom, the camp cat,
full of mice and moles, sleeping on the canvas top of the
Camp Loot's small red Fiat. I looked into his yellow eyes,
now flat and self-satisfied, now deep and mysterious, and

these eyes whispered to me: It's warm, we're full, relax awhile.

And I did. For the first time in several years I took a few weeks off from writing and began to get the camp office under control. If this particular paradise were Mt. Olympus, then I was Hermes — not quite a convict, certainly not an officer, but somewhere between, and this position was the physical expression of something I had always felt. I was often slightly removed, and this was beyond affectation or choice. It was my nature. I learned this position could be managed with a degree of gracefulness only if everything stopped at you. I knew guard secrets which I never passed to the cons, and I knew con secrets which I never passed to the guards. When clerks fell, and they crashed all the time, it was always because they tried to use the power they transmitted. The man I replaced had become confused by this illusion of power and oversported his own slender hand. He'd made deals with local vendors, who delivered directly to the camp, to bring him prime steak, fresh strawberries, whipped cream, which he paid for with padded purchase orders. But if strawberries entered camp and were paid for disguised as potatoes, this meant the potato ration suffered and there was less to eat for the men who actually did the work. When the crews returned from the roadhead — tired, muddy, hungry — they saw this great pig of a clerk eating strawberries soaked in imported brandy. No good telling the Camp Loot. He wouldn't have fired the clerk, not even when the crew arrived to install the clerk's private swimming pool, because the clerk did all the loot's work while the loot read detective magazines. But finally someone wrote a snitch letter to the captain of camps, who arrived one night to run a surprise inventory, chew out the loot and carry the clerk off in irons.

I ran the camp, in my turn, in the light of this example. There was no need to connive special goodies. I ate so well I immediately gained twenty pounds. The work was exacting, but hardly a full-time job, and I was paid in many ways. For one, I learned my precious number block I had prided myself on all these years was bullshit. I had claimed, and made it true, that I couldn't add a column of figures to the same sum twice. Now I found myself dealing with time sheets and wages per hourly rate and once a month a penny-by-penny account of all monies had to be submitted to the camp office, as well as an inventory of all supplies, and an account of usage. This was my essential job, mistakes were not tolerated, and if I wanted to continue my afternoon walks with the camp dog I had to do it. My number block vanished and this reality therapy had freed me from one more streak of romantic horseshit.

One morning at mail call I received six copies of my novel, which Gold Medal had titled *Felony Tank*. And there it was! It ran a hundred and seventy-five pages, and the running head on each facing sheet was my name — eighty-seven times in each copy. I immediately read the entire book. In print it seemed professional. But this, I knew, was all I would get. There would be no reviews, or special mentions. It was only one more paperback.

However, I had a taste for more, and, against the hope I might be mentioned in the *New York Times Book Review* by the department Criminals at Large, as Parson had been for his Gold Medal original, *Self-Made Widow*, I spent forty-five dollars to have the Sunday *Times* sent to me.

Every week this huge newspaper was shipped across the country to CC #42, Blue Lake, California, against the slender hope that a few lines in it might be about my first novel. I also subscribed to *Partisan Review* and *Encounter*, and as a result Margaret Sanger began to bum me for contributions.

My walking buddy, the camp dog, was named Pork Chop and he had had the emotional shit kicked out of him. He was a heavy, black, prematurely old dog, whose reddish eyes always had a speck of white in the corners. I think he once had the makings of a good dog, but the trip through a dozen masters had gutted him and left him listless to everything but red meat and sugar cubes.

I saw him lose his last master. For two years the laundry-man, Musgraves, whom we naturally called Muskrat, had been Pork Chop's friend. For two years Muskrat shared his food with Pork Chop, and bought him doggie bonbons with his canteen money, and every night Pork Chop slept at the foot of Muskrat's bed. Then one day, Muskrat went home on discharge.

Pork Chop cracked up. He wouldn't eat, he didn't sleep, and he sat all night at the foot of Muskrat's former bunk and howled his misery until the rest of the camp was on the point of mutiny. It wasn't until the loot had made up his mind Pork Chop would have to be shot that the dog came to his senses, absorbed his pain and decided to go on living, but he didn't have much left. He took up with no one else, and like any unhappy middle-aged person he began to eat all the time. I ate a lot myself.

One afternoon Pork Chop and I came on a swarm of ladybugs. They had just completed their metamorphosis, and for a hundred yards every tree and bush was covered with them.

The Sunday *Times* never reached me until Thursday. I opened it and went immediately to the book review section to turn to Criminals at Large. The week came when I was there. When I scanned the column and saw my own name it was if I had touched a charged wire. Something flared inside. The mention was richer than I had allowed myself to imagine and I found myself nominated by the Mystery Writers of America for their annual award for the best first novel in the suspense field. My reality had finally outpaced my capacity to produce fantasy.

The department began to realize what I was doing. They were shocked to it. Burger at Gold Medal had decided *Felony Tank* was soft for his line and he wanted to plug it as a prison novel. Since I was still a prisoner, the "tie" seemed sound to him, and I carelessly approved the idea. Fawcett's pub people naturally pushed their handout to any point where they thought they had a chance to claim some space, and one of these points was the San Rafael *Independent*, who ran the entire puff under a three-column photo of me. This was the thirty-six-point lead: SAN QUENTIN AUTHOR WRITES PRISON NOVEL!

Now imagine the warden reading the *Independent* at breakfast. His eye is as nicely tuned to SQ as mine is tuned to my own name. But when he sees his prison mentioned in association with a writer, already the associations aren't pleasant, and when he discovers the writer has written a prison novel . . .

"Holy shit! Those fools have let some mutt send out an exposé."

His first concern is for the director. The director and his men aren't indifferent to publicity, far from it, but they aren't happy with any form of publicity they can't control, and, doubtless, they have been dismayed to discover the public's ordinary taste to run more to an interest in the violent and unusual than to the pious recounting of good works.

The director does not like waves, and while this particular wave is only a ripple, who can ever tell? It might become tidal. Prisoners winning prizes, making statements to the press, it's all too unusual. The warden immediately jumps the assoc. warden of C and T and he jumps the librarian, who runs to his files, pulls my summary, and returns to say: the publisher is lying.

The first I know of any of this is when my new novel is suddenly confiscated. I had finished it and submitted it routinely for censoring. Instead of notice it had been mailed to N.Y.C., I received an interdepartmental stating that my ms. had been disapproved because it violated the Rules and Regs, article such-and-such, para so-and-so, by depicting a narcotics detective as addicted. Further, I had made antisocial attitudes appear attractive. The first charge was true, the second was scraped together.

I was dismayed. Clearly things had been going too smoothly. If the narc had to be rehabilitated my book was gutted. He was essential to the action — his addiction was essential to his motivation. I had already completely re-formed this book. Now I faced a second major revision, and as much as I liked the story, I had no illusion it was worth this kind of effort.

Things began to get silly. All my outgoing and incoming mail was rerouted to the mother institution where it was held. I didn't know this until I was suddenly ordered back. The camp steward, one of the road runners, drove me. "They just want to talk to you," he said nervously. "You'll be coming right back." But I knew the loot didn't expect me. He had been careful to make sure my files were in order and everything placed where he could find it.

We rolled east before heading south, then east across the edge of the Trinity Alps wilderness area, and into Redding. We passed the high school where I had learned to want to be a writer and rode down the street where I had walked to work on the *Record*, over the bridge above the Sacramento River.

I checked into Quentin, caught a cell and still another cell partner, and the next day I was called out to the ad building where I sat down with the assoc. warden of C and T and the librarian. The assoc. warden was determined to be civilized, but the librarian was furious. The buck had passed to him and he sat there with no place to lay it off but me. He chose to feel betrayed.

My dealings with the assoc. warden had always been pleasant, and this meeting was no exception, but I was never quite able to forget he was a politician. When I entered the room, he rose and shook my hand. The librarian gave me a curt nod.

The assoc. warden gave me the bad news. "We have a problem, Malcolm. I'm aware you weren't responsible for the manner in which your book has been publicized, but, things being as they are, you'll have to bear some inconvenience. On this second novel, we can't allow it. The character of Lieutenant Carver —"

I interrupted to say, "There are such men."

"We know that. But we can't allow *you* to say so. Particularly now that everyone has been told you're one of our prisoners. And you can thank Fawcett for that."

The librarian broke in to ask, "Why can't we sue this publishing house? They've engaged in an act of deliberate misrepresentation."

The assoc. warden waved this insanity away, and continued with me. "We have an opinion from the office of the state district attorney that we can require you to return the monies advanced to you under this second contract, or we can void the agreement by rescinding the specific return of state's rights which permitted you to sign the contract in the first place. We can do this, Malcolm, but we don't want to. I don't want to."

The assoc. warden pushed the letter from the D.A. out onto the table, but when I reached for it, the librarian snatched it away from me. "That's not for you!"

I looked helplessly at the assoc. warden, who said, "Let him read it."

The letter said in effect, subject inmate has no rights, none, not any.

The assoc. warden went on, "We've decided to leave this decision to you and allow you to revise your book to bring it into line with department standards, or return the money. I've read this book —" he shrugged slightly, "and I think it's a good book within its limitations, and if it hadn't been for this unfortunate publicity this question might never have been raised. But it has been raised and you are different because of it. Do you understand?"

I understood.

The assoc. warden thanked me for my cooperation, just

as if it had been volunteered, and then concluded, "With your talent, Malcolm, I don't see why you can't write pleasant stories."

I was returned to camp the next day. Rather than attempt "pleasant stories" I decided to quit writing until I was free. Knox Burger had become a regular correspondent and I wrote telling of the various actions taken against me, and he wrote back to say: Don't worry, we'll wait until you're free, even if we have to publish it as a historical novel.

The next time I rode to Quentin it was to appear before the Adult Authority. I had served three and a half years and earned a few thousand dollars, but the writing number, seen as theater staged for the Adult Authority, had blown up. First, there were my own troubles with censorship, and, second, another convict writer had just failed dramatically. He was one of my ed. dept. buddies, not Parsons, another man, who had published two mysteries with Mill-Morrow, which were extensively reprinted and translated into several languages. The late Erle Stanley Gardner threw his considerable weight behind this man and he was paroled to a glorious future. Ten months later, now drinking heavily, unable to write, he decided to fail. He had flown a lot of bad paper and knew it was only a matter of time before it drifted back to sting him. If he jumped parole, as most of us would have done, he blew his writing career. He decided on a bold save.

He called a press conference to say he found it confusing outside, there were too many distractions, and he couldn't work properly. He needed a quiet period in jail to reclaim his talent. Several large papers, including the San Francisco *Chronicle*, gave this space. The *Chronicle* ran a Sunday special complete with pictures of Dostoevski, John Bunyan, Mahatma Gandhi, Jeanne D'Arc and Jean Genet. There were only the slenderest grounds for this comparison. With the exception of Genet, the others were all political prisoners as most writing prisoners have been, and their intentions directed them to a higher level of sincerity. Still the comparison was made, and this other soul, having won his freedom with much the same kind of show I had imagined for myself, was shot down in flames, back in disgrace, and now while the memory was fresh was no time to try to revive this act in a slightly altered setting. I decided to soft-pedal the writing career. If the board mentioned it, I would dismiss it as something I had taken up to help pass the time.

Again I rode the gray goose to Quentin. The yard was abuzz. Seven inmates had been killed in the last ten days, and the smart heads said it had been because a bunch of gunsels had fallen out over a big heroin deal, but that the joint was filling with a violent spirit, and the morning before I went to the board I saw Conejo Rojos beaten to death by militant Indians armed with baseball bats. It took seconds. They hit him maybe five times, and he fell flat out, legs twitching. I turned and walked away. The blacks were angry. The Indians were angry. The gunsels arriving from Tracy were anxious to make reps as tough dudes.. There was a different spirit in Quentin. The blacks said, Why struggle and suck ass to make parole when they send you right back to the same mess that first put you in the Man's hand?

The Cynic said, You keep buttoned up and get back to camp. This joint is beginning to go hard rock.

When I walked into the boardroom I saw I had drawn

the one member who might be impressed with my writing. Clinton T. Duffy was the former warden of San Quentin, and the author of several books. When he greeted me by remarking that he "saw where I was a writer, too," associating us together, something shrewd whispered: *Now! Play this right and you're on your way home.*

Duffy was a good head. He was born and raised on the prison reservation and knew from long experience we weren't necessarily wild animals. When he became warden he defied tradition by walking openly and unguarded on the yard, stopping to talk to anyone with a problem. He brought in the movies, the school, the hobby program. He began many of the major reforms which later became pilot programs for the entire nation, and thousands of men have done easier and more productive time because of him, and to the extent that any single man can be responsible for what is essentially a historical process, Duffy deserves more credit for the reformation of the California prison system than he ever received, and it pleases me to be able to take this opportunity to tip my hat to him in passing and also to thank him for the parole.

My time was set at six years — four in and two out. So I served six months less than last time, and I salvaged between two and three years that might otherwise have been lost. Or so it seemed at the time.

I spent my last six months writing the very book the department had been afraid I would write, but not in the spirit they thought I might write it. I admitted to myself I was ambitious, and, having done what I had done, I wanted to do more, and I decided to write out of the only thing I knew well. I was a folklorist of the Quentin yard. I had been on it, but never quite of it, for years, and I knew dozens of stories. I began to weave some of these tales into a long collective novel. I was careful never to leave this book around where one of the guards might start reading it.

Meanwhile, from N.Y.C., Knox Burger was writing literally dozens of letters to his many friends trying to find someone who would give me a job. He contacted writers, producers, directors, agents, and several of these people offered to talk to me when I came out to see if we could put anything together.

One morning at mail call I had a letter from my sister. She was now twenty-eight, I was thirty-five, and we had been separated for twenty-one years. She drove the length of the state, seven hundred miles, to see me, and we knew each other. She wanted me to stay with her when I first came out, stay as long as I wanted, but at least until I knew what I was going to do. She made her home in a suburb of Los Angeles, and that was the next stop in my drift south.

"How did you find me?" I asked. "Did you see a copy of my book?"

She looked puzzled. "No, I hired a private detective. What book are you talking about?"

A few weeks before my parole, the Mystery Writers awarded me second honors for the year. I wasn't present at the ceremony. When the western-based Mystery Writers came to Quentin to make the award, the warden was happy to accept for me.

One morning I said goodbye to my friend the Chinese cook, and to my walking buddy, Pork Chop, and the loot drove me down to Eureka where I caught a plane to Los Angeles. It was spring, a lovely day, and I still wasn't bald.

Third Interlude

☗☗☗☗☗☗☗☗☗☗☗☗☗☗☗☗☗☗

I WAS NOW thirty-seven, close to two hundred pounds, beginning to gray. I was healthy, egocentric and there was little in my appearance to suggest how strange a man I had become. As this was hidden from others it was also hidden from myself. I didn't want to know.

I can now recover the simple arithmetic I ignored that day as I flew south along the Pacific coast — in the last twenty years I had been free ten months between Preston and the Nevada Prison, free eighteen months between my first and second jolts, and free eleven months between the second and the third. A month better than two and a half years. For over seventeen years I had been trained to dependence on a system which had casually sustained my physical survival while it had, with equal casualness, starved my every other need. Most of what I knew of this vivid and richly varied outside world and those mysterious others, women, I knew from the stories I had heard from my fellows. I had studied the world through magazines and television, through advertising. For years I had watched one or two movies a week and read as many novels. You may judge the quality of this education.

If we could ask this young/old man, staring at the stewardesses, what he wants his life to be, what vision he has of his personal future, he would probably get off some pious near-bullshit about working hard, writing well, earning recognition, but if he told the truth he would admit he mostly wanted excitement and romantic adventure. He wanted to swim in the ocean under the slowly beating sun and drive through the warm purple night, along the silver beaches, in an exciting car with the girl I had spent all those years perfecting in my imagination.

My sister lived near Compton, a suburb of L.A., with neat houses on wide streets, with shopping centers every ten blocks. In my need to have some attitude, I immediately saw it as the western version of the suburban nightmare mocked by oracles such as *The New Yorker* — you nodded, took the wrong freeway exit and entered another neighborhood superficially exactly like your own. Unable to discover your error you follow its logic into the "wrong" house where the wife and children you find there are also interchangeable. I saw this as stultifying, another triumph of mediocrity, for I had not been trained to see, nor could I imagine on my own, a world where friends would open every door.

But it is warm in Southern California, food springs from the ground, and people are not so anxious. My sister lived in one of hundreds of apartment courts, each court gathered around its expanse of lawn and its illusion of privacy and I spent those first pleasant afternoons lying out on a blanket, deepening my tan against my hopes of love, watching the children play. Two pretty blond little girls lived just next door, and when their mother came home from work she smiled at me, and, gratefully, I smiled back. She favored tight black skirts and sweaters, a thick rope of blond hair swayed against her slender back, and her ass moved like the most beautiful instrument I had ever seen. She looked as if she had just stepped off a sound stage to relax between takes. Many of the women I now saw around me seemed to have some share of this look, and it was difficult for me to understand how it was mass-produced and retailed in the discount stores that flourished in every shopping center.

When I asked my sister about her, Bobbie grinned and shook her head. "Are you sure you want to open that can of peas?" she asked me. She had survived the war of the sexes, picking up five beautiful children in the process, and I had been delighted to find her so level and straightforward.

"I like the way she walks," I said.

"That's artifice. Every girl learns that walk in the eighth grade."

I thought when I left the institution, I would also leave its censorship, but, as I learned on my first visit to the parole office, I had underestimated their arrogance. The Department expected to continue to censor anything I wrote. I thought this unconstitutional, I still do, but it was put to me flatly by a P.O., who made it clear he was just doing his job. There was no apparent appeal. The agreement we sign with the Department reads, in its most significant paragraph, ". . . any parolee may be violated at any time with or without cause."

One of my first free acts had been to mail my carbon

copy of the second novel to Knox Burger at Fawcett. Technically, I had already violated my parole. Formerly, I had thought little of these technical violations, they were nuisances everyone on both sides had apparently agreed to overlook, but I was no longer so sure, and, in significant addition, I now had more to lose. I was apprehensive — not toward any individual Department functionary, but against its aggregate spirit. It seemed to me the ways in which this organism, this machine, sought to insure its survival, and, inevitably, its growth, caused a certain numbness in many of the member cells. In the same way a soldier is able to dilute the casual atrocities of war in the larger spirit of his country, so the arms and legs of the Department took no responsibility for the occasional glow of madness lit in the forebrain. They often talked like old cons. "Yeah, they hatch a few strange ideas up there in Sacramento, and they don't want to hear what you think about them either, but, what the fuck, if it isn't one thing, it's another. Here, take a look at this —"

My new P.O. pulled a book-length ms. from his bottom desk drawer. "One of my other men submitted this for censoring. Read a little. Tell me what you think."

I sat there and read a few pages. It was a genre Western and not very skillful, but I thought of the man who had written it. Novels, even bad novels, don't write themselves. They take months, sometimes years, of effort. This was some man's bid to a larger fortune, and here it lay waiting for the P.O. to get around to it. The date on the title page was already six months old. I made up my mind to ignore this claim to the right of censorship. I determined to finish my novel set on the Quentin yard.

Her name was Lorna, and she wasn't quite as pretty as I first thought. She created the illusion with a consummate art she never quite stopped practicing, even in intimacy, and her impersonation of a beauty was very like my impersonation of an educated and experienced man. On this level, then, we were well enough met.

Our first date was a drive-in movie, and while her two little girls whispered in the back seat of her old Chevy, Lorna and I sat stiffly in the front watching the heroine simulate sexual ecstacy as the vampire placed his patently phony teeth to her throat. Lorna watched this with parted lips, and I watched her.

Later, in her apartment, the girls in bed, we continued to watch TV side by side on the couch, and I reached out, my heart in my throat, to smooth her lovely hair, and she turned in a single flowing motion to come into my arms. It was the nicest move she ever made toward me and she immediately began to subtract from it. After several urgent kisses, she drew back to tell me, "My body says Yes, but my mind says No."

I was dismayed at the suggestion this wasn't going to work. I couldn't know the degree to which it was form. She was twenty-seven, and her body must have been rich with experience, and she should have surely known, brain and belly, what she wanted to do. And, of course, she did. Her kittenish remark was only to urge me to create a situation where she could tell herself she had been carried away. My part was to produce fangs like the movie vampire and compel her to a passion, however horrid in its superficial elements, which she could not deny. She introduced, in effect, the whisper of rape.

But I thought her debate real, and I began to answer

temperately because I didn't want her to think I just wanted to fuck her, even though I did, and also because if the movie vampire were real he would be no more ashamed of his wounding teeth than I was of my wounding prick, and probably he would dream of the woman who would recklessly bare her throat with an instinct for pleasure as fierce as his own. But I cannot leave these considerations unbalanced by failing to remark that when I did meet just this fierce pleasure it frightened me.

I wanted to fuck, but, at the same time, I didn't. I sensed the test, smelled the risk, and beyond the possibility of pleasure I sensed the reality of responsibility. In addition, I was a derelict here, pulled into a feast, trembling with hunger, overwhelmed by the seeming richness, afraid he will eat himself sick, pass out on watered wine, to wake up once more on the street.

Meanwhile, my body, on its own program, continued after hers, and in a moment she pushed me back, shot me a single odd glance, and whispered, "Let me change."

She went into her bedroom and I sat listening to my heartbeat. Soon I heard her window open and began to tell myself the following story, where I imagined her as she slipped out the window to run barefoot through the cool grass to the corner Tio Taco stand to use the payphone to call one of her many boyfriends, who picks her up in an E-Jag, and they roar across to Hollywood, the real capital of her fantasy world, down the long curving sweep of Sunset Boulevard to Malibu to his pad, where they make love looking over the Pacific, and whenever their interest wanes they think of me still sitting here on her couch waiting for her to come back.

She came out of her bedroom wearing one of those short

nightgowns, the ruffled hem an inch below her crotch, and her legs were lovely, so white they seemed blue in the shadows. I reached for her, still almost unable to imagine I was actually going to fuck this beautiful girl, and, when I came to it, I doubled her, knees to shoulders, as some self-styled stud had told me to do (They love it, man) and pumped away rudely for a few moments before I collapsed into her incredibly soft and star-strung wetness. Later she told me the entire experience had been "awful."

I drove to Hollywood to talk to several of the agents Knox Burger had contacted for me, and they were cordial if not particularly enthusiastic. They suggested I make a systematic study of several television shows to determine what I might be able to write successfully and they supplied me with samples, a beginner's kit, to show how a premise should be framed for submission. It all seemed beyond me and I watched the particular shows they had recommended with the feeling I could never grasp the obvious flair and economy of the craft.

But my Quentin novel began to go well, and I worked on it with the feeling I was writing over my head. I had always hammered out my stories, stretching them across the weak spots, crudely fitting one piece to another, pumping up my own slender experience, stirring the whole dead mass into books that were more about other books than any real life I had experienced and understood, but this book seemed alive with possibilities. Finally I was drawing from a dependable source of inspiration, and each recovered detail led to a complex of further details. The characters seemed to take life to form themselves. I was thrilled, but certain I could never sustain — the better it began to go the more certain I was I would never be able to draw it all together and finish. One day I would sit down to work and my precious book would no longer make sense to me.

The time came when I felt I had enough to risk an outside opinion and I bundled it up and mailed it across the country to Knox Burger. He responded with enthusiasm and a contract. To the part of me that was tremulous he said, "Relax, you're a talented man, and you have a friend who's an editor." I would receive five hundred dollars a month for a year. This was real freedom, and I scarcely noted that when I signed this new contract I also violated my parole.

One of Lorna's friends told me, "Treat her like dirt. She loves it. But if you try to treat her as an equal she'll take it for weakness and begin to walk all over you."

I didn't take this advice. How could I? And Lorna began to walk all over me. I thought I loved her — and isn't that the same thing? — and I was obsessed with her body which drew at me like sweet warm cream. Her very richness gave me the power to return it, but when she came she twisted her face and made small rushing noises almost like distress, and once she told me, "I hate that moment, it makes me feel so vulnerable."

She was interested in power. In her fantasies she became Mrs. Howard Hughes or Mrs. Frank Sinatra, and once safely married to one of these rich and powerful men, she would find some way to manage their wealth and emerge, blond beauty intact, on the big board, like Evita Peron, the secret ruler of the nations of men.

Meanwhile, she had trouble simply holding a job because her ambition usually drove her into confrontations with middle management. The comfortable functionaries in the companies for which she worked sensed her intelligent and driving energy and felt the jungle breath of her intense sexuality and found reasons why she should be either transferred or fired. Her arrogance made her vulnerable.

I went the route with her. One day she moved me in. The next day she threw me out. A week later I was back. But she wouldn't fuck me. She told me it made too powerful a claim on her. I broke every glass in the house. Systematically, in an icy fury, I threw them one at a time into the baseboard. She stood watching, almost in shock, hanging there as if suspended, and when I finished my little demonstration I put my arms around her and she shoved her quim up against me as if it were on springs and I had tripped some delicate balance. I felt her moist heat, the mouth of her passion, and the intensity I sensed in her frightened me and I remained impotent while she hissed at me with withering contempt.

Another time we argued the entire night. She felt the highest aspiration of human ambition was manifested in the moon shots and it was my sense that this energy was either premature or entirely misplaced, that our mysterious future might be contained by this planet and even if it were not we should surely learn to live on it before we made plans to export our problems to the balance of the solar system. She was a resourceful and tricky debater, but I had logged thousands of undergraduate hours in San Quentin, one of the great bullshit academies of Western Civ., and I gradually sealed off the various avenues of her argument and beat her down. As the windows began to grow light I had exhausted her position and exhausted her. She lay back on the couch, loosened her hair, held out her arms to me and we fucked as nicely as we ever managed. I could have her sweet breath rushing next to my ear and know for the moment she really loved me — all I had to do was stomp the shit out of her every day to prove I was strong enough to protect her in this savage world.

One day, when she thought I was asleep, I overheard her talking to one of her girl friends. She was playing Lorna Lovely, soon to be spotted by Sinatra, and the friend asked, "What about Mal?"

"What about him? I don't love him."

"Come on, Lorna, why are you living with a man you don't love?"

"The girls like him. I feel I should make some effort to provide them with a father figure."

"And you don't love him at all?"

Automatically she lowered her voice as she neared the real truth. "How can it be a question of love? He's been locked up for years. How do I know what kind of man he may have become? What he might do?"

Oddly, I knew she did love me, she simply wouldn't admit the power I held over her and recognize it for the equal of the power she held over me, and our mutual failure shamed the magic we might have worked together.

When I left, I thought to spite her by moving to Hollywood into the heart of her fantasy, and, afterwhile, she did come looking for me, but it was, somehow, too late, and I was back floating on the warm river of my own dream.

I moved it seemed in a circle of golden light, without any strong sense of my past and even less of my future. For the first time in my life, except for those brief intervals when I had lived as a thief, I was free to go to bed when I felt like it and get up whenever I woke — then, more often than not,

I drove to the beach. A friend had sold me a monstrous old Cadillac convertible, strong as a tank, for two hundred dollars — a cherry with only 45,000 miles on the clock, and it is fair to say I loved it.

I swam, body surfed, lay in the sun with a gratitude I gradually stopped touching, but never stopped feeling, and in the afternoons I was usually in a bar. I had never been a drinker and I creamed off the pleasant part of this vice without particularly noticing the thickened skin and blurred reflexes of my drinking companions.

I worked less and less and the time came when my novel was almost as alien to me as I had feared it might become. There it sat beside my typewriter and I seldom looked at it, even though I was quick enough to show it to the girls I brought home. One was working as a secretary and, as proof of the quality of her love, she typed it on an IBM selectric, and the result looked as professional as print.

Knox Burger came out on a business trip, meeting writers and film people, and I found it exciting to sit around his suite at the Beverly Hills Hotel listening to book and movie deals being put together with some feeling this might be part of my real life. But my own book was sleeping and Knox was hardly impressed with the electric typing. It bothered him to find less than two hundred pages of a projected five hundred, most of which he knew had been written months earlier, while the advance was already more than half paid out. However, he felt we could offer this hunk to a hardcover house who might come in with a further advance to keep me while I finished if I could bear down and work as hard as I had worked in jail.

"What've you been doing?" he asked.

"Fucking around."

"I don't know anyone who has ever been able to write books in this town." He gestured off in the general direction of the Hollywood Hills. "Mailer went sour right up there."

But, once again, I couldn't worry as I lived out my grotesquely extended adolescence, and no amount of excellent advice could weigh beside the quality of this experience. It seemed always summer, that last summer after high school just before picking up the responsibilities of college. It was always a nice day, a little after noon and a bunch of us were driving up to the lake for a picnic where we would swim and play and engage each other in that delicious sexual fencing which often seems the only truly thrilling use to which we might put our lives. Here, then, was the same warm slow drift which had carried Judy and me, though I often had no special girl, and I floated along in a certain smug and not altogether attractive contentment, unable now — as before — to hear the cataracts roaring just ahead.

I should have heard something when I began to have a series of curious collisions with my current parole officer. When I had first transferred to the Hollywood office I had been assigned to the caseload of the sort of officer I was familiar with — you didn't give him trouble, he was willing to leave you alone. If you seemed to be going along reasonably well, he was willing to put you on "hold" in his mind and concentrate on those who were obviously failing. If you sent your reports in on time, lived quietly, didn't collect a wreath of traffic tickets, beat the shit out of your old lady or get picked up for D and D, you could wear out your parole with a minimum of interference.

But you were also, not infrequently, transferred from one caseload to another without notice, and this is what happened to me. For months the parole office had shown no interest in me, no one had even taken the trouble to come by to confirm I actually lived at the place where I reported my address. Then twice, ten days apart, I found the card of a new P.O. under my door. He had called, found me not home, and left his spoor. I called the parole office, asked for him, but he wasn't in. I left a message, but he didn't call back. I thought of going by to see him. It was a small ploy some of us used. Invent or exaggerate a problem, ask for advice, let him imagine he's helped you, and, meanwhile, he's reassured and isn't so likely to drop by your home unannounced. But I didn't get around to this. Then one night he caught me in.

I opened the door on a small, neat, comparatively young man and knew immediately who he had to be. He smiled, flicked a card at me with a jaunty two-fingered gesture, and said, "So you do live here."

"I called you," I said with some uneasiness, stepping back so he could enter. I still held his card.

"Yes, I know you did, but sometimes you fellows have more than one address —" He had been looking around, but he turned now, with a certain theatrical suddenness, to stare at me. "Isn't that so?"

"Well, I don't know. I guess it's possible."

He turned away and began to look around again. There was a studio portrait of a girl on the top of the television and he walked over to pick this photo up and stare at it briefly. Then he turned it to look at the back of the frame as if there might be some coded message there. He shot me a glance.

"Is this girl living here with you?"

"No, I live alone."

"If she were living with you, I could ask you to move. The bureau would back me."

"She doesn't live here."

"If I came here at four in the morning and found you in bed with this girl I could violate you. I don't say I would, but I could."

I stood there numbly and listened to this man, and could hardly hear what he was saying. I had had at least half a dozen parole officers on my three different paroles, and none of them had taken a line remotely like this. Obviously, he was reminding me how vulnerable I was, but at the same time he smiled a great deal and spoke almost idly as if his remarks were really designed to amuse me.

He began to go through my closet and emerged, in a moment, with several dresses and a nightgown. He displayed these trophies to me. "I thought you said you lived alone."

"I do. Those things just got left here."

"You're asking me to believe some girl came here with two dresses, wore one home and left the other? And this happened twice? Which still doesn't explain the nightgown."

"I didn't say I didn't have relations with women. I'm thirty-eight years old. Sometimes I think I'd like to be married."

"You can't marry without my permission."

"I know that."

As he was leaving he asked to read something I had written. My second novel, set in North Beach, had just been published and I gave him a copy. He tapped it with his finger. "This should tell me a lot about you."

He was back in a week, glancing at my ashtrays, looking, I supposed for lipstick-stained cigarette butts. He was casual, even cordial, but I heard in him the hum of some nasty energy, and still couldn't reflect what I supposed I knew. My gravest flaw was a quality of self-satisfaction, a light that seemed too bright after a long period of darkness, that prevented me from looking too closely at how others were now seeing me.

He told me, "This writing business seems a little shaky. I think you should give some thought to a regular job."

"That's not the opinion of the people who pay me."

I had to contest him. The writer persona was too precious not to defend.

"That may be —" he looked at me seriously — "but they're not responsible for you in the way I am, and I didn't see much in that book of yours."

"De gustibus . . ." I murmured.

"What?"

"Look, I only have a little over six months left on parole. Do you think, I mean, would you recommend me for an earlier discharge?"

He smiled at this. "I don't think so. It's good for you to have me breathing down your neck."

This exchange, as I considered it, seemed a clear admission our relationship was becoming unusual. Next he asked me to come into the parole office and bring my files. I had saved every scrap of paper relative to my writing and he prowled, with every sign of contentment, through this motley trove, while I sat, where I had always sat, by the side of his desk. When he came to the contracts on the prison novel, he asked, "Has this book passed the department censors?"

"In an earlier version," I lied.

"And when will this be published?"

"I can't say, it's not finished. Probably not for some time, and certainly not before I'm off parole."

"Your parole can be extended. I don't say it should be, but I can recommend it if I think best. The bureau would back me."

I sat in cold silence, wondering how I could free myself of this man.

He indicated my files. "This seems reasonably solid, but I know you've been over the line here and there. I know you've been driving. No one can live here and not drive. You must have permission. If I catch you driving, I can lock you up."

I nodded dismally.

I must try to explain why I drove without permission.

I would have to prove legality to the P.O. and I couldn't keep all the necessary papers in order — if I hadn't lost my license, I had mislaid the registration, or forgotten to pay the insurance premium. I was swamped in other ways. However harshly, the joint mothered us — fed us, kept us warm, treated our ailments — and now, away from home, I could hardly remember to pay the rent, and the gas bill and the phone bill, let alone take proper care of my teeth. So I drove without permission and sometimes came back to my apartment to find the electricity turned off for nonpayment, and none of this worried me.

I didn't seem able to worry. It was such a nice afternoon drifting here, beyond the confines of most normal lives. It was, I must suppose, too much. I lived like a man who has perfected a dangerous balancing act. Note his professional smile, his easy confidence, his marvelous grace as he mounts the slender platform, swaying above the abyss, to balance —

on one finger! — in the face of the unknown. *Bravo!* What an excellent show. Then one day there's an earthquake.

My earthquake was a young girl named Doris, who had slender shoulders, wide hips (her deep belly was traced with an arabesque of stretch marks, white on white) and no home. I had had some luck with girls this time, but, in the pimp's expression, I could catch, but I couldn't hold. My breath was too hot, my hand too heavy, and I fell in love with every girl I met. They reacted with instinctive alarm. They didn't know what was the matter with me, but they knew something was. Doris, however, was in a tight spot.

She'd impulsively married an acquaintance of mine. Quit her job, given up her apartment, and burned her bridges, only to discover her new husband was a dark and feckless man. Within ten days they had a violent fight. He threw her out, and I picked her up. She needed a place to stay.

Obviously, we couldn't live together in my apartment because the P.O. would be by any day to tell me what he could do and how the bureau would back him. Stalling for time, hoping for inspiration, I took her to a motel where we had a room by the week. Since so much lay against us, we hardly asked whether we really wanted to be with each other. I decided to confuse the P.O. with a devastating strategy — we went to the parole office and asked permission to marry. I assumed if permission were granted, we'd be allowed to live together, and that was soon enough to decide whether we really wanted to marry. At first, it seemed to go well.

The P.O. was delighted with Doris. She was tall, the kind of girl who almost imperceptibly leans toward men as she talks to them, as if unconsciously pulled by their male energies, and he was short and dark and it was apparent he liked having her here, dependent on his authority. He questioned her at length. "Are you aware of Malcolm's record?"

"Yes, I am."

"Are you aware of the true extent of it?"

She glanced at me. We didn't know each other well. I smiled to tell her nothing he might say would be dangerous to us. "We've discussed it," she said. "But I'm not interested in what Malcolm's done. I know what kind of man he is now."

It was nicely said, and I smiled again to express my gratitude. All these asides between Doris and me appeared to nettle the P.O.

"That's very trusting, I'm sure, but my responsibility is to protect both you and Malcolm, and I don't believe anyone should rush into marriage."

I decided to shoot my shot: "Yes, we understand how serious a step this is. However, if we could live together while we waited it would be much cheaper —"

He was shaking his head. "No, I won't allow that. I know you will be . . . together, but you must live separately."

The effort to be fair here is about to crack my teeth, but I must go on to say, the P.O.'s advice wasn't bad, for probably we wouldn't have found much happiness together. But it's also possible to be right for the wrong reason.

My first bold strategy having fluttered out to crash, I promptly devised another — I was nothing if not clever — and I decided to lose this particular parole officer by moving to San Francisco — with or without permission. When I asked permission, on the phone, he replied, "I think you should stick around and, if I didn't know better, I'd think you were trying to get away from me."

I couldn't afford a second apartment for Doris, and how

could I just turn her out? Further, I was disenchanted with Hollywood — there was no profit here for me. I was wasting valuable time. Drifting, as much as it suited me, was beginning to make me uneasy. I needed to lock up somewhere and finish my book, and I had always loved San Francisco. I didn't intend to jump my parole, but simply to misplace it for a month or so. It often happened, I had heard, that parolees began to drift away, then, coming to their senses, reported from wherever they had landed, and their paroles were simply transferred. I didn't believe there was the slightest possibility, despite the boiler plate in my parole agreement, I would or could be violated unless I was once again arrested for burglary.

So we drove the old Caddy to San Francisco, and had fun for a while, camping out, playing house. Then my money ran short, and Doris, who was a spender, grew restless. She took a job as a cocktail waitress and came home night after night to boast of the propositions put to her. Men wanted to take her to Europe, to Hawaii, while others wanted to establish her in luxurious apartments and only visit her once a month to chew her underwear. All the usual lines of bullshit. And, sometimes while she was at work, I walked the city as I had once walked looking for scores, and I felt some of my old uncertainty and anxiety.

Then I received a telegram.

> PO SAYS YOU'VE JUMPED. STOP PLAYING
> THE FOOL AND GET IN TOUCH WITH HIM.
> KNOX BURGER

When the P.O. had gone through my files, he'd noted all my connections. In the next few days I heard from my sister, my agent and my hardcover publisher. The P.O. had passed the word. If I didn't report, and report soon, I was violated. He wouldn't let go.

I was caught now by the part of me which had always yearned to belong to this ordinary world. I had wanted to be connected to others and was now being levered by the degree to which I had succeeded. At any time before I would simply have ducked my head and gone on running. But that time in my life was over.

Sadly, everyone responded to the P.O.'s official alarm by assuming I was dangerously out of control and about to crash. I was reminded of my responsibilities, and, while the reminders were just, I hadn't abandoned my work, but was only now returning to it. I composed a careful letter, putting my position as fairly as I could, and airmailed it to the P.O. I remember standing with the letter poised in the mail slot, half tempted to tear it up. Then I shrugged and let it fall.

Three days later, as we were eating breakfast, the bell rang. Doris wore only a robe and I was in my shorts, and we were talking over our problems. She had just said, "I know, honey, but the libraries are full of good advice." I walked to the door and opened it and, when I saw the hats, and their dense cop silhouettes, I knew.

"Malcolm Braly?"

Absurdly I said, "I am he."

"We have orders from the L. A. office to take you into custody."

They were not exactly cops but parole reps from the S.F. office, but the distinction was academic. They shoved into the apartment, and Doris cried out and ran into the bedroom. One of them immediately started after her, probably imagining she was off to dump our stash, or to get a gun from under a pillow. I tried to stop him.

"She's not dressed."

He paused in the bedroom door to watch as Doris, half hidden by the closet door, dressed. "Look," said the other one, "we don't know who you are. All we have on you is a teletype from L.A."

They turned out the apartment. We didn't have much. Doris sat at the kitchen table, her eggs drying on the plate, and began to cry. I was stunned. I had been warned if I didn't report I'd be violated. I had reported and I was violated anyway. In all that followed this casual betrayal was never noted.

When they were sure we had no dope, no guns, no money, one of them took a pair of cuffs from his belt. I looked at this restraining gear through a painful mist. "I swore I'd never wear those things again."

He snapped them open. "Sorry, it's regulations."

As we drove to the city prison, one of the reps said, "For a guy on a run, you didn't collect much."

"On a run" was the expression used to describe the time a parolee is out of sight, in violation, and assumed to be stealing with both hands.

"I haven't been on a run," I said.

And the rep replied, "It amounts to the same thing, doesn't it?"

Violation

━━━━━━━━━━━━━━━━━━━━━━━━━━━━

IT HAS TAKEN some time to deal with the parole rep's casual question, and it has only been in the retrospection of this account that I have come to see how he might have been right. The shaft, shaved to its finest point, which drives deepest, says I was indeed on a run, paid for by others with advances I wasn't earning, and whether I was entitled to this false youth, this period of carefree irresponsibility, is a question which can never be answered. However, I was living in a fashion I couldn't hope to sustain, and some period of reckoning and readjustment lay ahead for me. Perhaps it was only bad art and careless timing which allowed me once again to feed myself into the clumsy mechanism which had already ground at me for so long.

When I pulled up the dusty woolen blankets that first night, and turned my face to the scarred metal wall, I felt, straining beneath my control, the same agony which had scorched me six years before in Santa Barbara, but now it held no capacity to heal. I was sickened on my own foolishness.

Still, at first, I couldn't imagine they'd actually violate and return me to prison. I thought I was only facing a few days, a few weeks in the San Francisco jail. Just long enough to vividly remind me of the gravity of my position. Such shock treatment was a standard tactic. They pulled you back to let the brute breathe on you. Let you sense fully how precious it was simply to eat what you wanted, when you were hungry, simply to see that first star we were taught to wish on as children.

Doris was outraged. "I don't see how they can do something like this? Isn't this America?" She made a number of angry and desperate phone calls. First to the P.O. in Hollywood, who said, "I warned Malcolm, and he made the mistake of not taking me seriously." Then she called his superior, who said he wasn't familiar with the case. Then she called the department in Sacramento and they referred her to the local officer. She could have pursued this cycle forever and never cracked their routine. She didn't understand that our women always call to explain how their man is different, all the wives and the girls of the violators always call, and in the mind of the department they are little more than whores, otherwise they would love better men. Their despair, their loss didn't — and maybe it couldn't — count. The easy assumption was that we would lie to them and they would loyally repeat our lies. Or, at worst, they were no better than we — hookers, boosters, addicts, chippies and sluts, all trying to run a scam to break loose their old man. The fault, if there is one, rests deep in our customs.

At first Burger was disappointed and coldly furious, but when I was able to explain something of the mechanism which had closed on me, he began to try to pry me loose. His lever, stretching as it did from N.Y.C., was neither long enough, nor strong enough, but he waved it vigorously. He contacted his own friends in the Bay Area and asked them to help me and they asked Melvin Belli to look into it. Belli sent one of his people to see what they could do. I explained, with some anxiety, they could do almost nothing, and that little might be harmful. The violation process wasn't subject to judicial review, and I was certain the Adult Authority would resist fiercely any attempt to wrest the matter into the courts, and in any such game of legal badminton I was clearly the bird. My indeterminate sentence had been set, my discharge date now only five months away, but my time could be set and reset and set again. By law they had me, and, by law, they could keep me until I had served my max. And my max. was life.

And here I was once again in jail, the dismal climax of so many former failures, haunted now by the boy I had once been. The jail was here, unchanged, and, while I seemed to myself to be so different, the jail in its cold wisdom whispered to me there could have been little real change, or I should not still be here, defined by my situation, and the sympathy and the easy breaks given to the boy who didn't deserve them were denied to the man who did.

My prison persona slipped around me as I met others I knew and began, once again, to walk and talk. At the same time, my stomach went sour, my hair began to fall, and my spirit felt dusty and stunted. I was a weak and foolish man, of little value, who couldn't seem to understand the nature of the world he lived in. I forgot my dissatisfactions with Doris and began to imagine I loved her. I pounded the tier and wondered what she was doing.

After three weeks I began to realize the P.O. was completely serious. He intended to return me to Quentin if he could. His recommendation (and the bureau would back him) would have to be approved by the Adult Authority, but there was little chance they wouldn't simply rubber-stamp the action. Slight as the chance was, there I pinned my hope.

One morning they called me to roll it up, and, as I gathered my few things, I crossed my fingers in my most ancient charm, to pray they would set me free. Instead they locked me in irons and drove me across the Golden Gate Bridge to San Quentin. Looking down from the far end of the bridge, I saw a restaurant on the edge of Sausalito where we once had dinner, when I was still a real person, and I closed my eyes against my tears. I walked between gates and the prison closed on me. It was all exactly the same.

The Wit — he was always here — said, "You must be caught in a revolving door. What're you carrying this time?"

"A violation."

"That's lightweight. What're your charges?"

"Leaving the county without permission. Driving without permission. Shacking up."

"Don't shuck an old friend. They don't violate for that sort of nitshit."

"They do now."

I hit the yard. It looked the same, but a few things were different. There were rumors of strikes and riots, and I talked to one man who was suing the state for peonage because they forced him to work without pay. The Warren Court had filled everyone with writ fever. Twice a day the hardrocks and the psychos formed in a wavering line the length of the yard while an MTA issued them tranqs. They were now gentle as rabbits. But the blacks were salty and there were no tranqs for their problems. The official talk was still of rehabilitation but it had become the listless drone of a small-town minister approaching retirement.

I ran into Bob Grossbart, my former crime partner. After that first jolt, locked on Queen's Row, he had gone home to L.A. to try to become a pimp and had succeeded only in becoming addicted. He robbed a doctor for the drugs he thought he might be carrying and, in the course of the robbery, drove the doctor a few miles in the doctor's own car. Under California law, this is kidnapping, and Bob fell with straight life. All the time I had been bouncing in and out of San Quentin he had been pulling fifteen long ones in Folsom. Finally, reluctantly, they had released him to lifetime parole, and now, less than a year later, he was back for a list of small missteps similar to my own. Ironically, I couldn't believe there wasn't more to his violation than he was admitting. His foolish and boastful vigor was gone. His looks had faded with his youth. He was abject. How was I any different? Neither of us had traveled far from that moment twenty years before when we had bumped into each other on the streets of Sacramento. He told me he had heard Mick had been executed somewhere in the East for murder.

Dallas, another old and dear friend, was pounding the yard. He was also doing it all for third-offense sales of smack. "I know it sounds like bullshit," he told me, "but I was only trying to run my own habit. Compared to a dealer

I was a peddler with a pack. It's such shit. I really felt I might be outgrowing the stuff. Now it's over. I'm not getting out and if I do I'll probably be in a wheelchair or a box. Do you think the time will come when history will look back and judge us as we judge those who burned the witches?"

Dallas told me George had fallen again, for another clumsy burglary, and was now doing his time at the new Medical Facility at Vacaville. "How is he?" I asked, thinking of all George had known and taught to me and how little it had helped either of us.

"He's the same." Dallas smiled. "I suppose that's an indictment. We read that North Beach book of yours."

"Yeah, did George like it?"

"Pretty much, but I think he expected more of you."

The Librarian found me wandering through the stacks trying to find something to read, and I don't think he knew I had ever been gone. "How's your writing coming?" he asked.

I smiled with difficulty and told him I was under contract to one of the oldest and most respected publishers in the country, seeing in his eyes what this meant to him, while I was thinking of all those other failures recorded in his files. I couldn't imagine how I would ever be able to finish my novel.

Before my violation was official I was entitled to one final hearing before the Adult Authority, a personal hearing, and I now placed my hopes here. I was certain I could convince them, no matter how it had happened, I was truly rehabilitated. I had changed. From the time of my arrest in Santa

Barbara, now six years ago, I had been growing steadily, and I was no longer the man described in my file. To support this argument I asked my literary agent to send a summary of my earnings so it would be clear I had made more than enough to live on, and Knox Burger, ever energetic and faithful, wrote a long letter to the effect that while nothing in publishing was ever certain, he thought I could continue to earn a living if I continued to write, and he would be willing to sponsor me in New York if they would be willing to allow me to live there.

This seemed powerful to me. I had been able to make more writing than I had ever managed to steal. As Burger remarked in one of his notes to me: "Writing is probably no more honest than theft, but it's a great deal safer, and the retirement benefits, in any event, are the same."

Doris didn't hang in. How could I expect that? I had sprung myself on her, and she was hardly used to looking up from her breakfast to find armed men carrying off the man she happened to be living with. The right or the wrong of it, assuming any clarity could ever be brought to the discrimination, was pale beside the blunt fact.

The Adult Authority, expanding as every organ and limb of the correctional establishment continued to expand, had swollen to a panel of nine members, and there was reason to hope I might appear before some of the newer and more liberal appointees, but when I walked into the boardroom for my hearing I was dismayed to find Cletus J. Fitzharris. The names we called this man are both obscene and libelous and I must content myself by saying his reputation on the yard was by far the most sinister of any Adult

Authority member. We hated and feared him, and his personal percentage of denials was significantly higher than the board average.

"Sit down, Mr. Braly."

I sat in my chair, sharply diminished, but still determined to fight. Fitzharris was a tall, thin, sour man, a Catholic moralist stamped out of a mold now broken, who still wore the rimless glasses fashionable two decades before.

He began with the empty form, "We're sorry to see you back." He tapped my file, now the size of a phone book. "You've collected a substantial list of charges here. Apparently you didn't respect the agreement you signed with us."

How to explain how distant that agreement began to seem after eighteen months out there, and how difficult it was to keep a steady focus on your special situation when you were beginning to feel, finally, just like anyone else.

He went on. "And this paramour of yours —" his mouth flexed in disgust. "Why did you treat her with such disrespect?"

How to explain to this Dickensian anachronism, or anyone still using words like paramour, that this was the seventh decade of the twentieth century, and ordinary people, in increasing numbers, were beginning to consider the content more important than the form?

"I asked permission to marry. The parole officer's reaction was tantamount to refusal."

"And did it occur to you his judgment might be superior to yours?"

"He was playing with me."

Fitzharris stared at me bleakly. He had heard this story, in a thousand variations, before. He went on. "How do you plead to these charges?"

This was the form. A mock trial before absent witnesses. If we were not guilty we wouldn't be here, and if we didn't plead guilty we would be found guilty. In my case the substance was accurate and I could make no defense at this point.

"Guilty."

"Very well," he began in a tone that sounded like the prelude to my exit music, and I interrupted desperately.

"Mr. Fitzharris, doesn't it mean anything to you that for the first time in my life I've been able to earn my own way? I had a job where I made decent money."

"That's noted. In this one area you've done well. But this writing business comes and goes, doesn't it?"

I could hardly say it didn't.

"And you're an old con. How can we trust you? How do we know what you've been up to? You vanish for months at a time. Then there's this violence in your record."

"That was twenty years ago."

He had the grace to look down. "I know. But that was you out there in Nevada, not someone else."

"It was not me. I am someone else. In the twenty years since that happened I have never stopped trying to change myself."

"How can we know that?"

That was it, wasn't it? They didn't know. How could they know? And since anything I might find to say was selfishly inspired, designed to free me, it had to be discounted. Only the file could be trusted, and here the ink never faded.

When I played this scene over, as I did again and again, the feeling that came over me was the horror of total impotence. There was nothing I could do. No way to demonstrate my sincerity. I had moved beyond the usual pattern and was now abandoned there.

I left the boardroom sure of several things. I was denied. The Adult Authority were probably poorer judges of who would make it and who wouldn't than the average con on the yard. They were taking fifty thousand dollars a year to sit in those big leather chairs and wing it. And, finally and most demeaning, I knew it was somehow more agreeable to Fitzharris to deny me than it would have been to set me free.

What could I do? Go to court with Melvin Belli? Return to camp, escape and make my way to the Magic City to write a book — *J'accuse!* — exposing this sorry mess? Or hang myself wtih my belt? All these things occurred to me, but what I actually did was crawl around the yard whining bitterly to anyone who would listen to me. There was cold comfort there.

The Cynic said, "An ace? That's no hill for a stepper. A year ain't shit. Tighten up and walk it off. Injustice? You've been dealing with these assholes most of your life and you still believe in justice?"

But, you see, I did believe in justice and this belief had formed the last stronghold of my idealism. I never felt I was right, the world wrong. I felt if I straightened my own hand, the deal would then always be square. True to Goethe's telling homily, I had cleaned my own doorstep only to be buried in another's trash. And when I accepted this, tightened up and began to walk it off, I was no longer young.

Since I was now a trusted old con, a willing mule, I was shipped off to one of the new conservation centers. These are modern units, designed to service and man the camp programs. No walls, no cells, no guns anywhere in sight. We lived Army style, sixteen to a barracks, and every barracks had a rec room and a TV, and if you wanted to watch *Make Room for Daddy*, instead of *The Man from U.N.C.L.E.*, you walked around from barracks to barracks until you found one where this show was playing.

The old-timers scorned these new prisons and dismissed them as Holiday Motels. We couldn't be conned by departmental window trimming. We were still under the Man, and the Man still had a gun locked away somewhere nearby. The rest was bullshit. Essentially, it was only Folsom with Muzac. We see old prisons as scars because they whisper to us of that which is ugly in our spirit, but old monasteries look much the same, and it's possible this glistening tile and gleaming Formica will someday communicate the same message we now hear from stone walls and iron bars. Those who thrill over these new prisons and exclaim, "You can do everything but go out for a pizza!" will never understand this until they've served in one. The ways in which we are denied our own free choice are finally all the same. Simple fairness compels me to admit it's better than being beaten with a rubber hose, but not much better.

I had seldom pulled time as hard as this. I had always had my real life to look forward to. Now it seemed it might well be behind me. The waste of this precious time appalled me. I couldn't put it out of my mind, and, at the same time, I couldn't remember the time I had already served. But my number — A-8814-B — which had trailed me all these years was a constant reminder. They were now issuing numbers in the late seventy thousands, and a number as low as mine was a curiosity. It was obvious to anyone who heard it I had built a lot of time, but I refused to remember the total of the years, and so I was no longer quite sane. But if I entered this area to truly consider it I could only discover what a desperate freak I had made of myself.

Most never risk prison and of those who do only a few are ever actually locked up, and of these few only a tiny minority return again and again. Statistically, I was a monster and, judged by any average, I had delivered myself to a fate as narrow as if I had been born with a crippling birth defect.

A buddy, who worked in records, got his hand on my file for a few moments and, thinking it would please me to have it, he lifted a copy of my earliest mug shot, taken that day I had first entered Q with Gerry to be advised so aptly *Illegitimus non carborundum,* and I stared at this boy who had wanted to be a poet, and wondered, if I could have known what I was going to have to walk through, would I have bothered?

As I avoided the message held in the total of the years, so I tried to avoid the message implicit in this violation. I no longer held Truth Court. I could no longer endure the cold light, but I could not stop thinking. Plato causes Socrates to say: The unexamined life is not worth living. And a quarter of the way around the earth Krishna was telling Arjuna: You must do your work without hope of reward. My work, for which I had little relish, was to attempt to understand why these things had happened to me. One of the last poems I wrote, when Crazy Smith and I were in love with *mpi,* contained these lines:

FALSE STARTS

> *My passion was seeing*
> *and I became an enormous eye*
> *which can not close ...*

Now it seemed clear to me I had always known I was going to jail. When I had bolted Redding to try to join the Navy, I had known. When I had told Percy, "We'll be back," I had known. When I had followed George into the all-night diner, I had known. Not so clearly in my intuition, which had probably given up, but even more certain in the mechanism I set for myself. I proved it again when I dropped my address on the floor of the doctor's office and went home to wait for the police. Finally, I had cheerfully provided the P.O. with the rope he needed to hang me.

I had served more time for a handful of inept burglaries than most men would have served for killing a police officer, and the prison, which I had hated so deeply and scored so bitterly for its every failing, was only my chosen instrument in the willful destruction of my own life.

I didn't know why I had done this to myself. I couldn't guess at the hidden etiology or the mysterious *primum mobile* — There were, finally, too many possibilities and no one more compelling than the rest. As much as I felt I might have learned, which was always more a process of discarding the clearly false than securing the clearly true, I still knew no more of what motivated me than I had the night I followed the boy whose coat I had stolen out of the pool hall and into the hands of the police. And if I didn't know, who did?

Discharge

>=========================<

AFTER A YEAR, I returned to the board. The Adult Authority had once again performed mitosis, adding still more representatives to handle their swelling caseload. Now we appeared before a full member and a sort of *aide-de-camp*.

I drew two men I had never seen before, but they knew me. My file, still stamped *Special Interest*, was before them, and because of this they took their time and picked at every old scab. Once again they asked if I was homosexual, and once more, I wearily denied this pointless charge. Why did they ask? They weren't dull men. But if this was my problem, they could hardly imagine all these years in prison had cured me. And if I had said, "Yes, I am. I admit it." Would they have said, "Well, don't be like that"?

One member, since I was now a writer, whipped off a literary reference, misquoting Voltaire: "Once an artist, twice a pervert." Voltaire, in his turn, was also in the file, secured against any casual reexamination.

The aide, an obviously careful and clever young man, climbing the ladder, looked at me with a kind of theatrical shrewdness and said, "I get the distinct feeling we'll see you again. You're the kind who will always outreach and out-smart himself."

I understood that this was designed to make me think. To shock me from any complacency I might have generated. But what I truly understood was that here in this final dia-logue neither of us knew what to say. We looked at each other and each saw the other to be bankrupt. Everything had been said and the simple moral issues were no longer compelling. How could anyone, much less myself, know whether I would survive? Whether I wanted to? No con-vincing case could be made that it was even important to anyone but myself. I still hoped to do well, I still nursed my dreams of the magical reversal that would ultimately reveal me to be the moral superior of these self-satisfied function-aries, but I had always hoped to do well. I had never planned to harm anyone. And if I failed again and returned again, what difference would that make to anyone else on the planet? I would probably end in one of the small grave-yards that are part of every prison reservation.

They looked at me and found me disagreeable and dis-turbing because, finally, there was no reason why I should have taken this long and difficult journey. And I looked, in my turn, and found them disagreeable because they wouldn't admit they knew this.

I left this hearing with a discharge. No parole. When I hit the bricks I was as free as anyone else. And they proved me right when I had judged the smallness of their spirit because they gave me a final kick. They were handing out a number of discharges that year, they needed the room for fresh meat, and most were effective in three to six months. Mine was eighteen months away. And during that eighteen months I would turn forty. The officer who handed me the result was shocked by it and thought there might have been a clerical error, but when he checked with the Board Recorder he was told it was accurate. I could imagine why they might have given the screw this last turn, but I was as weary of making excuses for them as I was weary of making them for myself. It costs several thousand dollars to confine a prisoner for a year and I wondered if they truly thought this money would be well spent.

I was assigned to another camp — again as camp clerk — and began taking walks with another camp dog. Gradually my native hopefulness wore away my depression, and I began the long countdown until I would finally be as free of the state as any other citizen, however free that was. For six months I took care of my assigned work and did little else but play bridge. I lost myself in the intricate and abstract patterns of those fifty-two cards, and, one day, against creditable defense, I engineered a perfect Vienna Coup, and vanished beyond another of those seeming boundaries which have defined my life.

I sent for a Xerox of my prison novel, and working each night when the office was dark, I gradually brought it to conclusion. If I had been tunneling out of the big yard I couldn't have generated any more apprehension. I was certain if the department ever stumbled across this book they would keep me for the rest of my life. They would bury me in the darkest hole of their deepest prison. I'm sure my fear was exaggerated, but it was real to me. They had kicked me, however casually, until I was cowering, but I would have my say. If any of the camp personnel understood what I was doing they were willing to look the other way. We were all small fry in a remote outpost of the same vast machine, and many of these camp bulls had their own problems with the department. Still I guarded my manuscript as nations guard their codebooks and as the total of the pages swelled my apprehension matched it. I finished six days before my discharge, and reading over my work from this terminal vantage I was satisfied to discover I had put in little of my bitterness and less of myself. It was the story of an alien land where I had been visiting for some time, which I held to be not alien at all.

My last day I received this telegram:

> STAY COOL OUT HERE.
> WARMLY,
> KNOX BURGER

When you have a discharge, you're free at one minute after midnight. You can if you wish start walking down the road just like any other citizen. I dressed carefully in slacks and a sweater my sister sent me, gave away my canteen and caught a ride to the nearest town with the guard going off duty at midnight. We were friends and he bought me a companionable beer before he dropped me off at the Greyhound bus depot. I had an hour to wait for the southbound express. I thought of walking around to look for something to eat. I wasn't hungry. I simply needed to exercise my right to buy and eat whatever I wanted. But I was sure nothing would be open this late. Instead I bought a cup of chocolate from a vending machine.

The chocolate was watery and the depot depressing. I was the only one waiting and I sat there under the cold blue lights, my cardboard box at my feet, with the feeling I was suspended. I hadn't expected to be excited. I'd hit the bricks five times now, and I understood how a life of narrow certainty was opening to a richer world of greater risks. I was a zoo-bred monkey suddenly released to sit here on the edge of the jungle.

I was discharged. Finally free. Free to be lonely. Free to go broke. Free to fail. Free to deal with the still ominous mysteries of my own most intimate nature. Still I was free. Unless I went back to my old trade no one could lock me in handcuffs and carry me off to jail, and I couldn't imagine I'd ever steal again.

Still some weight pressed and my struggle had left me exhausted. It was over, I had survived, but in some way I can't satisfactorily explain this final experience had broken my heart. And left it easier for me to live.

The Real World

===

I'M SITTING ACROSS from Stella Stevens. She's beautiful, as artfully worked up as any portrait, and the man with her, obviously her man of the moment, is tall, deeply tanned, with thick yellow hair, and it's easy to imagine these two are visiting here from another planet where life is more generous.

I'm trying to contain my nervous apprehension, trying to remember not to fold my arms protectively across my chest, trying to assure myself I won't do anything to expose myself as an asshole in front of the entire country. Rich Little sits beside me. He watches the monitor for a while, then stares at his hands as they make Here is the church, here is the steeple.

Beverly, my wife of a few weeks, sits calmly, also watching the monitor. This is a taping of the Tonight Show where

I'm scheduled to be one of the guests, and we're waiting here in the greenroom. My novel, *On the Yard*, has been issued a few weeks earlier, and my publisher's publicity people have arranged this important appearance.

The first guest, now on, styles himself Lonesome John. John's spent fifteen years in the far north of Alaska where he passed the long arctic nights teaching himself to play the guitar with his feet. He's pretty good, up there on the monitor, and if it had occurred to him to play with his hands he might well have become virtuoso.

The parallel between the two of us is obvious, and I'm still relishing this irony, amazed at how life supplies details so audaciously neat no artist could feel comfortable at having imagined them, when I'm signaled for my own appearance.

It's now over eighteen months since I left camp on discharge, rolling down the length of California on the Greyhound, over ground I had ridden years before with my wandering family, into a limbo that almost swamped me. I took a room near my sister (who loved me no less for my apparent foolishness, but who was deeply involved in a new marriage) and spent most of my time in bed. I knew no one and I had neither the courage nor the interest to try to meet people. The door of my room may as well have been locked as the door of my cell had always been. My novel had disappeared into the mysterious process which had claimed it from me and the thought of it held little power to help me in this time. I no longer trusted myself, nor knew with any clarity what I really wanted. I lay in bed. When I woke I would read until I became sleepy again. I ate canned soup and peanut-butter sandwiches, and, once in a while, I went out to a neighborhood bar where I drank beer and watched others play pool. Once again I was drifting, but now the water was dark and, despite my strange paralysis, I was frightened.

I went broke and convinced myself it would be a small risk to take something easy, just enough for food and rent, and I was out in the night, prowling a nursery and garden supply house, when the lights of a squad car washed over me, and I was sure they had spotted me crouched there in the underbrush. I bolted in an instant panic to run stumbling and frequently falling across a large empty lot, expecting at any moment to see spotlights ahead. I would be snared from the darkness like a terrified rabbit.

The last time I fell I landed in a small stand of underbrush, and crawled deeper into this thin cover to lie gasping with exhaustion. My throat burned with a deep and painful fire and I was far more alarmed at the erratic hammering of my own heart than I was at the possibility I might be questioned by the police.

How grotesque I seemed to myself. The boy who had climbed the sides of buildings with such a reckless heart was gone, and in his place had appeared this middle-aged man who knew only one way to fail. I sensed then in some clarity how that part of me which had always been fearful was once again trying to return me to the safest place I had ever found. Some primitive center, some ur-self, who still refused to recognize that life was always a gamble.

I decided that night on the boldest move I thought possible and I wrote Knox Burger asking him to loan me the fare to New York, to the Magic City, and this good man telegraphed me the money within an hour of receiving my plea for help. Once more I set off in pursuit of my real life.

I stepped into the bright lights and the polite applause while the studio band played a chorus of "Birmingham Jail," and there was Johnny, half-rising, smiling, holding out his hand. This was *it*, wasn't it? Finally, as I had so often imagined, my photo was appearing on the cover of *Life*. The concrete symbol of my personal worth. It was part of my earliest understanding to believe this admiration, this attention, was the most valuable gift I could ever receive.

But I'm on this talkshow not because I've written a useful novel, but because I'm a former prisoner, and Carson leads the talk not to writing, but to jails. I'm naturally pleased and excited to be here — as the Cynic has always said: It beats a poke in the eye with a sharp stick — but I've begun to sense a fundamental error. As a child of my times I had never questioned my yearning for fame, but I was now beginning to realize I had taken the container for the con· tents. It was not fame I had yearned for, but excellence — this was the evolutionary energy made manifest in me, and I yearned for excellence because I wanted to be worthy of love.

I told canned stories on the Tonight Show, set pieces I had often heard on the yard, but I told them as if they were my own coin and not the folklore of those I had left behind. A few days later, one of my former Quentin supervisors, a decent, patient and hopeful man, wrote to tell me how disappointed he had been in my appearance. He had watched, he said, "a self-satisfied egotist" who had selfishly ignored the opportunity to say something that might help those still pounding the yard. To give some small boost to those who had not had his advantages.

It was true. I didn't think of the friends I had left behind in the clumsy hands of the department. I thought only of my own small success and I used the opportunity to sneer at the department and ventilate my continuing bitterness at the process which had robbed me of my youth.

I was out, but they still had me. My file, that idiot double of my life, was not destroyed, but held in limbo in some basement room in State Office Building Number One, and a new file — in the tax bureaus and the computers of credit raters and insurance companies — was now growing on me. And I further realized the extent to which I was already caught up in the steady institutionalization of our society as one by one we barter our free initiatives in the name of convenience and for the illusion of security.

That evening our apartment filled with friends who came to watch me watch myself on the Tonight Show. There was a lot of good-natured kidding and not much respect for the phenomena. I was doing my turn. I had found a life here in the Magic City, a life among peers, and I had also found some part of the love I had always yearned for.

But when I saw myself walk across the stage to the tune of "Birmingham Jail," there was something about that dude up there who strongly reminded me of the emcee on the Warden's Show. I still looked like a waiter. I was still appearing in flea circuses. And the Wit, always my constant counsel, whispered: Jesus, buddy, don't you ever learn.

That happened eight years ago, and it's now almost ten years since the department discharged me. The pattern is clearly broken. Except when I have been working on this book, I seldom think of San Quentin or the Department of Corrections and the Adult Authority. It seems long ago, in another lifetime. I no longer brood over the right or the wrong of what was done to me — it happened — and I wonder if it isn't the effort to contain our lives in a morality so simple which leads some of us into such terrible trouble. I can't answer my own question. At the end of his long life, Jung wrote that the individual was the only reality. If I sense this truth precisely, it says my life, as all lives are, is unique. For myself, I would change nothing because it has all led me to become the man I hoped to be.

It's pleasant to end this account by thanking all those — Howard, George, Veto and Steven, Judy, Bobbie, Nimar and Knox — whose positive influence helped me to survive.